Global Issues in Income Taxation

By

Daniel Lathrope
Professor of Law
University of California
Hastings College of the Law

AMERICAN CASEBOOK SERIES®

Mat #40678030

© 2008 Thomson/West
          610 Opperman Drive
          St. Paul, MN 55123
          1–800–313–9378

Printed in the United States of America

ISBN: 978–0–314–18806–9

TEXT IS PRINTED ON 10% POST
CONSUMER RECYCLED PAPER

To my mother, Wanda J. Lathrope,
for her love and support

—D.J.L.

*

Preface

The cases, items, and text in this book are designed to provide students in a basic federal income taxation course with both comparative and international perspectives on tax issues. The book is accessible to students early in the course. An introductory chapter covers the structure of global tax systems and income taxes, as well as the various concepts of "income" employed by different tax systems. Coverage also includes chapters exploring the comparative tax treatment of in-kind benefits, gifts and inheritances, deductions, the taxable unit and income splitting rules, and capital gains. A separate chapter explores the issues raised when income is earned in international transactions. Basic international tax coverage includes an introduction to taxation based on source or residence/citizenship, avoidance of double taxation, tax deferral, transfer pricing, and tax treaties.

The book includes both domestic and foreign cases, authorities, and statutes, as well as explanatory text. Because of its coverage, this text also is an excellent vehicle for exploring tax policy issues.

I want to thank Brian Coughlan, Kathryn Dery, Courtney Nash, and Stephanie Perez, who are J.D. graduates of Hastings, for their assistance in preparing the manuscript and publishing this book. I also wish to thank Antoine Veysset, a LL.M. graduate of Hastings, for his work on the book and his special assistance in the translation of French materials.

Daniel J. Lathrope

March 2008

*

Global Issues Series

Series Editor, Franklin A. Gevurtz

Titles Available Now

Global Issues in Legal Ethics by James E. Moliterno, College of William & Mary, Marshall-Wythe School of Law and George Harris, University of the Pacific, McGeorge School of Law
ISBN 978–0–314–16935–8

Global Issues in Property Law by John G. Sprankling, University of the Pacific, McGeorge School of Law, Raymond R. Coletta, University of the Pacific, McGeorge School of Law, and M.C. Mirow, Florida International University College of Law
ISBN 978–0–314–16729–3

Global Issues in Tort Law by Julie A. Davies, University of the Pacific, McGeorge School of Law and Paul T. Hayden, Loyola Law School, Los Angeles
ISBN 978–0–314–16759–0

Summary of Contents

Table of Contents

*

Table of Cases

The principal cases are in bold type. Cases cited or discussed in the text are roman type. References are to pages. Cases cited in principal cases and within other quoted materials are not included.

Global Issues in Income Taxation

*

Chapter 1

INTRODUCTION TO GLOBAL TAX SYSTEMS AND INCOME TAXES

A. INTRODUCTION

Governments impose taxes to raise revenue in order to provide general public services and finance their operations. In their search for revenue, governments impose taxes on a variety of bases, including income and profits, consumption, property, and payroll. These tax bases may be further segmented and variations in tax systems abound. For example, income taxes typically apply separately, and with different rates, to individuals and business entities, such as corporations. The specific treatment of particular items of income or deduction also may differ greatly from one income tax to another. Taxes on consumption may apply broadly across the economy (e.g., general consumption taxes such as value-added taxes and sales taxes), or be targeted at specific goods or products (e.g., gasoline taxes and tobacco taxes). Property taxes may apply different rates or different valuation methods, depending on whether the property being taxed is real, personal, commercial, or residential. Additionally, the tax rates that apply in a particular tax may be flat or steeply progressive.

The overall level of taxation and the mix of taxes employed by a country may have important consequences for its development. The Organization for Economic Co–Operation and Development (OECD) is a forum where the governments of 30 countries work together to address the economic, social, and environmental challenges of globalization. In that role, the OECD develops data on the tax levels and tax structures in OECD countries. The members of the OECD generally include most European countries, Turkey, Canada, Mexico, the United States, Australia, Japan, Korea, and New Zealand.

1

One measure taken by the OECD of a country's tax system is the ratio of its total tax revenues to its gross domestic product. The ratio is basically the share of the economy that the government uses to support governmental services, and that ratio differs considerably among OECD countries. Tax levels, of course, vary among countries for many reasons, including international economic conditions, the strength and performance of the country's economy, and political decisions about the level of governmental services. In 2004, the overall OECD tax ratio was 35.9%. Three countries (Belgium, Denmark, and Sweden) had tax ratios of 45% or more, with Sweden having the highest ratio at 50.4%.[1] Two OECD countries (Korea and Mexico) had tax ratios below 25% in 2004, and Mexico's tax ratio of 19% was the lowest of any OECD country.[2] The United States had a tax ratio of 25.5% in 2004.

Long-term trends in tax ratios are also instructive. The overall tax ratio for all OECD countries increased 6.2% (from 29.7% to 35.9%) between 1975 and 2004.[3] That cumulative figure conceals significant differences in the change in the tax ratios for different regions. For example, in Canada, Mexico, and the United States, the cumulative tax take from GDP rose from 25.2% in 1965 to just 26% in 2004. Compare that with the increase in tax take by OECD European countries, which rose from 26.4% to 38.3% over the same period. The overall tax ratio for Australia, Japan, and New Zealand went up from 21% to 29.4% in the same years. The OECD summarizes the long-term data on overall tax ratios as follows: "The trend towards higher tax levels over this period reflects the sizeable increase of public sector outlays in almost all industrialized countries, with recourse of governments to alternative ways to finance their spending—non-tax revenues, borrowing, and printing money—being limited for a variety of reasons."[4]

Overall levels of taxation provide one perspective on a country's tax system. The mix of taxes that generate the government's revenue provides another. The OECD tracks the tax structure of its member countries and measures the percentage of tax revenue raised specifically through personal income taxes, corporate income taxes, social security contributions (for pensions, unemployment, health care, etc.) paid by employers and employees, payroll taxes,

1. OECD, Revenue Statistics, pp. 18–19 (2006 ed.) (all overall OECD figures are unweighted). For detailed information compiled by the European Union on the tax systems of EU countries, see Taxation Trends in the European Union—Data for the EU Member States and Norway (2007 ed.) at http://ec.europa.eu/taxation_customs/resources/ documents/taxation/gen_info/economic_analysis/tax_structures/Structures2007.pdf.

2. OECD, Revenue Statistics, pp. 18–19 (2006 ed.).

3. Id.

4. Id. at 22.

property taxes, and consumption taxes. In 2004, the mix of revenue raised by all OECD countries was:

Tax	Percentage of Total Tax	
Personal income tax	25%	
Corporate income tax	10%	
Social security contributions[5]	26%	
(Employer)		(15%)
(Employee)		(9%)
Payroll taxes	1%	
Property taxes	6%	
General consumption taxes	19%	
Specific consumption taxes	11%	
Other taxes	3%	

The OECD reports that this mix of taxes has remained stable, but the trends reveal interesting information. Personal income taxes were once the largest source of revenue (at 30% in the 1980s) but that tax is now surpassed by the revenue generated through social security contributions and total consumption taxes. The share of revenue produced by general consumption taxes has risen from 14% in the 1970s. The growth in revenue from general consumption taxes has been the result of the increased importance of value added taxes in many OECD countries.

The significance of revenue from personal income tax in OECD countries varies widely. For example, in 2004, the Slovak Republic raised just 9.3% of its tax revenue through the personal income tax. Other countries that do not rely heavily on personal income taxes as a source of revenue include the Czech Republic (12.7%), Korea (13.6%), Greece (13.8%), Turkey (14.9%), the Netherlands (16.4%) and France (17%). On the other end of the spectrum are Denmark, which raised 50.7% of its revenue from the personal income tax in 2004, New Zealand (41%), and Australia (40.2%). The comparable figures for the United States and Canada are 34.7% and 35.1%, respectively.[6]

An additional factor that may significantly affect a country's tax system is the structure of its government. In federal systems, the different levels of government may have more or less autonomy in designing and operating their tax systems, or one level of government may collect tax revenues for use by other levels of government. For example, in OECD countries with a federal system, the shares of total tax revenues in 2004 going to the central government varied from 80% in Mexico to 29.5% in Germany. In

---

5. Id. Self-employed persons also pay social security contributions so the employer and employee contributions are less than the total.

6. Id. at 75 (Table 11).

the United States, the federal government's share of total tax revenue for 2004 was 38.5%, the states received 20.8%, and local governments received 8.1%.[7]

B. THE STRUCTURE OF INCOME TAXES

Income taxes are commonly categorized as either "global" or "schedular." Global income taxes have a comprehensive base and apply a single rate structure to determine a taxpayer's tax liability. In a global income tax, all allowable deductions are taken in calculating the tax base. In contrast, a schedular income tax operates on the basis of different categories, or "schedules," of income that are grouped together with related deductions. Tax rates for the different schedules may vary, the ability to take particular deductions on a schedule may be limited, and the ability to offset one schedule's income with a loss from another schedule may be restricted. Interestingly, the possibility exists in a schedular system for a particular form of receipt or benefit to fall outside of the defined schedules, thereby becoming tax-exempt.[1]

Income tax systems typically have characteristics of both global and schedular systems. No system is purely one form or the other. The United States income tax is, in large measure, a global income tax. Taxpayers are taxed on "taxable income," which is measured by first determining "gross income," a broad term which the Supreme Court, in *Commissioner v. Glenshaw Glass Co.*,[2] tells us is employed by Congress to exercise, "the full measure of its taxing power." But students of the federal income tax should be able to quickly compile a list of provisions in the Internal Revenue Code that are schedular in nature. The passive activity loss rules in Section 469 of the Internal Revenue Code, which combine income and deductions from passive activities and restrict the deductibility of losses from such activities against non-passive income, is one schedular feature of the income tax. Similarly, the restriction on the deductibility of investment interest in Section 163(d) of the Code and the taxation of capital gains and losses are additional examples of schedular-type provisions that operate within a tax system that is primarily global in nature.

7. Id. at 27–29. The OECD separately classifies 22.7% of United States tax revenue as from social security funds that it does not attribute to the federal government.

1. See generally, Hugh J. Ault & Brian J. Arnold, Comparative Income Taxation—A Structural Analysis 167 (2d ed., 2004); Victor Thuronyi, Comparative Taxation 233–34 (2003). A "composite" structure also exists where flat tax rates are first applied in a schedular system and then a progressive surcharge is applied to the combined schedules of income. Lee Burns & Richard Krever, "Individual Income Taxation," Ch. 14, p. 496, in Victor Thuronyi, Tax Law Design and Drafting (2000).

2. 348 U.S. 426, 75 S.Ct. 473, rehearing denied, 349 U.S. 925, 75 S.Ct. 657 (1955).

The Netherlands income tax provides an example of a tax system with schedular features and some interesting substantive provisions. Taxable income is grouped into three "boxes." Box 1 generally includes income from labor, business and professional income, pensions, and income from owner-occupied dwellings. For owner-occupied housing, a taxpayer who owns a house or apartment used by him or his household includes a percentage (up to 0.55%) of the market value of the dwelling in income. Income in box 1 is reduced by various deductions and allowances and taxed at progressive rates of 33.65% to 52%. Box 2 consists of income (dividends and capital gains on disposition) from substantial shareholdings in companies. A taxpayer generally is regarded as having a substantial shareholding if he owns, alone or together or with his spouse or partner, at least 5% of the shares in a resident or nonresident company. Capital losses and expenses relating to substantial interests reduce the income in box 2 and 25% of a box–2 loss may be credited against tax on income in box 1. Box 2 income is taxed at a flat 25% rate. That tax is in addition to the corporate-level tax paid by the company. Box 3 operates as a surrogate tax on investment income. After 2001, investment income that is not from a substantial interest, such as dividends, interest, and royalties, is not taxable. In box 3, the value of investment assets is deemed to produce a 4% net yield that is taxed at a 30% flat rate. Thus, a 1.2% tax is imposed on the net value (net of certain liabilities) of such assets. Investments in certain "green funds" and "social ethical projects" are exempt from the box 3 tax. Under the Dutch income tax, losses in one box may not offset income in another box. Capital gains that are not derived in the course of a business and not in box 2 are exempt from taxation.[3]

France also employs a schedular income tax. The French income tax, however, plays a reduced role in the county's overall revenue scheme. The French value added tax and a separate tax to support the social security system both raise more revenue than the general income tax.[4] There are six specific categories of taxable income in the French income tax: real estate income, industrial and commercial profits, wage income, farming income, dividend and bond income, and income from the sale of appreciated property (real estate and stocks). A seventh category, that applies to non-commercial profits, is a catchall category. Each category of income has its own rules for deductions and taxable income is the aggrega-

3. Regarding the Netherlands income tax, see IBFD, Global Individual Tax Handbook 2007 383–90 (2007); http://ec.europa.eu/taxation_customs/re sources/documents/taxation/gen_ info/economic_analysis/tax_structures/ Country_tables/NL.pd.

4. In 2005, 53.8% of taxed households paid the income tax. Annuaire statistique, Direction générale des impôts, 2006, Paris.

tion of all of the categories. Intricate rules determine whether an overall loss in a category may be used to reduce income in another category. In some instances, an overall loss in a category will not offset income in another category and in other situations an overall loss may be partially or fully deductible against another category of income. Aggregate taxable income is taxed at progressive rates. Capital gains and, in some situations, interest are taxed at flat rates.[5]

C.   THE NATURE OF "INCOME"

To state the obvious, an income tax taxes "income." But what is "income?" The answer to this question depends on who is responding to the inquiry. The definition of income provided by economists is known as the "Haig–Simons" definition of income, in recognition of the two theorists most associated with developing the concept.[1] Under the Haig–Simons definition, income is defined as: (1) the market value of rights exercised in consumption, plus (2) the change in the value of the store of property rights between the beginning and end of the period in question. Every income tax departs substantially from the Haig–Simons definition. Typically, various consumption expenses receive preferential tax treatment (e.g., the home mortgage deduction and deductions or credits for child care). And, income taxes normally do not tax mere apprecia-tion in the value of property. Instead, taxation of a gain in property generally is deferred until the taxpayer sells or disposes of the property (a "realization" event). Thus, the Haig–Simons definition stands as an economist's ideal, rather than a practical guide for the design of an income tax. A variation of the Haig–Simons definition is employed in some income taxes. Referred to as the "accretion" concept of income, that definition requires inclusion in income of realized accessions to wealth.[2] The United States income tax gener-ally operates on the accretion concept of income.[3]

A different concept of income derives from the notion that income comes from an earning event and must be produced by a "source." The idea of the source concept of income is that income is the product of labor (e.g., salaries and wages), capital (e.g., interest and dividends), or both.[4] The notion is frequently expressed in

5. See generally, IBFD, Global Indi-vidual Tax Handbook 181–186 (2007).

1. See Henry C. Simons, Personal Income Taxation 50 (1938).

2. Victor Thuronyi, Comparative Taxation 235–36 (2003).

3. I.R.C. § 61; see Commissioner v. Glenshaw Glass Co., 348 U.S. 426, 75 S.Ct. 473, rehearing denied, 349 U.S. 925, 75 S.Ct. 657 (1955).

4. See generally, Peter W. Hogg, Joanne E. Magee, & Jinyan Li, Princi-ples of Canadian Income Tax Law 82–86 (5th ed. 2005); Victor Thuronyi, Com-parative Tax Law Ch. 7.2.2 (2003); Rob-in Woellner, Stephen Barkoczy, Shirley Murphy & Chris Evans, Australian Tax-ation Law ¶¶ 7–3–040 (17th ed. 2007).

terms of income being likened to "fruit" or a "flow:"[5]

> The fundamental relation of 'capital' to 'income' has been much discussed by economists, the former being likened to the tree or the land, the latter to the fruit or the crop; the former depicted as a reservoir supplied from springs, the latter as the outlet stream, to be measured by its flow during a period of time.

The relationship between "income" and "capital" in the source concept of income also derives, in part, from the distinction in trust law between the interests of a life tenant (income) and the remainder (principal).[6]

The concept of income that underlies an income tax system may or may not produce different results for a taxpayer. For example, most common forms of receipts, such as wages, rents, dividends, and interest would be equally taxable under both an accretion concept of income or a source concept of income. Alternatively, consider the potential tax treatment of a "windfall." Under an accretion concept of income, the taxpayer is clearly wealthier as a result of the windfall and should be taxed on the benefit. Under a source concept of income, the question is whether the windfall is from a taxable source. If it is not, the windfall should be received tax free. Also, consider the taxation of a capital gain from the sale of property. The realized gain is clearly an increase in wealth that is taxable under the accretion concept of income. But under the source concept of income, the gain is not a "flow" from the taxpayer's capital. Rather, the proceeds from the sale of the property merely represent the seller's capital, albeit in different form, and should not be taxable.

Once again, tax systems do not purely follow one theoretical model or the other. Thus, while the United States' income tax generally follows the accretion concept of income, some items are excluded from income due to their source.[7] Similarly, tax systems based on the source concept of income may also tax capital gains.

The Australian income tax is based, in part, on the source concept of income. A taxpayer in Australia is taxed on "income according to ordinary concepts" and other amounts statutorily included in assessable income.[8] The case that follows explores the concept of "income according to ordinary concepts." Consider how

---

5. Eisner v. Macomber, 252 U.S. 189, 40 S.Ct. 189 (1920).

6. Robin Woellner, Stephen Barkoczy, Shirley Murphy & Chris Evans, Australian Taxation Law ¶ ¶ 7–3–040 (17th ed. 2007).

7. For example, Section 103 of the Internal Revenue Code excludes from income interest on any State or local bond.

8. §§ 6–5, 6–10 (Income Tax Assessment Act 1997) (Australia).

the taxpayers in this case would be taxed under an accretion concept of income.

COMMISSIONER OF TAXATION
v. COOKE & SHERDEN*
Australian Tax Court, 1980.
10 ATR 696, 29 ALR 202, 80 ATC 4140.

* * *

THE COURT delivered the following written judgment.

THE BACKGROUND

The taxpayers, two married couples, were engaged in the selling of soft drinks on a door-to-door basis. * * *

* * *

Each couple carried on the business of selling the manufacturer's drinks in the area assigned to that couple. Each chose to hire from the manufacturer the truck on which the bottles were carried and each of the male respondents habitually drove the truck and delivered bottles to the customers' residences. * * *

In the winter of each of the three years of income under consideration each couple took a holiday of about a week's duration at a place in Queensland, or outside Australia in the Pacific Ocean. The manufacturer offered to pay the charges for transportation and accommodation and, in fact, did bear those charges. Each holiday was taken by the respondents, and provided by the manufacturer, by way of participation in a "holiday scheme" controlled by the manufacturer. The manufacturer claimed to exercise a discretionary and gratuitous benevolence to those who satisfactorily performed agreements of the kind to which the respondents were parties. Each of the manufacturers published at different times within the relevant period statements about the schemes. One example will indicate the terms on which holidays might be offered:

Rules for Holiday Scheme

* * *

The island holiday scheme is designed to encourage every retailer to do his best to promote his sales during the year commencing 1st July, 1970, and although this is purely a gratuitous gesture by the management and no legal rights are conferred upon any retailer by reason of the scheme, the management is anxious to see that the efforts of retailers who reach their allotted quotas of sales are recognized.

---

* Footnotes with case citations omitted.

The following general rules have been prepared to cover the arrangements: 1. The holiday period is to be approximately one week taken during the months of June and July unless the committee otherwise determines. 2. No cash payment in lieu of the holiday trip will be made. 3. Each retailer, in order to be considered, must be a fully effective retailer at the time of the holiday trip. 4. Each retailer accepted by the committee will receive one ticket for himself and one ticket for his wife for the holiday trip. He is not at liberty to transfer either ticket to any other person but must go himself and take his wife. This is only a discretionary holiday scheme for retailer and wife, not a negotiable reward. Our objective is to give the retailer's wife a holiday as much as the retailer. If the wife cannot go or if a retailer is single (unattached) a second ticket may be issued to a lady companion in lieu of a wife, provided the committee considers that this person is genuinely in lieu of a wife and not just a fill-in for someone because the retailer thinks there is a free ticket to be used. 5. Any retailers who negotiate any transferring of stock or trading in sales between one another in order to indicate an apparent increase in individual sales or otherwise take part in any practice considered unfair by the committee will be automatically disqualified for two years. 6. The committee will exclude from further participation in the scheme any individual or individuals reported by the manager of a scheme holiday resort to have misconducted or misbehaved in any way. 7. The committee may, without notice, exclude any individual or individuals from the scheme. 8. The decision of the committee on any matter arising in connexion with the scheme shall be final.

* * *

The male respondents ... believed the assertion to be true which is contained in the manufacturer's "Rules for Holiday Scheme," that "No cash payment in lieu of the holiday trip will be made," and the parties to the appeals made their submissions on the assumption that those persons for whose transportation and accommodation in connexion with a holiday the manufacturer offered to pay had no means of obtaining any other benefit in lieu of what was offered.

The taxpayers could not hope to receive money from the manufacturer if they did not take the benefit, and they acquired no rights against the carriers or resort proprietors which they might convert into money. Nevertheless, the holiday was paid for by the manufacturer, and satisfied a desire of each taxpayer, and the Commissioner contends that the value of that benefit is part of the income of each partnership, and thus increases the assessable income of each taxpayer.

* * *

p∿c.

The Commissioner adjusted the net income of the respective partnerships to include the amounts paid to provide the respondents' holidays. The respondents each objected to the inclusion in his or her assessable income of his or her individual interest in the increased amount of the net partnership income. Each objection was disallowed and each objection, at the instance of the taxpayer, was referred to a Board of Review. The Board unanimously upheld the objections, directing that the assessments be amended by excising from the income of each partnership for the years in question the sums included by the Commissioner as the cost of the holidays and that each partner's assessment be consequentially amended.

From these decisions the Commissioner appealed to the Supreme Court of Victoria. The appeals were heard together and dismissed. From that judgment the Commissioner sought and obtained leave to appeal to this Court.

THE ISSUES

Issue

The Commissioner seeks to uphold the assessments by reference both to § 25(1) and § 26(e) of the Income Tax Assessment Act 1936 (Cth). He contends that the value of the holidays constitutes income according to ordinary concepts, and furthermore that it is a benefit given to the taxpayers in respect of, or for or in relation directly or indirectly to, services rendered by them.

THE CONCEPT OF INCOME

*income
def.*

It is convenient first to look at the concept of income, to which the Act frequently refers but which it does not define. Whether a receipt is to be treated as income or not is determined according to "the ordinary concepts and usages of mankind" * * *, except where statute sweeps in particular receipts or amounts which would not ordinarily be taken to fall within the concept.

Although income is not defined by the Act, its provisions give some indication of its meaning. Thus, an indication may be found in the definition in § 6(1) of "income from personal exertion": "... income consisting of earnings, salaries, wages, commissions, fees, bonuses, pensions, superannuation allowances, retiring allowances and retiring gratuities, allowances and gratuities received in the capacity of employee or in relation to any services rendered, the proceeds of any business carried on by the taxpayer either alone or as a partner with any other person, any amount received as a bounty or subsidy in carrying on a business ..." "Income from property" is defined simply to mean "all income not being income from personal exertion".

In Federal Commissioner of Taxation v. Dixon, Dixon C.J. and Williams J. commented: "The definition in § 6 of 'income from personal exertion' or 'income derived from personal exertion' has always been used as a possible guide or test in cases where the question is whether a particular receipt is income or not. It is true that the definition is concerned only or chiefly with the difference, for the purposes of the rates of tax, between income from property and income from personal exertion, but, where any of the expressions contained in the definition are relevant, it is logical enough to use them as an indication that a given receipt is income". But the definition does not bring into the statutory concept of income what would not be found within the concept according to ordinary notions. As Windeyer, J. pointed out in Scott v. Federal Commissioner of Taxation: "The definition does not I think bring anything into charge as income. It refers to what is already by its nature income.... By describing what 'income from personal exertion' is, the definition is indirectly indicative of what income is. That is all: but otherwise it is irrelevant."

There are other provisions which indicate the nature of an income receipt. By § 25, the gross income of a taxpayer is divided into assessable income and exempt income; by the definition of taxable income in § 6(1), taxable income is assessable income reduced by allowable deductions; and by § 17 income tax at the rates declared by the Parliament is levied upon taxable income. The operation of this complex of provisions requires that taxable income must be, or be expressed as, a pecuniary amount. An item of income which could not be reckoned as money could not find its way into taxable income so as to be subjected to tax at a rate declared by the Parliament. And § 20 requires that income wherever derived and expenses wherever incurred be expressed in terms of Australian currency. So the Act sufficiently shows that the items of income are to be money or to be reckoned as money. Consistently with this notion, the Act makes particular provision for some non-pecuniary receipts by including within assessable income the value to the taxpayer of those receipts (see § 26(e) and (ea)), and thus brings a pecuniary amount to tax. The notion that the items of income are money or are to be reckoned as money accords with the ordinary concepts of income as "what comes into (the) pocket" to adapt Lord Macnaghten's phrase in Tennant v. Smith, [1892] AC 150 at p. 164. That is not to say that income must be received as money; it is sufficient if what is received is in the form of money's worth (Cross (Inspector of Taxes) v. London & Provincial Trust Ltd. per Greene M.R.) Nor is it necessary that an item of income be paid over to the taxpayer: it is sufficient, according to ordinary concepts and usages, that it be dealt with on his behalf or as he directs, as § 19 of the Act recognizes.

Smith

Although Tennant v. Smith was concerned with the operation of legislation different in structure from the Income Tax Assessment Act, some parts of their Lordships' speeches applied ordinary conceptions to the construction of the terms of the Act there under consideration. Thus Lord Halsbury L.C. said

> "I come to the conclusion that the Act refers to money payments made to the person who receives them, though, of course, I do not deny that if substantial things of money value were capable of being turned into money they might for that purpose represent money's worth and be therefore taxable.

> The illustration given in the argument of the mode of arriving at a trader's profits, and the mode of treating his stock-in-trade, suggests that money's worth may be treated as money for the purposes of the Act in cases where the thing is capable of being turned into money from its own nature."

And Lord Watson held that

> "profits ... in its ordinary acceptation, appears to me to denote something acquired which the acquirer becomes possessed of and can dispose of to his advantage—in other words, money—or that which can be turned to pecuniary account."

Lord Hannen said:

> "That which could be converted into money might reasonably be regarded as money—but that is not the case before us."

If a taxpayer receives a benefit which cannot be turned to pecuniary account, he has not received income as that term is understood according to ordinary concepts and usages.

The conversion of an item into money may occur, of course, in a variety of ways. It is not desirable (even if it be possible) to define in advance the ways in which conversion may possibly occur in order that a non-pecuniary item of receipt might be treated as an item of income. However, it will not often occur that a benefit to be enjoyed by a taxpayer cannot be turned to pecuniary account if the benefit be given up, or if it be employed in the acquisition of some other right or commodity.

If one were so to vary the facts of the present case that the tickets with which the taxpayers were provided could be surrendered by them for cash, the benefit which, on that hypothesis, the taxpayers would have received would have been converted into money, and would have constituted income if the origins of the receipt gave that character to it. Indeed, as the authorities show, it is not necessary that the pecuniary alternative be available by way of direct conversion of the benefit received (Heaton (Inspector of Taxes) v. Bell; Abbott v. Philbin).

In _Heaton v. Bell_ the taxpayer was an employee of a company which had introduced a voluntary car loan scheme for certain employees. Under the scheme the company bought cars, insured them, paid road fund tax and lent them to employees from whose weekly wages money was deducted according to the type of car on loan. If an employee cancelled the arrangement, as he was free to do on notice, the deduction from his pay ceased. By a majority it was held that on the true interpretation of the arrangement between company and employee, the monetary wage remained unaltered and that accordingly the respondent's emoluments, taxable under Sched. E of the Income Tax Act, 1952 (UK) were his gross wage before deduction. On that footing, of course, the relevant receipt was the monetary wage, part of which was applied to the hire of the car. But an alternative basis of assessment was upheld by a majority of their Lordships who held that the free hire of the car was a "perquisite" of the taxpayer's employment because he could have surrendered the free hire of the car and become entitled to a higher monetary wage than he was receiving.

Abbott v. Philbin was another example. There, the taxpayer, the secretary of a company, was granted an option to purchase shares in the company at a certain price, then the market price. The taxpayer exercised the option when the market price of the shares had increased, and he was assessed to tax on the difference between that market price and the sum of the option price and the cost of the option. This basis of assessment was rejected, and it was held that the monetary value (if any) of the option when granted was taxable. Although the option was not assignable, it was a benefit capable of being turned to pecuniary account as Lord Radcliffe explained: "That right is, in my opinion, analogous for this purpose to any other benefit in the form of land, objects of value or legal rights. It was not incapable of being turned into money or of being turned to pecuniary account within the meaning of these phrases in Tennant v. Smith merely because the option itself was not assignable. What the option did was to enable the holder at any time, at his choice, to obtain shares from the company which would themselves be pieces of property or property rights of value, freely convertible into money. Being in that position he could also at any time, at his choice, sell or raise money on his right to call for the shares, even though he could not put anyone he dealt with actually into his own position as option holder against the company. I think that the conferring of a right of this kind as an incident of service is a profit or perquisite which is taxable as such in the year of receipt, so long as the right itself can fairly be given a monetary value, and it is no more relevant for this purpose whether the option is exercised or not in that year, than it would be if the advantage received were in the form of some tangible form of commercial property."

In the present case it is unnecessary to answer the questions which his Lordship asked: "Must the inconvertibility arise from the nature of the thing itself; or can it be imposed merely by contractual stipulation? Does it matter that the circumstances are such that conversion into money is a practical, though not a theoretical, impossibility; or, on the other hand, that conversion, though forbidden, is the most probable assumption?" Whatever be the answer to these questions, and whether their answers depend upon principles universally applicable or upon the circumstances of particular cases, the respondents in the present cases could not have turned the benefits in fact received by them to pecuniary account. It is immaterial that the respondents would have had to expend money themselves had they wished to provide the holidays for themselves. If the receipt of an item saves a taxpayer from incurring expenditure, the saving is not income: income is what comes in, it is not what is saved from going out. A non-pecuniary receipt can be income if it can be converted into money; but if it be inconvertible, it does not become income merely because it saves expenditure.

The holidays which were enjoyed by the taxpayers in the present case provided them, at a cost to the manufacturers, with a non-convertible benefit. It seems curious that a benefit which has cost money is not convertible into money, either by sale or by some less direct mode of realization, and it may be that cases of this kind are to be found only where the benefit is gratuitously provided. If this be so, the inconvertible benefit falls outside the revenue net not because it is a gratuity, for a taxpayer may receive as income a benefit gratuitously provided (Federal Commissioner of Taxation v. Dixon); it falls outside the revenue net because it is not money or money's worth, and there is no statutory provision which widens the net to catch it. In particular, it falls outside § 20 which brings to tax the money value of consideration which is paid or given upon any transaction otherwise than in cash. In the present case, the Commissioner disavowed any reliance on that section.

If the definition of income from personal exertion in § 6(1) of the Act is referred to as a description of income, a question may arise whether the benefit of a holiday may be seen as the "proceeds of a business". The gratuitous provision of the benefit does not necessarily preclude its characterization as the proceeds of a business (Squatting Investment Co. Ltd. v. Federal Commissioner of Taxation and, on appeal, Federal Commissioner of Taxation v. Squatting Investment Co. Ltd.). But the inconvertibility of the benefit, which prevents it from falling within the general notion of income, takes it outside the proper ambit of the proceeds of the

business. Just as inconvertibility limited the connotation of "prof- ~~Comparison~~
its" in Tennant v. Smith, and was apt to limit the connotation of
"perquisite" in Heaton (Inspector of Taxes) v. Bell, so it limits the
connotation of "proceeds of a business" in § 6(1), for that term
does not go beyond proceeds which would be held to be income
according to ordinary concepts (Colonial Mutual Life Assurance
Society Ltd. v. Federal Commissioner of Taxation).

The benefit not being convertible into money or money's
worth, there was no receipt of income according to ordinary concepts, and the assessments are not supported by § 25(1). The
alternative foundation is § 26(e).

Section 26(e) of the Act

It is conceded that the relationship between retailer and manufacturer was not that of employee and employer, and that aspect of
§ 26(e) may be omitted from consideration. Omitting that aspect,
§ 26(e) includes in assessable income: "the value to the taxpayer of
all allowances, gratuities, compensations, benefits, bonuses and
premiums allowed, given or granted to him in respect of, or for or
in relation directly or indirectly to, any ... services rendered by
him, whether so allowed, given or granted in money, goods, land,
meals, sustenance, the use of premises or quarters or otherwise."

It has been suggested that § 26(e) applies only to receipts
within the general conception of income. See for instance Hayes v.
Federal Commissioner of Taxation per Fullagar, J.; Scott v. Federal
Commissioner of Taxation per Windeyer, J. Or as was said by
Bowen, C.J. in Eq. in Donaldson v. Federal Commissioner of
Taxation: "Perhaps the proposition is not so much that § 26(e)
applies only to income and not to capital items, but rather that it is
so worded that there is nothing it covers which would not be of an
income nature in any event."

Section 26(e) was explained by Windeyer, J. in Scott v. Federal
Commissioner of Taxation in this way: "As I read § 26(e) its
meaning and purpose is to ensure that certain receipts and advantages which are in truth rewards of a taxpayer's employment or
calling are recognized as part of his income. In other words the
enactment makes it clear that the income of a taxpayer who is
engaged in any employment or in the rendering of any services for
remuneration includes the value to him of everything that he in
fact gets, whether in money or in kind and however it be described,
which is a product or incident of his employment or a reward for
his services. If, instead of being paid fully in money, he is remunerated, in whole or in part, by allowances or advantages having a
money value for him they must be taken into account. The enactment does not bring within the tax-gatherer's net moneys or

moneys' worth that are not income according to general concepts. Rather, it prevents receipts of moneys or moneys' worth that are in reality part of a taxpayer's income from escaping the net."

Whether or not § 26(e) widens or strengthens the net cast by § 25(1)—a question which it is unnecessary now to resolve—the former provision applies, in the circumstances of the present cases, only if the benefit received by the taxpayers was in respect of or for or in relation directly or indirectly to services rendered by them.

The dual reference in § 26(e) to employment and services rendered conjures up the distinction between a contract of service and a contract for services to be found in decisions on workers' compensation legislation. Whether or not that is the distinction intended here, the expression "services rendered" must draw in situations not encompassed by the term "employment".

There is a general sense in which the giving or rendering of services may be used, in which case it is a term of wide import: Employers' Mutual Indemnity Association Ltd. v. Federal Commissioner of Taxation per Starke, J. But it must be read in the context of § 26(e). It may be, as Jenkinson, J. suggested in the judgment under appeal, that the expression should be understood in the way in which "work and labour done" is understood by lawyers.

In Employers' Mutual Indemnity Association Ltd. v. Federal Commissioner of Taxation the court held that when a company limited by guarantee, empowered to carry on all kinds of insurance business, investigated and adjusted and either resisted or paid claims made under policies issued by it, it did so on its own account in the course of its business and did not thereby render services to its members even though policies issued by the company were only to members.

Various views were expressed by the members of the court as to the notion of giving or rendering services.

They were analyzed subsequently by McTiernan, J. (himself a member of the court) in Revesby Credit Union Co-operative Ltd. v. Federal Commissioner of Taxation: "I consider that 'the rendering of services' should consist of the doing of an act for the benefit of another, which is more than the mere making of a contract and which goes beyond the performance of an obligation undertaken in the course of an ordinary commercial contract."

Here the parties were in the position of manufacturer and retailer. One sold and the other bought bottles of soft drinks. The retailer paid to the manufacturer a price for those drinks.

There were no services which the respondent retailers rendered to the manufacturers. Although the successful conduct of the retailers' respective businesses enhanced the sales by the manufac-

turers to the retailers, and added to the notoriety of the manufacturer's products, the conduct of the retailers' businesses was not a
service rendered to the manufacturers. The businesses were conducted for the benefit of the retailer, and the advantages which
thereby accrued to the manufacturers were not the product of
services rendered to the manufacturers. Advantages accrued to the
manufacturers because the retailers, independently of any obligation owed to the manufacturers, conducted their businesses in a
way which yielded advantages to both. It is true that the retailer
was required to keep a round book containing a record of customers, but we agree with Jenkinson, J. that this was no more than the
"performance of an obligation ancillary to the agreement for sale
and resale of the products."

The relationship was essentially one of seller and buyer. The *rationale*
taxpayers did not render services to the companies with which they
had contracted. The provision of holidays was not part of any
contractual relationship and in our view the provision of holidays
could not be said to have been directly or indirectly for services
rendered by the taxpayers.

Neither of the foundations relied on by the appellant supports
the assessments. The appeals should be dismissed with costs.

Chapter 2

BENEFITS IN KIND

A. INTRODUCTION

EXCERPT FROM THE REPORT OF THE ROYAL COMMISSION ON TAXATION

Volume 3, pp. 43–46, 1966.

Benefits that "save the pocket" obviously increase the economic power of the recipient, just as do cash receipts that go into the pocket. One of the areas of inequity in the present system is the fact that many such benefits, which are untaxed or partially taxed, are available to some taxpayers and not to others. If benefits in kind are not taxed, the buyer and seller in a transaction can arrange that the seller be remunerated with tax-free benefits in kind with the tax saving divided between them.

Benefits in kind take many forms, ranging from substantial items like the use of a car or a house, life insurance, retirement benefits, provision of board and lodging, discounts on merchandise, and interest-free loans, to trivial items like a free Christmas turkey. Most such benefits arise from employment or from the operation of a business. The gross gain from any transaction can take the form of goods, services or the use of property.

The failure to tax benefits in kind gives tax units that can obtain their remuneration in this form an advantage over others. Furthermore, if some forms of benefits in kind are not taxed, it is equivalent to subsidizing the goods and services that are available free of tax, relative to all other consumer goods and services that can only be purchased from tax-paid income. The subsidized goods and services will be substituted for other goods and services.

When benefits in kind have an established market value, their taxation is a relatively simple matter. The form of the benefit is frequently the result of a specific deal between the buyer and seller

18

and is not shared with others. Frequently, however, these conditions do not exist.

Some of the relevant circumstances cannot be ascertained objectively because it will always be in the interest of the parties to these arrangements to understate the benefits for tax reasons. Because the possibilities of abuse are so great, we are firmly convinced that a very hard line must be taken towards the taxation of benefits in kind. This involves the adoption of several rules:

1. Ordinarily the recipient of benefits in kind should bring into his tax base what the benefits would cost if purchased in the market.

2. The tastes and preferences of recipients of benefits in kind should be ignored for tax purposes. It must be assumed that the recipient had a choice between the benefit itself and the receipt of a cash payment that would have enabled its purchase in the market. To the extent that the benefit is worth less to the recipient than its market costs, he should arrange to receive his remuneration in a different form or obtain additional remuneration to compensate for the tax liability implicit in the receipt of the benefit in kind.

3. Benefits in kind can be received in the course of performing services for a net gain, for example, the food and shelter consumed while out of town on a legitimate business trip. The objective here must be to bring into the individual's tax base:

   a) the extra cost of providing food and shelter that is of better quality or in greater quantity than would usually be purchased by the individual from tax-paid income;

   b) any reduction in personal expenditure that is made possible by way by being away from home;

   c) any expense incurred to satisfy the individual rather than to produce income.

   Because the tax administration cannot possibly determine the style or preference of each individual, and therefore cannot determine in an objective fashion the value of these benefits, arbitrary standards should be adopted and the value of benefits in kind in excess of the standards should be brought into the tax base of the recipient.

4. Where a common facility provides benefits in kind to a number of individuals simultaneously, the benefit should be apportioned among them, failing which, a special tax should be imposed on the party providing the benefit.

While we recognize that the application of these rules would not be easy or costless, we are convinced that such benefits have thus far not been dealt with adequately. The result has been a lessening in taxpayer morale and loss of faith in the integrity of the tax system. The revenue loss may not be great, but to those who are able to obtain them, tax-free benefits may be very significant. We feel that the law should be made more explicit and that greater administrative effort should be devoted to enforcing the law dealing with benefits in kind. We also recommend later more stringent reporting requirements in this connection for businesses and organizations.

Note

The Royal Commission on Taxation Report, commonly known as the "Carter Commission Report" in honor of the Commission Chair, Kenneth Carter, was the product of an extensive study of tax reform options in Canada.[1] The Carter Commission Report has been described as "the high-water mark of pragmatic thinking about a comprehensive tax base . . ."[2] and "the high water mark of egalitarian, redistributive tax policymaking in Canadian history."[3]

The excerpt from the Carter Commission Report describes the policy considerations in taxing "in kind benefits," also commonly referred to as "fringe benefits." Fringe benefit taxation raises some of the most fundamental questions about tax "fairness," protection of the tax base, maintaining respect for the tax system, and administrative concerns such as valuation of benefits and reporting requirements. These questions may be addressed through legislation or administratively by the agency charged with enforcing the revenue laws. The following two decisions deal with the taxation of employer-provided educational benefits. See if you agree with each court's approach.

DETCHON v. HER MAJESTY THE QUEEN*
Tax Court of Canada, 1996.
1 C.T.C. 2475, 11 C.C.P.B. 291.

Rɪᴘ J.T.C.C.:

1. The appellants Eric Detchon and Clifford Goodwin appeal income tax assessments for the 1985 and 1986 taxation years on

---

1. See generally, Boris Bittker, "Income Tax Reform in Canada: The Report of the Royal Commission on Taxation," 35 U. Chi. L. Rev. 673 (1969).

2. Charlotte Crane, "Government Transfer Payments and Assistance: A Challenge for the Design of Broad–Based Taxes," 59 SMU L. Rev. 589, 590 n.3 (2006).

3. Lisa Philipps, "Public Perspectives on Privatization: Taxing the Market Citizen and Inequality in an Age of Privatization," 63 Law & Contemp. Prob. 111, 114 (2000).

* Some footnotes omitted.

the basis neither of them received a benefit in respect of employment pursuant to paragraph 6(1)(a) of the Income Tax Act, R.S.C. 1985, c. 1 (5th Supp.) (the "Act")[1] as a result of their children attending their employer's school, and alternatively, if a benefit was conferred, the value of the benefit received by each of the appellants was less than determined by the Minister of National Revenue (the "Minister").

2. In assessing the appellants, the Minister considered that each of them received an employment benefit the value of which was equal to the tuition fees that the parents of other students were required to pay Bishop's College School ("BCS"). Detchon had one child attending BCS for the whole of 1985 and two other children for the term September to December 1985. All three children attended BCS during both terms in 1986. The Minister added the amounts of $9,355 and $16,116 to his income for 1985 and 1986 respectively.

* * *

6. During the years in appeal the appellants were employed as teachers at BCS in Lennoxville, Quebec. BCS is a private educational institution incorporated as a non-profit corporation under the provisions of the Quebec Companies Act. It offers courses to males and females at the secondary level (grades 7 to 11) and grade 12. The school has both day students and boarding students.

7. Lawrence Sakamoto was Treasurer and Director of Finance at BCS in 1985 and 1986. At time of trial he was Treasurer. He stated BCS caters to people who in 1995 can afford to pay tuition and board aggregating $23,000 for their child's education. Students from Mexico, Japan, Venezuela, Spain, United States and Canada and other countries attend BCS.

8. For the years in appeal the teachers at BCS had no "formal" contract said Sakamoto. They simply received a letter setting out their salary for the year. Although it was not stated in writing, Sakamoto testified, the teachers at BCS had certain obligations due to the fact BCS was primarily a boarding school: the teachers had to live on campus, attend chapel every morning, be available 24 hours a day, seven days a week and send their school age children to BCS. The teachers were also expected to eat at the school cafeteria since a "family atmosphere" was encouraged. BCS employed "about 40 teachers" during the years in appeal.

---

1. Paragraph 6(1)(a) provides:

6(1) There shall be included in computing the income of a taxpayer for a taxation year as income from an office or employment ...

(a) the value of board, lodging and other benefits of any kind whatever received or enjoyed by him in the year in respect of, in the course of, or by virtue of an office or employment ...

9.   On the other hand, Sakamoto explained, the teachers were aware of the school's policy of free tuition to children of staff. He described the free tuition as "part of the culture" of BCS. He stated staff "knew what is required of you by the nature of the place and what you are entitled to." Staff entitled to free tuition for their children included administrators, including Sakamoto who sent his child to BCS.

10.   Sakamoto insisted that teachers' children were obliged to attend BCS. This was due to "the nature of the school." He explained members of staff live on campus with their families and would not be "good for our image if [teachers'] children of school age go to a public school".

11.   "BCS" he said, "had no other choice." For a child to go to a public school would mean, Sakamoto declared, "the staff child [is] playing for the opposition".

12.   Sakamoto said that if a teacher, for example, did not send his or her child to BCS "the teacher would have to think it over carefully." He stated BCS did not have a policy of dismissing a teacher if a child did not attend the school, but suggested the teacher would be reprimanded by the school's headmaster.

13.   It was advantageous to BCS for the staff to send their children to the school, Sakamoto declared. Traditionally, he said, children of BCS staff do better academically than other students and so raise the average of the school. They also participate more actively in extra-curricular activities. These children are role models. He also stated that if the children attend BCS the staff is better able to devote their time to the school; their time is not disturbed with their child's daily travel to school in Lennoxville.

14.   BCS has never achieved full capacity and its cost of having its staff's children attend is "virtually nothing," Sakamoto stated. These children, he said, "do not take places of other children." The children of BCS staff are fully integrated in the school's general population. They attend the same classes and follow the same programs as paying students.

15.   Salaries are not dependent on whether their child is attending BCS, Sakamoto stated. There is no increase in a salary paid to a teacher, for example, once his or her child leaves the school. A staff parent cannot transfer his or her right to send a child to BCS to another person, for example, to a niece or nephew.

16.   Sakamoto acknowledged that in 1985 and 1986 BCS incurred losses from its operations. "The school," he said, "has more deficits than break-even or income." BCS is a registered charity.

17.   Sakamoto estimated that 14 or 15 children of BCS staff attended the school during 1985 and 1986. Approximately 300

students attended BCS during those years of which 240 were boarders and 60 were day students. Children of staff were day students. Fees for room and board were $11,000 for the 1984–1985 term and $11,950 for the 1985–1986 term. Fees for day students for the 1984–1985 term and 1985–1986 term were $6,900 and $7,470 respectively.

18. The financial statements of BCS for financial years ending June 30, 1985, 1986 and 1987 were produced as evidence. Respondent's counsel calculated that for the period ending June 30, 1985, the cost of instruction and "instructional administration" to BCS was $1,503,894. Based on a student population of 300, including staff children, the cost of instruction and related administration for each student was $5,013. Similar costs per student for 1986 and 1987 fiscal years were $5,504 and $5,023 respectively.

Costs

19. During 1985 and 1986 Detchon's salary from BCS was $25,582 and $30,621 respectively and Goodwin's salary was $28,675 and $26,619 respectively.

20. Neither Detchon nor Goodwin paid any tuition for their children. They did, however, pay personal service fees for each child in the amount of $300 for the 1985–86 school year and $500 for the 1985–86 school year. These fees covered transportation costs and rental expenses for school athletics, accident insurance, cadet fees, student identification cards and costs of movies and dances. Sports were compulsory at BCS. Detchon added he also paid for school uniforms, trips and books; these expenses were approximately $1,500 a year.

21. Respondent's counsel asked Sakamoto "What is so special at BCS you'd want to pay so much?" Sakamoto replied BCS provides a "traditional, safe education [with] old values". He also stated that if a child is barred by Quebec law from attending an English school in Quebec, that child may attend BCS.

22. Sakamoto explained that the high tuition fees at BCS are the result of the school not receiving financial assistance from the government of Quebec. * * *

23. The children of the appellants received certificates of eligibility to be educated in English since the appellants received their elementary education in English in Quebec: section 73 of the Charter. Thus, the appellants' children had the right to attend English public elementary and high schools in Lennoxville at no cost.

24. Detchon testified he is in his twenty-sixth year of teaching at BCS. His wife also taught at BCS in the years in appeal and at time of trial was the school's Director of Admissions. Detchon confirmed that no formal employment contract existed between him

and BCS for the years in appeal. At the beginning of the year the headmaster sent a letter outlining salary for the upcoming year. There were no written terms or conditions of employment, Detchon stated, but a teacher was "expected to be there the whole working day (and) work hard ... attend chapel ... [coach] sports ... [eat] meals on campus," at least breakfast and lunch, and "dinner, if on duty." Teachers may also be "on call." Detchon stated teachers are on duty one out of every three days. Teachers were expected to be on campus, or "on call," in the event, for example, a child "required help" during the evening. "When you live on campus, your house is not your house ... You have children coming and going all the time."

25. In Detchon's view he had to send his children to BCS. Before attending BCS, Detchon's children attended Lennoxville Public School, an elementary school in Lennoxville.

26. Detchon acknowledged that he was not in a financial position to pay tuition fees to BCS for his children. His last child graduated from BCS three years ago, he said, and he "finished paying BCS this past year."

* * *

Analysis

49. It is quite a stretch to consider that only BCS obtains a benefit when its teachers' children attend the school. While it may be useful for its purposes to have its teachers' children attend BCS, it is no less an advantage for the employees of BCS to avail their children of a product that demands a good amount of money in the education marketplace.

50. There is simply no evidence that the appellants were legally obligated to send their children to BCS or horrendous consequences would ensue. The appellants would not have been discharged from their teaching positions. There may have been professional and community pressure to send the children to BCS, but nothing more. The appellants may have been obligated under their contract with BCS to do certain things, such as live on campus, eat in the cafeteria, be available at all times, but sending their children to BCS was not one of the obligations.

51. I agree * * * that the free tuition was a benefit for purposes of paragraph 6(1)(a). The free tuition represented something of value in a material or economic sense to the appellants. The appellants, as a result of the free tuition, were not being returned to a previous economic state, as in Huffman v. R. (sub nom. Huffman v. Canada), [1990] 2 C.T.C. 132, 90 D.T.C. 6405

(F.C.A.), at page 6407, for example. To put it succinctly: the appellants got something for nothing.

52. The free tuition arose by virtue of the contract of employment; the circumstances here are different from those in McNeill v. R. (sub nom. McNeill v. The Queen), [1987] 1 C.F. 119. The arrangement for free tuition was part of the terms of employment. The tuition was received by the appellants by virtue of their employment with BCS. The employer was in fact paying for an ordinary personal expense of the appellants: Krull v. Canada (Attorney General) (sub nom. Canada (Attorney General) v. Hoefele), [1996] 1 C.T.C. 131, 95 D.T.C. 5602 (F.C.A.) per Linden, J.A., at page 8. Were they not employees of BCS they would have to pay the regular tuition fees for their children to attend the school. The free tuition offered by BCS is no different from a manufacturer, for example, giving a product to an employee. The employer is giving something of value to its employee at no cost. If another employer in Lennoxville offered its employees free tuition at BCS for their children, such advantage would surely be a benefit to the employees. I see no reason why the appellants should be treated differently. It is clear the free tuition was a benefit from employment contemplated by paragraph 6(1)(a) of the Act.

53. I do not agree with appellants' counsel that the value of the benefit is the additional or incremental cost to BCS of having the appellants' children attend the school. In cases such as Houle, supra, and Wallace, supra, the courts recognized the value of a benefit to the shareholder to be the operating costs of the boat to the corporation and the operating costs incurred by the corporation were market costs. I have been cited no Canadian authority permitting me to value the benefit to the appellants at BCS's incremental cost of having additional students and ignore both the average cost to BCS of teaching a student and the price paid to BCS.

54. I do not agree * * * that the value of the benefit is the cost of obtaining education elsewhere in Quebec. The evidence of Sakamoto was that the tuition fee at BCS would be significantly reduced if it had received provincial grants. Other private schools in Quebec receive provincial government grants which permit them to charge low tuition fees. The appellants educate their children at BCS and it is the value of the benefit at BCS which is to be considered. One must consider facts as they exist. For example, to reduce the value of the benefit to the difference between the average cost per student at BCS and the grant per student other private schools receive is a hypothetical exercise.

55. The true value of the benefit received by the appellants a year is the economic value of the one year's education at BCS. This, of course, is difficult, if not impossible to determine. Who can say

what a year's education is worth? That is an exercise for economists and educators. I am left with a more mundane challenge: to value for tax purposes the value of the free tuition.

56.   There is no evidence before me that parents who are not employed by BCS, but who earn similar income to the appellants, may send their children to BCS for free or reduced tuition. If there was such evidence, I would be inclined to value the benefit to the appellants at the amount of fees, if any, paid by such parents.

57.   There is no obligation for an employer to charge its employees for a good or service any more than its actual costs of the good or service. The employer need not add any profit element and indirect overhead costs to any good or service it provides to its employees: ABC Steel Buildings Ltd. v. Minister of National Revenue, [1974] C.T.C. 2176, 74 D.T.C. 1124 (T.R.B.). Respondent's counsel stated that an analysis of the financial statements of BCS suggest the average cost per student for fiscal years 1985, 1986 and 1987 was $5,013, $5,504 and $5,023 respectively. (Each fiscal year of BCS straddles two taxation years of the appellants.) These amounts are close to the amounts applied by the Minister in valuing the benefits and, in the circumstances, valuing the benefit at the average cost per student is an appropriate method of valuation. My conclusion may appear harsh to the appellants. Unfortunately education is not a product, such as a suit, that is to be valued in the hands of the recipient of the gift and not what it cost the donor: Rogerson, supra. In Pepper v. Hart, supra, Lord Griffiths, at page 618, noted:

> it is surely common knowledge that the provision of free or subsidised education for the children of those teaching in independent schools was part of their usual terms of employment and that the salaries paid would be wholly insufficient to meet a charge to tax based on the full fees of the school.

58.   Here, too, it is obvious that the salaries of the appellants are insufficient to meet the tax assessed on the value of the benefit added to their incomes. However, it would not be just and reasonable to other Canadian taxpayers that employees, solely because of their occupations and low level salaries, obtain a tax free benefit from an employer who does not pay a higher wage. To permit such a tax advantage to one group of taxpayers is not within the object and spirit of the Act. The average cost to BCS of educating a student is a sensible method of valuing the benefit.

* * *

60.   I propose to allow the appeals only for the purposes of referring the assessments back to the Minister to reassess on the basis the value of the benefits was the lower of the average cost per

student to BCS for each year and the value actually assessed. I think this is fair in the circumstances. * * *

* * *

Appeals allowed.

GUAY v. HER MAJESTY THE QUEEN*
The Federal Court of Canada, 1997.
97 D.T.C. 5267, 3 C.T.C. 276.

DÉCARY, J.A.:

1. The applicant is a federal public servant employed by the Department of Foreign Affairs and International Trade (the Department). He is part of the group of employees known as rotational employees, who must perform their duties both in Ottawa and at Canada's missions abroad and who may spend half to two thirds of their careers abroad. A rotational employee who begins to work for the Department is immediately informed that he or she must accept "the principle of rotational employment inherent in such work" and be prepared "to accept any assignment that the Department considers useful or necessary, either in Ottawa or at any of Canada's diplomatic or consular missions abroad."

2. Rotational employees face a significant problem when it comes to obtaining French-language primary and secondary education for their children. There is no equivalent abroad of the French-language public education available in Quebec and Ontario; children who begin or continue their education in French in Quebec or Ontario or who wish to begin or continue it abroad have no real choice but to attend, both in Canada and abroad, one of the network of French-language institutions under the French Agence pour l'enseignement français à l'étranger. That network includes about 400 lycées or schools in 127 countries (according to 1995 figures) and, in all those countries, uses the curriculum of the French Ministry of Education.* * *

3. Accordingly, because their children, when abroad, must attend an institution that is part of the network of French-language institutions, rotational employees who have returned to Ottawa or are in Ottawa pending an assignment abroad prefer to send their children to the Lycée Claudel. The evidence shows that it is difficult, and often impossible, to enrol a child in one of the network's institutions abroad if the child has not already begun or continued his or her education in Canada at an institution that is part of the network.

* Some footnotes omitted.

4. The problem, of course, is that the Lycée Claudel in Ottawa is a private institution, that an education there is not free and that the cost is very high. Thus, it cost the applicant $9,735.00 in 1991 to send his two children there, whereas he would not have had to spend anything if his children had attended public school in Gatineau, Quebec, where he lived.

5. To remedy this financial disadvantage for the Department's rotational employees, the Treasury Board Secretariat has adopted the following directive.

33.01. The provisions of this directive are available to career foreign service employees as defined in FSD 3.01(a) and to RCMP Liaison Officers, while serving in the headquarters city, in order to ensure continuity in French language education for their dependent children while serving outside Canada.

33.02. The deputy head may authorize payment of the cost of tuition, prescribed textbooks (up to the equivalent of Ontario Grade 12/OAC) and school supplies (up to the equivalent of Ontario Grade 8) incurred at the Lycée Claudel in Ottawa in respect of:

(a) children who were registered in the French lycée system during the assignment of the employee abroad;

(b) children who commence primary schooling in the first year of the lycée system during the assignment of an employee in Ottawa following an assignment abroad; and

(c) children who are enrolled in the Lycée Claudel where an employee has not been offered an initial assignment outside Canada.

33.03. Payment authorized in accordance with Section 33.02 shall normally be limited to the two-year period immediately following:

(a) the employee's assignment to Ottawa from abroad, and/or

(b) the date on which the employee commences rotational employment.

33.04. Exceptions to the limitations prescribed by Section 33.03 may be considered on an individual basis by the deputy head of the employing department, who may approve extensions of up to one year at a time as a result of operational requirements. This deputy head discretion would also extend to situations where an employee is assigned to or from Canada during the academic year.

6. In practice, parents who send their children to the Lycée Claudel in Ottawa pay the cost themselves and are then reimbursed

by the Department. If they remain in Ottawa for more than two consecutive years, they are told that "you are required to furnish a letter from your assignment officer stating that you have not been offered a posting or that you did not refuse a posting. Reimbursement can only be authorized upon receipt of this letter".

7. In his assessment for the 1991 taxation year, the Minister of National Revenue (the Minister) included in the applicant's income the $9,735.00 the applicant had received in 1991 from his employer, the Government of Canada, to reimburse him for the expenses he had incurred to send his children to the Lycée Claudel in Ottawa. The Minister initially characterized the amount received by the applicant as an "allowance", which made paragraph 6(1)(b) of the Income Tax Act (the Act) applicable, but later changed his mind and is now arguing that the amount is a reimbursement of actual expenses incurred by the applicant and hence a benefit received by the applicant by virtue of his employment within the meaning of paragraph 6(1)(a) of the Act. The introductory portion of that paragraph reads as follows:

6(1) There shall be included in computing the income of a taxpayer for a taxation year as income from an office or employment such of the following amounts as are applicable:

(a) the value of board, lodging and other benefits of any kind whatever received or enjoyed by him in the year in respect of, in the course of, or by virtue of an office or employment....

8. After an exhaustive review of the case law, the Tax Court of Canada Judge confirmed the notice of assessment. His conclusion reads as follows:

From the foregoing analysis, I am inclined to conclude that the reimbursement by the Government of Canada of the appellant's expenses with respect to his children's education falls within the "fiscal scope" of paragraph 6(1)(a) of the Act. This conclusion is based on the following factors:

(a) these expenses have to do with a personal matter, i.e. the education of an employee's children;

(b) they were incurred as a result of the appellant's decision to enrol his children in a French-language education system, even though that decision was entirely understandable in the circumstances;

(c) they were incurred in anticipation of the appellant's being posted outside Canada.

All things considered, the relationship between these expenses, which were reimbursed by the Government of Canada, and the appellant's employment, although a close one, does not seem to me to be close enough to place the reimbursement of those expenses beyond the fiscal scope of paragraph 6(1)(a) of the Act. Furthermore, the appellant has not shown that the reimbursement of the expenses here in issue did not, under certain circumstances, provide him with an economic benefit. . . .

9. With respect, we are of the view that this conclusion is inconsistent with the finding of fact made earlier by the Judge, namely:

First of all, the tuition fees of an employee's dependent children are indisputably expenses of a personal nature. In paying those expenses, parents are discharging a personal obligation which, in principle, is incumbent upon them in their capacity as parents. The reimbursement of those expenses by an employer at first glance constitutes a benefit within the meaning of paragraph 6(1)(a) of the Income Tax Act. However, there is something particular about this expense in this case. These fees were paid by the appellant as a result of the condition regarding the rotational nature of his position. That condition was inherent in the appellant's employment with the Government of Canada. His children's attendance at the Lycée Claudel was the only realistic option if the appellant decided that his children were to continue their education in a French education system when outside Canada.

10. Once the only realistic option available to an employee, because of the rotational nature of his or her employment, is to enrol his or her children in the only institution in Ottawa that offers the French education system recognized throughout the world, it can no longer be concluded that there is an insufficient relationship between the expenses incurred by the employee and the employee's employment.

11. The ultimate decision is, of course, made by the employee, but in reality the decision is imposed on the employee by the very nature of the employment. The employer has itself recognized the exceptional situation faced by its rotational employees. In the fulfilment of his legal duty to ensure that his children receive an education, and for the perfectly legitimate purpose of ensuring continuity in that education, the applicant was for all practical purposes compelled by the requirements of his employment to decline the free education available in the public system and to pay the cost of a private education system, a cost the Department's non-rotational employees do not have to pay.

12. The Minister made much of the choice open to the applicant not to take his children abroad with him or to enrol them in public school when his duties kept him in Ottawa. This is not a realistic argument. The Minister of National Revenue seems in this

regard to be going directly against the policy of the Department of Foreign Affairs and International Trade. The applicant's choice in this case is dictated by the interests of his children, which require that they accompany their parents abroad and that their parents' relocation compromise, slow down or disturb their education as little as possible. The Minister also argued that the expenses were incurred not because of an actual change in the applicant's place of work, but in anticipation of an uncertain event, namely the posting of the applicant abroad. However, the evidence shows that the applicant's status as a rotational employee makes his posting abroad unavoidable and that if he is not posted within two years or if he refuses a posting, the steps necessary to prevent any abuse have been taken by the Department in section 33.03 of the directive referred to above.

13.   We therefore conclude that the relationship between the reimbursed expenses and the applicant's employment is sufficient to exclude the reimbursement from the tax field of paragraph 6(1)(a).

14.   To determine whether a reimbursement is a benefit within the meaning of paragraph 6(1)(a), it must be ascertained whether the applicant's net worth increased following the payment or, rather, whether the payment simply restored the taxpayer to the position he would have been in had it not been for the expenses incurred because of the requirements of his employment. This principle was expressed as follows by our colleague Linden, J.A. in Canada (Attorney General) v. Hoefele:[7]

> Therefore, the question to be decided in each of these instances is whether the taxpayer is restored or enriched. Though any number of terms may be used to express this effect—for example, reimbursement, restitution, indemnification, compensation, make whole, save the pocket—the underlying principle remains the same. If, on the whole of a transaction, an employee's economic position is not improved, that is, if the transaction is a zero-sum situation when viewed in its entirety, a receipt is not a benefit and, therefore, is not taxable under paragraph 6(1)(a). It does not make any difference whether the expense is incurred to cover costs of doing the job, of travel associated with work or of a move to a new work location, as long as the employer is not paying for the ordinary, every day expenses of the employee.

15.   In the case at bar, the reimbursement by the Government of the cost of the applicant's children's education at the Lycée

---

7.   (1995), [1996] 1 F.C. 322 (Fed. C.A.), at page 332, leave to appeal refused by the Supreme Court of Canada on (1996) (sub nom. Minister of National Revenue v. Hoefele), 204 N.R. 398 (note) (S.C.C.).

Claudel in Ottawa in no way increased the applicant's net worth; the reimbursement put him in the same position as if he had not been compelled by the nature of his employment to send his children there.

16.   The application for judicial review will be allowed, the Tax Court of Canada's decision set aside and the case referred back to the Tax Court of Canada with the instruction that the taxpayer's appeal must be allowed and the matter referred back to the Minister of National Revenue so that he can reassess the taxpayer on the basis of these reasons.

Application for judicial review granted.

Note

The taxation of fringe benefits in the United States is largely codified in the Internal Revenue Code.[4] Section 132 sets out a basic framework for the taxation of fringe benefits and an array of other sections deal with the tax treatment of certain specific benefits such as employer provided life insurance,[5] health insurance,[6] dependent care assistance,[7] and retirement benefits.[8] To see how the taxpayers in the *Detchon* and *Guay* cases would fair under the Internal Revenue Code, read Section 117 and Regulation § 1.117–4(c).

B.   TAXATION OF FRINGE BENEFITS

Tax systems generally tax fringe benefits under one of three approaches.[1] The first is to begin by viewing fringe benefits as part of an employee's compensation that are presumptively included in income, subject to specific exclusions and administrative considerations regarding valuation and other matters. A second approach selectively denies the employer a deduction for providing the benefit, thereby taxing it at the employer's tax rate. The United States employs a combination of these two approaches through Sections 61, 132, and 274 of the Internal Revenue Code.

A third approach to the taxation of fringe benefits is to exclude the benefit from the employee's calculation of income and impose a separate tax (a "fringe benefits tax") on the value of the benefits at the employer level. Australia and New Zealand are two countries that have adopted this approach.[2] In Australia, the fringe benefits tax was enacted in response to widespread use of untaxed or low-

---

4. See generally, Boris Bittker & Lawrence Lokken, Federal Taxation of Income, estates and Gifts ¶ ¶ 14.01–14.02 (1999).

5. I.R.C. § 79.

6. I.R.C. §§ 105, 106.

7. I.R.C. § 129.

8. I.R.C. §§ 401–436.

1. Victor Thuronyi, Tax Law Design and Drafting 516–517 (2000).

2. Id. at 517.

taxed fringe benefits in the country. Taxation of fringe benefits at the employer level was also viewed as helping to address many of the most nettlesome administrative problems resulting from attempting to tax each individual employee receiving a particular benefit.[3]

Theoretical and administrative issues still remain under the fringe-benefits-tax approach. For example, it still must be determined which particular benefits are subject to the separate tax at the employer level and which benefits excluded from tax at the employer level should be taxable to the employee. Thus, detailed guidance is needed to determine the benefits subject to the fringe benefits tax and those that are totally exempt from taxation. Benefits also must still be valued, albeit at the employer level. What should be the relationship between the rates for the fringe benefits tax and the income tax? Should the fringe benefits tax rate be higher, lower, or the same as the employee's tax rate? Does the answer to that question depend on whether the goal of the tax is to discourage employers from providing fringe benefits or simply to remain tax-neutral as between cash and in kind compensation? If employees are taxed at graduated rates, is it possible for the fringe benefits tax to reach the same result as taxing the benefit directly to the employees? Should adjustments be made in the fringe benefits tax to take account of the fact that the employee is not taxed or that the employee might have been entitled to a deduction if the benefit had been acquired directly?

The Australian fringe benefits tax (FBT) is detailed and illustrates many of the issues presented by implementation of such a tax.[4] The FBT is an employer-level tax levied at the highest marginal tax rate applicable to individuals plus the Australian medicare tax rate. The base for the tax is the employer's "fringe benefits taxable amount," which is calculated on the "taxable values" of the fringe benefits provided during the year, plus a "gross up" (an increase in the tax's base) that accounts for the fact that the employer is entitled to a deduction for payment of FBT.[5] Taxable values are calculated under various methods (e.g., market value, cost to employer, or by formula) depending on the particular fringe benefit, and reduced by any payment made by the employee. Employees exclude covered fringe benefits from income but the fringe benefits are accounted for in determining related benefits, such as entitlement for other social benefits or medicare levies.

---

3. Hugh Ault & Brian Arnold, Comparative Income Taxation–A Structural Analysis 174 (2d ed. 2004).

4. See generally, Robin Woellner, Stephen Barkoczy, Shirley Murphy & Chris Evans, Australian Taxation Law Ch. 26 (17th ed. 2007).

5. The amount of the gross up depends on whether the employer also receives a credit in calculation of the Australian goods and services tax. Tax-exempt employers may receive a rebate of FBT. Id. at ¶ 26–000.

Twelve specific fringe benefits are identified for purposes of the FBT and there is a residual category designed to catch other benefits not included in another category.[6] The specific fringe benefit categories include the personal use of an employer car, employer loans, debt forgiveness by an employer, the provision of housing by an employer, stand-by airline transportation provided to airline employees, parking for an employee's vehicle, and discounts on employer provided property.[7] The residual category of fringe benefits catches items such as employer-provided insurance, and free or discounted employer services.[8] Specific exclusions from the FBT are provided for several items and there are rules designed to help coordinate the FBT with the income tax. Thus, exclusions from the FBT are provided for salary and wages, dividends and employee share plans, pension contributions, items of small value, and certain items with a work connection.[9]

RULING 1999/6

Australian Tax Office, 1996.

What this Ruling is about

1. This Ruling sets out the tax implications of flight rewards (see paragraph 2) received from consumer loyalty programs (see paragraph 3) following the decision of Foster, J. of the Federal Court in Payne v. FC of T (1996) 66 FCR 299; 96 ATC 4407; (1996) 32 ATR 516 (Payne's case). Rewards other than flight rewards, are not considered in this Ruling.

2. For the purposes of this Ruling, a "flight reward" has the following characteristics (being the characteristics of the program considered in Payne's case):

(a) the reward consists of a free flight (including a free holiday package), a flight upgrade, or free hotel accommodation or car hire that may attach to such free flights or paid flights;

(b) a flight reward can only be taken by the member or an immediate family member (i.e., spouse, child, grandchild, parent, grandparent, etc.);

(c) a flight reward is not transferable for cash; and

(d) a flight reward is not redeemable for cash.

3. For the purposes of this Ruling, a "consumer loyalty program" is a marketing tool operated by a supplier of goods or services (including credit card providers), or a group of such suppli-

---

6. Id. at ¶ 26–040.

7. Id. at ¶ ¶ 26–400–26–555.

8. Id. at ¶ 26–650.

9. Id. at ¶ ¶ 26–110, 26–170.

ers, to encourage customers to be loyal to the supplier(s). The standard features of these programs are:

(a) the customer is dealing with the supplier in a personal capacity, that is, in accordance with the normal arm's length commercial relationship that exists between consumers and suppliers;

(b) membership is restricted to natural persons;

(c) membership of the program is usually by application, which may require an application fee and/or annual fees;

(d) points are received with each purchase of goods or services;

(e) members and non-members pay the same amount for the goods or services purchased; and

(f) points are redeemable for goods or services.

4.   The taxation implications considered by this Ruling are:

(a) whether there is a liability for fringe benefits tax ("FBT") under the Fringe Benefits Tax Assessment Act 1986 ("FBTAA") for employers in respect of flight rewards received by employees; and

(b) whether a flight reward received by a recipient is assessable under section 6–5 or 6–10 of the Income Tax Assessment Act 1997 ("the Act").

Class of person/arrangement

5.   This Ruling applies to:

(a) persons in receipt of flight rewards wholly or partly derived from tax deductible expenditure; and

(b) employers who incur expenditure in such a way that it may allow an employee to access flight rewards.

6.   In this Ruling, "employer" extends to associates of an employer, and "employee" extends to relatives and associates of an employee.

Ruling

Flight rewards received under a consumer loyalty program

Employer

7.   Flight rewards, with the following exceptions, are not subject to FBT as they result from a personal (that is, non-employment) contractual relationship. The first exception is where the person with the personal contract is also an employer and provides the flight reward received to an employee in respect of the employment. That is, under the conditions of the flight reward program,

FBT only applies where the employer and employee have a family relationship and the flight reward is received in connection with the employment. The second exception is where, in respect of the employment of an employee, a flight reward is provided to an employee, or the employee's associate, under an "arrangement" for the purposes of the FBTAA, that results from business expenditure. It should be noted the Commissioner has determined that flight rewards accrued from membership of consumer loyalty programs are distinct and separate from any benefit resulting from the payment by the employer of membership fees.

Employees

8. Flight rewards received by employees from employer-paid expenditure are not assessable income.

Individuals rendering a service or in business

9. Flight rewards that are received by an individual who renders a service or has received the flight reward as a result of business expenditure are, with the following provisos, not assessable as the flight rewards arise as a result of a personal (that is, non-service/non-business) contractual relationship. The provisos are where the person renders a service on the basis that an entitlement to a flight reward will arise (e.g., a person enters into a secretarial service contract with an understanding that a flight reward will be received) or, in a business context, where the activities associated with the obtaining of the benefits amount in themselves to a business activity.

Value of flight rewards

10. In respect of free air tickets and ticket upgrades, the Commissioner accepts a valuation method based on a percentage of the full published fare (referred to in the industry as the full undiscounted fare) for economy, business and first class travel of the relevant airline. * * *

* * *

Explanations

16. In Payne's case, Mrs. Payne joined the consumer loyalty program without her employer's knowledge. Mrs. Payne was unable to cash in the flight reward (airline tickets) or transfer it to anyone else, but she was able to have the flight reward made out in the name of family members. The reward points Mrs. Payne accrued from employer-paid travel (and some privately-paid travel) were used to acquire airline tickets in the name of her parents who travelled from England to visit her. The Commissioner assessed

Mrs. Payne on the value of the airline tickets that accrued from employer-paid travel. The Federal Court held Mrs. Payne was not assessable in respect of the flight reward as she received the flight reward as a result of the personal contract she established with the airline on payment of the membership fee.

Ordinary income

17.　　The first consideration is whether the flight reward has the characteristics of ordinary income. The Note in subsection 6–5(1) of the Act requires section 10–5 to be consulted as specific provisions may affect the treatment of some ordinary income. Section 10–5 has a listing for "non-cash benefits" that directs one to "benefits" and "employment". Under "benefits" is a listing for "business, non-cash" that directs one to section 21A of the Income Tax Assessment Act 1936 ("the 1936 Act"). Under "employment" is a listing for "allowances and benefits in relation to employment or rendering services" that directs one to paragraph 26(e) of the 1936 Act.

18.　　In Payne's case, Foster, J. considered whether the flight reward was income according to ordinary concepts. He determined it was not income, based on the reasoning of the Full Federal Court in FC of T v. Cooke and Sherden 80 ATC 4140; (1980) 10 ATR 696; (1980) 29 ALR 202. The key findings were the flight reward was not "money" or "money's worth" (characteristics listed by Halsbury LC in Alexander Tennant v. Robert Sinclair Smith (Surveyor of Taxes) [1892] AC 150 at 157) and the flight reward was not convertible into cash. Hence, for an employee, the flight reward was not income.

19.　　Section 21A of the 1936 Act requires that "in determining the income derived by a taxpayer, a non-cash business benefit that is not convertible to cash shall be treated as if it were convertible to cash". The issue of whether there is a "non-cash business benefit" is considered in paragraphs 22 to 25. For a flight reward to be assessable to a business taxpayer, it must have the characteristics of ordinary income with the exception that it is not convertible to cash.

* * *

21.　　It is concluded only a business taxpayer could have a flight reward assessed as ordinary income under section 6–5 because only a business taxpayer can have a non-cash benefit treated as if it were cash and, hence, be ordinary income. Other taxpayers must be considered under section 6–10 (statutory income) which directs one to paragraph 26(e) of the 1936 Act. Paragraph 26(e) is discussed in paragraphs 22 to 25.

Employment or business relationship

22. In determining the tax implications of rewards received from consumer loyalty programs, a consideration common to both the income tax and FBT provisions is to identify whether, in the provision of the reward, there exists the necessary employment or business relationship. * * *

23. The identification of the relationship, if any, between the giving of the benefit on the one hand and the taxpayer's employment or business activities on the other, is crucial to determining whether the taxpayer receives a benefit in any capacity other than that of employee or business operator and whether it can be said the benefit is in consequence only of the taxpayer's employment or business activity or of some other consideration. Although Payne's case dealt purely with an employment situation, it is considered the following comments apply equally in a business context, except where the activities associated with obtaining the benefits have a business character.

24. In Payne's case, the matter of identifying whether an employment relationship existed, i.e., whether the provision of the free travel was "in respect of ... employment", attracted considerable argument. The Federal Court decided if there was a benefit given, it was given as a result of the personal contract between the taxpayer and the consumer loyalty program provider, notwithstanding the benefit arose as a "consequence" of the employment. The Court found paragraph 26(e) of the 1936 Act did not apply as the points were not earned because of the employment relationship but because of the relationship between the passenger and the airline, a relationship that was not productive of income for the passenger.

25. The Court further found the flight tickets were provided in "consequence" of the taxpayer's employment in that the flights that earned the necessary points were undertaken in the course of her employment and paid for by her employer. The employment was, therefore, an indirect or "contributory cause" of the receipt of the benefit. However, this was not sufficient for the benefit to be taxable under paragraph 26(e) as, per Foster, J. (FCR at 321; ATC at 4425; ATR at 535), "for a benefit, etc., to be caught by the section, there needed to be a role played by the employer in the giving, etc., of the benefit". This is lacking where the employee is the person who makes the decision to join or not join the loyalty program. In Payne's case, the taxpayer's employer had no part in the program and did not encourage, arrange or pay for the employee to participate.

Alternative views

26. It has been argued that flight rewards received by an employee from employer-paid expenditure are assessable to the

employee. This is based on the propositions that the employer is aware the employee can obtain a flight reward from the employer-paid expenditure if the employee is a member of a consumer loyalty program or the benefit is received in relation to employment. These propositions formed the basis of our previous Rulings.

* * *

28. In view of Payne's case, the term "given or granted" requires the employer and employee to have an understanding that the employee will receive an entitlement to flight rewards from employer-paid expenditure. The fact that an employer may have a policy that allows employees to use points acquired from employer-paid expenditure for private purposes is not, of itself, enough to demonstrate that an employee will receive flight rewards as it is up to the employee to determine if they will receive flight rewards by becoming a member. Similarly, just because an employer has paid the membership fee for a consumer loyalty program, does not mean the employee will ever receive flight rewards unless the employer has agreed that sufficient employer-paid expenditure will occur to result in flight rewards. In any event, the flight rewards must be received in respect of employment and Foster, J. found that not to be the case.

Note

In an administrative announcement,[10] the United States Internal Revenue Service has stated its position on the taxation of benefits from frequent flyer programs:

> The IRS will not assert that any taxpayer has understated his federal tax liability by reason of the receipt or personal use of frequent flyer miles or other in-kind promotional benefits attributable to the taxpayer's business or official travel. Any future guidance on the taxability of these benefits will be applied prospectively. The relief provided by this announcement does not apply to travel or other promotional benefits that are converted to cash, to compensation that is paid in the form of travel or other promotional benefits, or in other circumstances where these benefits are used for tax avoidance purposes.

An additional issue under the Australian FBT is whether the employee's potential tax results should affect the employer's tax result under the tax. To prevent overtaxation of a benefit, the taxable value of a fringe benefit under the FBT is reduced by the so-called "otherwise deductible" rule. In general, if the employee would have been entitled to a deduction if he or she had incurred the cost of the benefit, then the benefit is not included in the employer's FBT base. To illustrate the

10. Announcement 2002–18, 2002–1 C.B. 621.

purpose of the rule, assume an employer provides a benefit to an employee and there is no fringe benefits tax. The employer generally would receive a deduction for providing the benefit. If the employee would also have been entitled to a deduction if he or she had incurred the cost of the benefit, the income from the receipt of the benefit should be offset by a deduction and the employee should not have to pay additional tax. Neither the employer nor the employee would bear a tax on the benefit if it were deductible to both. The "otherwise deductible" rule is designed to achieve the same result under the FBT. The two administrative rulings that follow illustrate the operation of the rule and the need for planning.

INTERPRETIVE DECISION 2005/219
Australian Taxation Office, 2005.

Issue

Does the "otherwise deductible rule" (ODR) pursuant to subsection 19(1) of the *Fringe Benefits Tax Assessment Act 1986* (FBTAA) apply to reduce the taxable value of a loan fringe benefit to nil, where the employer provides a low interest loan jointly to the employee and their spouse and where the proceeds of the loan are used to jointly acquire an income producing property?

Decision

Yes. Subsection 138(3) of the FBTAA applies so that the loan is deemed to be provided to the employee alone. The same fiction is maintained for the purposes of paragraph 19(1)(b) of the FBTAA so that the employee is deemed to be entitled to a "once-only" deduction.

The employee provides the employer with a declaration pursuant to paragraph 19(1)(c) of the FBTAA and the ODR applies in accordance with subsection 19(1) of the FBTAA to reduce the taxable value of the loan fringe benefit to nil.

Facts

The employer, a financial institution, provides staff loans to certain employees at a lower interest rate than it charges its customers. One of these staff loans is provided jointly to an employee and their spouse.

The spouse is not an employee of the employer.

The loan is wholly used by the employee and the spouse to jointly acquire a rental property. The property is rented to a third party at a commercial rate.

In accordance with subparagraph 19(1)(c)(ii) of the FBTAA, the employee provides the employer, before the declaration date, with a declaration in a form approved by the Commissioner.

Reasons for Decision

Subsection 19(1) of the FBTAA was the subject of detailed consideration by Ryan, J. in *National Australia Bank v. Federal Commission-*

er of Taxation (1993) 46 FCR 252; 26 ATR 503; 93 ATC 4914, (*NAB Case*). The *NAB Case* established the following propositions in relation to a staff loan provided to Mr. and Mrs. Heskett, "The Heskett Loan":

1.   That the mechanism chosen by the draftsman (under subsection 138(3) of the FBTAA) to avoid the result of double taxation in the circumstances of a single benefit provided jointly is to deem it for all the purposes of the FBTAA to have been provided to a single recipient.

2.   That the loan provided jointly to Mr. and Mrs. Heskett is deemed to have been provided to Mr. Heskett alone and on that basis paragraph 19(1)(a) of the FBTAA is satisfied.

3.   That the same fiction is maintained for the purposes of paragraph 19(1)(b) of the FBTAA, so that Mr. Heskett, as the sole recipient of the loan and the sole investor of the proceeds, would have been entitled to a once only deduction in respect of the whole of the gross interest had he paid it in the relevant tax year.

4.   That paragraph 19(1)(ba) of the FBTAA was satisfied including the taking into account the amount of interest actually paid to the Bank.

5.   That there was sufficient information contained on Mr. Heskett's declaration form so that paragraph 19(1)(c) of the FBTAA was satisfied.

In the present case the facts are analogous to "The Heskett Loan" and the *NAB Case* decision can be applied. Subsection 19(1) of the FBTAA is therefore satisfied and the ODR applies to reduce the taxable value of the loan fringe benefit to nil.

DETERMINATION 93/90

Australian Tax Office, 1993.

Income tax: does the "otherwise deductible rule" apply to reduce the taxable value of fringe benefits provided to associates of employees?

1.   No. The "otherwise deductible rule" does not apply to benefits provided to associates of employees. The operation of the "otherwise deductible rule" is limited to benefits provided directly to employees.

2.   The term "associate" is defined in subsection 136(1) of the *Fringe Benefits Tax Assessment Act 1986* (FBTAA). It carries the same meaning as subsection 26AAB(14) of the *Income Tax Assessment Act 1936*. The definition is very broad and includes relatives, partners, trustees, beneficiaries and related companies.

3.   This determination does not deal with fringe benefits provided jointly to employees and their associates.

Example:

An employer provides two low interest loans which give rise to loan fringe benefits, one to an employee and one to the employee's spouse. Both the employee and the spouse invest their loan monies in shares.

Treatment of the employee's loan: A declaration is provided by the employee to his employer stating that the loan was used wholly for income producing purposes (as required by paragraph (c) of subsection 19(1) of the FBTAA). The "otherwise deductible rule" enables the taxable value of this loan fringe benefit to be reduced to nil.

Treatment of the spouse's loan: Even though the spouse's loan is also used for income producing purposes, there is no reduction in the taxable value of this loan fringe benefit. The "otherwise deductible rule" does not apply because the spouse is not an employee, but is an associate of the employee.

Chapter 3

GIFTS AND INHERITANCES

A. INTRODUCTION

The income taxation of gifts, whether made *inter vivos* or at death, presents a number of theoretical questions.[1] The donee of a gift receives additional wealth that can be consumed. Should that make the donee taxable on the gift? If the donee is taxable, should the donor, who parts with wealth, receive a deduction as a result of the transfer? And if the tax system has an estate and gift tax or an inheritance tax, should that affect the income tax treatment of gifts? Despite the theoretical arguments for taxing gifts in an income tax,[2] gifts generally are not treated as income to the donee. The exclusion of gifts from an income tax may be the result of either an express statutory exclusion or because gifts are not included within a taxable category in a schedular income tax.[3]

If gifts are excluded from income, the important question becomes: What qualifies as a "gift?" Is the concept of a gift limited to just "personal" gifts between family, friends, and long-term acquaintances at birthdays, holidays, celebrations, and the like? Or can transfers in a quasi-business setting, such as a "gift" to celebrate the completion of a successful business venture, the transfer of an award to a top producing employee, or the gold watch given to an employee for years of devoted service, qualify for the exclusion? Students of the United States federal income tax know that the Internal Revenue Code provides limited statutory guidance

---

1. See generally, Boris Bittker & Larry Lokken, Federal Taxation of Income, Estates and Gifts ¶¶ 10.01–10.03 (1999).

2. See Joseph M. Dodge, "Beyond Estate and Gift Tax Reform: Including Gifts and Bequests in Income," 91 Harv. L. Rev. 1177 (1978).

3. Hugh J. Ault & Brian J. Arnold, Comparative Income Taxation—A Structural Analysis 183 (2d ed., 2004); Lee Burns & Richard Krever, "Individual Income Taxation," Ch. 14, p. 527, in Victor Thuronyi, Tax Law Design and Drafting (2000).

on these questions.[4] Instead, the guiding principles come from the Supreme Court in *Commissioner v. Duberstein*,[5] where we are told that the primary factor in ascertaining whether a transfer is a "gift" is the intent of the transferor. Specifically, a transfer is a gift if it is given "out of affection, respect, admiration, charity or like impulses."[6]

Other tax systems may use different standards for ascertaining whether a transfer is a gift. The following two Canadian cases deal with the taxability of payments that are made voluntarily to the recipient. See if you can reconcile the results in these decisions.

CAMPBELL v. MINISTER OF NATIONAL REVENUE
Tax Appeal Board, 1958.
21 Tax A.B.C. 145, 59 D.T.C. 8.

THE CHAIRMAN:

1. This appeal was heard in Toronto. The appellant, who is now a married woman living in Renfrew, Ontario, has enjoyed a wide reputation as a professional swimmer. The appeal is for the taxation year 1956 and is from an assessment made by the Minister of National Revenue wherein a tax in the sum of $945.34 was levied in respect of income for that year. The matter in issue is whether the sum of $5,000 received by the appellant in 1956 from The Toronto Daily Star is subject to tax as income in that year.

2. * * * In the year 1955 the appellant made her first attempt to swim across Lake Ontario. In preparation for that event The Toronto Telegram made a certain payment for training expenses which amounted, according to the appellant, to $55 per week for a period of seven weeks. She failed by a distance of one and one-half miles to complete the swim across Lake Ontario in 1955. Shortly after this experience the appellant was approached by two reporters from The Toronto Daily Star who suggested to her that she make another attempt to swim across Lake Ontario in 1956 and that she do so under the auspices or sponsorship of The Toronto Daily Star. This resulted in the appellant—who at the time was under twenty-one years of age—together with her mother, Mrs. Florence E. Campbell, of Fergus, entering into a contract with the Toronto Star Limited. This contract was made as of September 2, 1955. The contract set out that in consideration of the sum of $600 the appellant granted to the Toronto Star Limited the sole and exclusive option for her services as a professional swimmer. It is to

4. See, e.g., I.R.C. §§ 74(c) (employee achievement awards); 102(c) (no gift exclusion for transfers to an employee); 132(e) (exclusion for de minimis fringe benefits).

5. 363 U.S. 278, 80 S.Ct. 1190 (1960).

6. Id.

be noted that this sum of $600 was actually received by Shirley Campbell in the year 1955 and was duly reported as income received by her in that year. In this contract Shirley Campbell covenanted and agreed with the Toronto Star Limited to attempt to swim across Lake Ontario in 1956. It was agreed that all details having to do with the projected swim should be taken up by the publishing company with Shirley Campbell herself and with her advisory committee consisting of Messrs. Samuel M. Irwin, Paul L. Fox and Arthur Maloney, Q.C. Certain exclusive rights were given under this contract by Shirley Campbell to the Toronto Star Limited and, in return, the Toronto Star Limited agreed with Shirley Campbell as follows:

> To pay Shirley the sum of $5,000 if she shall complete the aforesaid long distance swim. In the event Shirley shall fail to complete the aforesaid long distance swim, no further sum shall be payable by the publisher but Shirley shall be entitled to retain the said sum of $600 given as consideration for the granting of the option and the expenses hereinafter mentioned.

> To pay Shirley's necessary expenses (including a coach's fee not to exceed $500) and the out-of-pocket expenses of her coach incurred after receipt of notification from the publisher of the date, time and place of the aforesaid long distance swim ...

3. The appellant continued with her evidence to relate that in the summer of 1956 she engaged in a further attempt to swim across Lake Ontario in accordance with the terms of her contract with the Toronto Star Limited. The witness said that she had almost completed the swim across Lake Ontario when, only about one-half mile from the Toronto shoreline, her coach directed that she be taken out of the water. She stated that while she was recovering in a room in a downtown Toronto hotel from the effects of her grueling and disappointing ordeal Mr. Hindmarsh, Jr., of the Star, came to her hotel room and said that although she had not completed the swim in accordance with the terms of contract it was felt that she had made such a good attempt that the Toronto Star was going to make her a gift of $5,000. The next day she received a cheque from the Toronto Star Limited for the sum of $5,000 which she considered as a gift. She said that since this attempt in the summer of 1956 she has not engaged in further marathon swimming and was married in October, 1956. The witness emphasized under cross-examination that when Mr. Hindmarsh, Jr., came to see her in the hotel room he made it plain that, although the Toronto Star Limited was under no obligation to pay the sum of $5,000, they were going to make the payment notwithstanding because she had made such a good attempt to complete the swim across the lake.

* * *

5. It will be readily seen that the problem posed in this appeal falls within a narrow scope. The appeal will be determined by a decision as to how this sum of $5,000 should be classified. There is no question that Shirley Campbell received the sum of $5,000 from The Toronto Star Limited in the year 1956. The simple question is whether this sum was income to Miss Campbell in that year and thus assessable to income tax or whether the whole amount was something other than income. What has to be settled is whether the payment to Shirley Campbell of $5,000 was in the nature of a personal gift or whether it was remuneration. It is the kind of question that has been before the courts on many occasions and it is helpful to have the benefit of judicial observations and decisions in similar cases heard in the courts of Canada, England and Ireland.

issue

6. The Income Tax Act defines what is income for income tax purposes and one cannot give to "income" a meaning contrary to that given by the statute. It is to the real nature of the payment that one must look in cases of this kind. It may be taken as well settled that it is always to the true nature of the payment that the courts must look in determining whether or not a receipt of money is "income".

7. Section 3 of the Income Tax Act provides as follows:

> The income of a taxpayer for a taxation year ... is his income for the year from all sources inside or outside Canada and, without restricting the generality of the foregoing, includes income for the year from all
>
> (a) businesses,
>
> (b) property, and
>
> (c) offices and employments.

8. "Business" is defined in Section 139(1)(e) of the Act as including a profession, calling, trade, manufacture or undertaking of any kind whatsoever as well as an adventure or concern in the nature of trade, but does not include an office or employment.

* * *

10. The Act describes sources of income and describes methods of computing income but, in determining the nature of the payment under consideration herein, it is to the decided cases that one must go for guidance. While each case is found to turn upon its own facts and no infallible criterion emerges, nevertheless the decisions are useful as illustrations and as affording indications of the kind of considerations which may relevantly be borne in mind in approaching the problem. Some things are so obviously income that their nature is unchallengeable. The commonest examples are

the wages and salaries received by employees, the fees received by professional practitioners from their patients or clients, the commissions received by agents from their principals. Remuneration is mostly, but not necessarily, governed by agreement as in the present case so that default in payment would furnish ground for legal action. Sometimes, however, it is in a form quite outside any contractual right, for example periodical bonuses to employees, which being a part of their remuneration are undoubtedly part of their income. The simplest concept of remuneration probably does not look beyond what is customary, but the principle has been extended to cover rewards which are merely occasional. Thus, a gift of money by a horse owner to a jockey who has won a race has been held to be part of the jockey's income. In fact it may be accepted that the courts are agreed in holding that the remuneration for personal efforts associated with a calling is income. Thus the character of a particular receipt is not governed by the fact that there is no likelihood or possibility that it will recur.

11. In reviewing and evaluating the facts of this appeal it is to be observed that in giving her evidence the appellant said that she became a professional swimmer in 1952. * * *

12. The appellant was asked by counsel for the Minister of National Revenue as to whether she could give any reason why The Toronto Star would want to pay her $5,000 if she did not complete the swim. The answer of the appellant was that she thought it would be good publicity for The Toronto Star.

13. When officials of The Toronto Star Limited were successful in obtaining Shirley Campbell's consent to become a party to the contract they were, in effect, securing the services of Shirley Campbell as a professional swimmer. It was already widely recognized that Miss Campbell's best known trade or calling was that of a professional swimmer. It should be readily apparent from the wording of the contract that the whole scheme or arrangement was entered into as a promotion enterprise by The Toronto Star Limited. * * *

* * *

15. The only reasonable conclusion to be drawn from the arrangement entered into is that the Star, for promotional purposes, contracted with Shirley Campbell for the exclusive use of her services as a professional swimmer. True, Miss Campbell may have been a secretary or stenographer at the time but she was widely known in all circles by reason of her trade or calling as a professional swimmer.

16. Although there may not have been any legal obligation on the part of The Toronto Star Limited to pay the sum of $5,000 to

Miss Campbell when she failed by such a narrow margin to swim across the lake, nevertheless the prestige of the publication, under the circumstances, would have been sorely lessened in public opinion if there had been strict adherence to its technical legal position as a party to the contract. Thus the promotional aspect and value of the enterprise would have been jeopardized. If the promotion was to have the effect of enhancing good public relations then the Star would have to pay Miss Campbell for the services which she had rendered to the Star and to the Star exclusively. In fact on the day after the swim the Star reported as set out above that although she did not complete the swim Shirley Campbell's magnificent effort to conquer Lake Ontario was recognized by the Star with a cheque for $5,000. The Star had agreed to pay Shirley upon the completion of the swim but felt that as it had ended so heartbreakingly one-half mile from shore she had earned the $5,000. The assistant managing editor gave evidence that this sum of $5,000 was charged to promotion.

17. Under the circumstances can there be any conclusion other than that the Star felt obligated to pay Miss Campbell the sum of $5,000 for the services which she had rendered exclusively to that publication? It must be held that the true nature of this transaction was the performance of services for which payment was made. The money was paid in respect of services performed by Miss Campbell in a business context.

18. In Herbert v. McQuade, [1902] 2 K.B. 631, Collins, M.R., said, at p. 649:

> A payment may be liable to income tax although it is voluntary on the part of the persons who made it and the test is whether, from the standpoint of the person who receives it, it accrues to him in virtue of his office; if it does, it does not matter whether it was voluntary or whether it was compulsory on the part of the persons who paid.

19. In Henry Goldman v. Minister of National Revenue, [1953] 1 S.C.R. 211, Kellock, J., said as follows:

> The appellant having succeeded in obtaining the remuneration he set out to obtain ... I do not consider the form by which that result was brought about is important ... What the appellant received, he received as remuneration as he intended.... This was not received by him as a testimonial nor as anything but remuneration for the services which he had performed. That the services had been completed when payment was made or that there was no assurance from the beginning that the services would be remunerated do not prevent the amount in question being taxable income.

* * *

22. The finding that the $5,000 was paid and received as remuneration for services concludes the matter against the appellant's plea. Nor does it matter whether the payment was made pursuant to an enforceable obligation or was voluntary. The amount of $5,000 which Shirley Campbell received from The Toronto Star Limited, and which the Star itself said was earned by her, was income resulting from the services which she rendered and, as such, is assessable to income tax.

23. The personable appellant in the present appeal may derive some small satisfaction in knowing that since the hearing of the appeal there has ensued a completely sympathetic consideration of her claim. Everything that could be advanced in her behalf was ably set forth by her counsel. On the other hand counsel for the Minister of National Revenue took a very strong stand that the sum received by Miss Campbell constituted income subject to taxation.

24. It must be admitted that there has been a desire, if possible, to afford Miss Campbell some relief in her taxation difficulty. However, bearing in mind the inflexible rule that "there are no equities in a taxing Act" it is apparent that no avenue is open to justify interference with the assessment made by the Minister of National Revenue. Indeed there exists a preponderance of legal authority against the view urged on behalf of the appellant.

25. In Partington v. Attorney–General, [1869] L.R. 4 H.L. 100, the following is set out as a criterion:

> If the person sought to be taxed comes within the letter of the law he must be taxed, however great the hardship may appear to the judicial mind to be.

26. Although it is done with considerable reluctance there is no alternative but to record that this appeal fails.

Appeal dismissed.

McMILLAN v. MINISTER OF NATIONAL REVENUE
Tax Review Board, 1982.
C.T.C. 2345, 82 D.T.C. 1287.

1. Point at Issue

2. The point at issue is whether the appellant, a former employee and manager of Cox and McMillan Limited which operated a general insurance agency, is correct in considering, a "windfall", the amount of $5,000 received in 1978 from Marsh & McLennan Limited, an insurance broker. The latter, in 1976, became the new broker of The Canada Life Assurance Company. This company

had been the client of Cox and McMillan Limited from 1931 to 1976.

* * *

28.   4.03. Analysis

Facts

29.   4.03.1. On the one hand the outline of the facts is as follows:

30.1. The appellant was an insurance broker who operated his own agency through the facilities of Cox and McMillan Limited, an insurance broker company * * *. The appellant was, in fact, the only broker working for the two agencies * * *;

31.2. In 1973, the appellant was shareholder of 50% of the shares of Cox and McMillan Limited * * *;

32.3. The Canada Life Assurance Company, a client of Cox and McMillan Limited for 40 years, decided in 1976 to change its insurance broker to Marsh & McLennan Limited * * *;

33.4. After a meeting with the representative of Marsh & McLennan Limited (Mr. Band), the representative of Canada Life (Mr. Fraser) and Mr. McMillan, it was decided that the appellant would be treated as a sub-agent to whom a subcommission would be given—$5,000 per year over three years. This was confirmed by a handshake agreement * * *. This type of agreement is commonly used in this kind of business * * *. The said subcommission of $5,000 over three years was roughly 10% of the commission of Marsh & McLennan Limited in the Canada Life file * * *.

34.5. The appellant would not have received the subcommission if he had not held a valid insurance broker's licence and if Marsh & McLennan Limited itself would not have received commission * * *.

35.   4.03.2 However, on the other hand it is also true that Marsh & McLennan Limited was not obliged to pay the said subcommission to the appellant. However, because the decision of Canada Life to put its insurance business in the hands of only one insurance broker would substantially cut the Cox and McMillan income, "the paternalistic Canada Life Insurance Company" * * * wished to find a way to help the appellant personally.

36.   The suggestion of subcommission in a handshake agreement was made by Mr. Band of Marsh & McLennan Limited * * *.

37.   4.03.3 In substance there was no relation between the new broker and the former broker Cox and McMillan Limited. Moreover, personally the appellant had not helped the new broker to obtain the file of Canada Life. It was not a finders fee. The former broker, Cox and McMillan Limited, was the loser. The amount paid personally to the appellant by the new broker was to

satisfy Canada Life. The new broker considered this delicacy of "the paternalistic Canada Life" towards the appellant as a kind of obstacle to complete a transaction with Canada Life. It was a good suggestion from the new broker to treat the appellant "as a sub-agent" because, once again, this permitted him to complete this important transaction. However, the appellant was not, in fact, a sub-agent. The said "subcommission" was not actually a subcommission. No service was requested of or performed by the appellant subcommission. No service was requested of or performed by the appellant to help the new broker to complete the transaction. No assistance was provided by him to Marsh & McLennan Limited either before or after the change of business. In fact, the only thing that the appellant did to help the new broker was to accept the $15,000. Moreover, as he had no right to this amount or to any other amount, if he had not accepted he would have received nothing.

38. 4.03.4 In my opinion "sub-agent" and "subcommission" are only words to cover a gratuity payment for which the appellant had no legal expectation and this is a windfall. Even if the hand-shake agreement would have been a written agreement, this would not have changed the substance.

39. 4.03.5 One could not say that the $15,000 is a payment indirectly made by Canada Life for long service. The payment indeed was not made, even indirectly, by Canada Life * * *.

5. Conclusion

40. The appeal is allowed and the matter is referred back to the respondent for reassessment in accordance with the above Reasons for Judgment.

Appeal allowed.

Note

So Ms. Campbell is taxed on the $5,000 that she receives from The Toronto Star while Mr. McMillan escapes taxation on the $15,000 he is paid by Marsh & McLennan. Can these decisions be harmonized? Or must one of them be wrong? Perhaps paragraph 10 of the *Campbell* decision provides a clue about what is going on. Notice the reference in paragraph 10 to the "sources of income?" The Canadian income tax is built on a source theory of income.[7] That is, "income" derives from some taxable "source." So a receipt classified as a "windfall," like Mr. McMillan's payment from Marsh & McLennan, has no taxable source and, consequently, is not income. You might recall that the taxpayers

---

7. See Peter W. Hogg, Joanne E. Magee & Jinyan Li, Principles of Canadian Income Tax Law 82–86 (5th ed. 2005); Vern Krishna, The Fundamentals of Canadian Income Tax 138–40 (9th ed. 2006).

in *Commissioner v. Glenshaw Glass Co.,*[8] relying on an earlier statement by the Supreme Court that income is "the gain derived from capital, from labor, or from both combined,"[9] argued that the recovery of punitive or exemplary damages was not income because the damages were neither derived from capital nor receipts from the performance of services. In *Glenshaw Glass*, the Supreme Court rejected the taxpayer's argument about the nature of income and, instead, adopted an "accessions to wealth" approach for determining when a taxpayer has gross income under section 61 of the Code. *Campbell* and *McMillan* illustrate how a different approach might work. In that regard, consider how Mr. McMillan would have faired under the standard in *Glenshaw Glass*.

B. GIFTS AS REALIZATION EVENTS

If a donor makes a gift of noncash property, should the gift be treated as a taxable disposition of the property? In answering that question, should we care that a gift of property does not produce cash that the donor may use to pay her tax liability? Or is the fact that a gift is voluntary and the donor was free to sell the property for cash a sufficient response to the donor's potential liquidity problem? If a gift is a taxable event, determining the donor's gain or loss will require us to value the gifted property. Should the difficult valuation issues that will surely arise affect the decision about whether to tax gifts? If an *inter vivos* gift is a taxable event, should the same rule apply to gifts made at death? Should the existence of an inheritance or estate tax at death affect the income tax consequences of property passing at death?[10] If gifts generally are taxable, should the same rule apply to gifts between spouses? And what about the donee? What basis (i.e., tax cost) should the donee take in the transferred property?

With so many variables to consider, it is not surprising that tax systems reach different conclusions to these questions. In the United States, *inter vivos* gifts and gifts at death generally are not taxable events to the donor. A special rule also makes all transfers of property between spouses tax free. In addition, a transfer of property between former spouses may be tax free if the transfer is incident to divorce.[11] The donee of property received as a result of an *inter vivos* gift generally takes the donor's basis in the gifted property, i.e., a transferred basis.[12] A spouse receiving property

---

8. 348 U.S. 426, 75 S.Ct. 473, rehearing denied, 349 U.S. 925, 75 S.Ct. 657 (1955).

9. Eisner v. Macomber, 252 U.S. 189, 40 S.Ct. 189 (1920).

10. See generally, Lee Burns & Richard Krever, "Individual Income Taxation," Ch. 14, p. 651–52, in Victor Thu-

ronyi, Tax Law Design and Drafting (2000).

11. I.R.C. § 1041.

12. I.R.C. §§ 1015(a), 7701(a)(43). Section 1015 has a special rule that limits the donee's basis in the transferred property for purposes of determining loss to the property's fair market value from his or her spouse also takes a transferred basis in the property.[13] But, a recipient of property acquired from a decedent generally takes a basis in the property equal to its fair market value at the date of the decedent's death.[14] Under this rule, all of the appreciation (or depreciation) in the value of the transferred property escapes the income tax. That rule, however, is scheduled to be replaced with a modified-transferred-basis rule that will apply in the case of a decedent who dies between January 1, 2010 and December 31, 2010. The new provision employs a transferred-basis provision but also includes a generous $1.3 million basis increase (up to fair market value) for property passing from a decedent and an additional $3 million basis increase (again, up to fair market value) for property passing to a surviving spouse.[15]

In Australia, a taxable event occurs upon the disposition of an asset, which is deemed to occur when there is a change in the beneficial ownership of that asset. This provision applies to *inter vivos* gifts, where the property is deemed to be disposed of by the donor for its fair market value and the donee receives a cost base equal to such value.[16] A special rule applies at death, which is generally not considered to result in a disposition of the asset and where the donee generally takes the donor's tax base.[17] Contrast the Australian treatment of gifts to the rules that apply in France. In France, neither *inter vivos* gifts nor gifts at death are taxable events to the donor under the income tax, the donee does not have income, and in both situations the donee receives a tax base in the property equal to its fair market value![18] The ability to use gifts as a tax avoidance strategy in France is limited somewhat by inheritance and gift taxes that have modest allowances and steep rates.[19]

Note

Following are excerpts from the Canadian income tax statutes that deal with taxation of the donor when noncash property is given *inter*

at the time of the transfer, if such value is less than the donor's basis.

13. I.R.C. § 1041(b)(2).

14. I.R.C. § 1014. A special rule allows the basis of the property to be determined with reference to its fair market value six months after the decedent's death. §§ 1014(a)(2), 2032(a).

15. I.R.C. § 1022.

16. §§ 104–10, 110–25(2), 116–20 (Income Tax Assessment Act 1997); see Robin Woellner, Stephen Barkoczy, Shirley Murphy & Chris Evans, Australian Taxation Law ¶¶ 7–120, 7–610, 7–625, 7–645 (17th ed. 2007).

17. §§ 128–10, 128–15(4) (Income Tax Assessment Act of 1997). The donor's tax base may be the property's fair market value if the donor originally acquired the property prior to the enactment of the capital gains tax. See generally, Robin Woellner, Stephen Barkoczy, Shirley Murphy & Chris Evans, Australian Taxation Law ¶¶ 8–520 (17th ed. 2007).

18. Article 150 VB (French Tax Code).

19. See IBFD, Global Individual Tax Handbook 2007 189–90 (2007).

vivos or at death. Note, that these statutes represent the "general rules." The exceptions and special provisions would take up many more pages. For example, an array of statutes permit tax-free transfers of farming property from parents to their children. Also, note that these statutes deal only with the tax consequences of the gift. The taxation of any income from the gifted property and the taxation of any appreciation on the subsequent sale of the property are separate issues which are considered in a subsequent chapter.[20] Following the statutes is a case that presents an interesting valuation issue that arose when property passed at death under Section 70(5).

S. 69(1) Inadequate considerations

Except as expressly otherwise provided in this Act,

* * *

(b) where a taxpayer has disposed of anything

* * *

(ii) to any person by way of gift *inter vivos*, * * *

* * *

the taxpayer shall be deemed to have received proceeds of disposition therefor equal to that fair market value; and

(c) where a taxpayer acquires a property by way of gift, * * * the taxpayer is deemed to acquire the property at its fair market value.

S. 70(5) Capital property of a deceased taxpayer

Where in a taxation year a taxpayer dies,

(a) the taxpayer shall be deemed to have, immediately before the taxpayer's death, disposed of each capital property of the taxpayer and received proceeds of disposition therefor equal to the fair market value of the property immediately before the death;

(b) any person who as a consequence of the taxpayer's death acquires any property that is deemed by paragraph (a) to have been disposed of by the taxpayer shall be deemed to have acquired it at the time of the death at a cost equal to its fair market value immediately before the death;

* * *

S. 70(6) Where transfer or distribution to spouse [or common-law partner] or spouse trust

Where any property of a taxpayer who was resident in Canada immediately before the taxpayer's death that is a property to which

---

20. See Chapter 4, infra.

subsection (5) would otherwise apply is, as a consequence of the death, transferred or distributed to

(a) the taxpayer's spouse or common-law partner who was resident in Canada immediately before the taxpayer's death, or

(b) a trust, created by the taxpayer's will, that was resident in Canada immediately after the time the property vested indefeasibly in the trust and under which

(i) the taxpayer's spouse or common-law partner is entitled to receive all of the income of the trust that arises before the spouse's or common-law partner's death, and

(ii) no person except the spouse or common-law partner may, before the spouse's or common-law partner's death, receive or otherwise obtain the use of any of the income or capital of the trust,

if it can be shown, within the period ending 36 months after the death of the taxpayer or, where written application therefor has been made to the Minister by the taxpayer's legal representative within that period, within such longer period as the Minister considers reasonable in the circumstances, that the property has become vested indefeasibly in the spouse or common-law partner or trust, as the case may be, the following rules apply:

(c) paragraphs (5)(a) and (b) do not apply in respect of the property,

(d) * * * the taxpayer shall be deemed to have, immediately before the taxpayer's death, disposed of the property and received proceeds of disposition therefor equal to

(i) where the property was depreciable property of a prescribed class, the lesser of the capital cost and the cost amount to the taxpayer of the property immediately before the death, and

(ii) in any other case, its adjusted cost base to the taxpayer immediately before the death,

and the spouse or common-law partner or trust, as the case may be, shall be deemed to have acquired the property at the time of the death at a cost equal to those proceeds, * * *.

* * *

S. 70(6.2) Election

Subsection (6) * * * does not apply to any property of a deceased taxpayer in respect of which the taxpayer's legal representative elects, in the taxpayer's return of income under this Part * * * for the year in which the taxpayer died, to have subsection (5) * * * apply.

S. 73(1) *Inter vivos* transfers by individuals

For the purposes of this Part, where at any time any particular capital property of an individual (other than a trust) has been transferred in circumstances to which subsection (1.01) applies and both the individual and the transferee are resident in Canada at that time, unless the individual elects in the individual's return of income under this Part for the taxation year in which the particular property was transferred that the provisions of this subsection not apply, the particular property is deemed

(a) to have been disposed of at that time by the individual for proceeds equal to,

* * *

(ii) in any other case, the adjusted cost base to the individual of the particular property immediately before that time; and

(b) to have been acquired at that time by the transferee for an amount equal to those proceeds.

S. 73(1.01) Qualifying transfers

[P]roperty is transferred by an individual in circumstances to which this subsection applies where it is transferred to

(a) the individual's spouse or common-law partner;

(b) a former spouse or common-law partner of the individual in settlement of rights arising out of their marriage or common-law partnership; * * *

* * *

S. 248(1) Definitions

In this Act,

* * *

"common-law partner", with respect to a taxpayer at any time, means a person who cohabits at that time in a conjugal relationship with the taxpayer and

(a) has so cohabited with the taxpayer for a continuous period of at least one year, or

(b) would be the parent of a child of whom the taxpayer is a parent, * * *

* * *

THE QUEEN v. MASTRONARDI
Federal Court of Canada (Court of Appeal), 1977.
1 F.C. 399, 77 D.T.C. 5217, 16 N.R. 323, C.T.C. 355.

1.   This is an appeal by the Crown from a judgment of the Trial Division in which the learned Trial Judge allowed the respon-

dents' appeal from the reassessment for income tax for the 1973 taxation year in the estate of Umberto Mastronardi, deceased.

2. The respondents are the executors and trustees of that estate.

3. At the time of his death, the deceased was the owner of the majority common shares of Mastronard: Produce Ltd., (an Ontario Corporation), and by virtue of section 70(5) of the *Income Tax Act*, * * * and by section 19(1), * * * he was deemed to have disposed of those shares immediately prior to his death and to have received as proceeds of disposition an amount equal to their fair market value * * *. At the time of the death of the deceased, Mastronardi Produce Ltd. was the owner of a term life insurance policy which provided for the payment to the company of the sum of $500,000 on the death of the deceased. This policy was dated September 25, 1972 and was for a term of five years, with the face amount reducing by $100,000 on each anniversary date. The policy was non-convertible and non-participating. The policy had no cash surrender or other value prior to death. The deceased was required by the insurance company to have two independent physical examinations which he had on August 28, 1972. The deceased died suddenly and without warning of cardiac arrest on February 20, 1973 at the age of 51 years. Neither the deceased nor his immediate family were aware prior to his death that he was a likely or suspected candidate for the heart attack brought on by arteriosclerotic cardiovascular disease and from which he died.

4. The parties agree that the fair market value of the shares of Mastronardi Produce Ltd. would be $323.58 per share, if no account was taken of the insurance policy, which is the value used by the respondents in calculating the taxable capital gain arising on the deemed disposition of the shares of Mastronardi Produce Ltd. The parties also agree that if the shares were to be valued on the basis of taking into account the policy at the instant of death, the value would be $778.59 per share which is the figure used by the Minister of National Revenue in calculating the deceased's income for his 1973 taxation year.

5. In my view, the learned Trial Judge correctly stated the problem facing him in interpreting section 70(5) (*supra*) when he said [[1977] 1 F.C. 234 at p. 238]:

> ... it is apparent that there is a two step fiction enacted by section 70 subsection (5) of the Act. The first fiction is that the taxpayer after he dies is deemed to have disposed of the subject property "immediately before his death".

> The second fiction is that he is deemed "to have received proceeds of disposition therefor equal to the fair market value of the property at that time".

The problem is to determine what was the legislative concept of section 70 subsection (5) of the Act and apply such to the facts of this case.

After summarizing the submissions of the parties, the Trial Judge then reached the following conclusions [at page 239]:

> The words "immediately before his death" in section 70 sub-section (5) of the *Income Tax Act* should not be construed as meaning the equivalent of the instant of death; and also those words do not import a necessity of valuing capital property taking into account the imminence of death.

And, in conclusion, he stated [at page 239]:

> In my view, therefore, in this case, both such valuations * * * must be considered as having taken place at some other time rather than at the instant of death of the deceased and no premise of imminence of death of the deceased should form any part of such valuations.

6. We have carefully reviewed all of the authorities to which reference was made by counsel during the course of argument and can find nothing therein which has persuaded us that the learned Trial Judge erred either in the conclusions which he reached or the reasoning which he followed in arriving at those conclusions. To ignore the plain meaning of a statute in the context of a given set of facts and to substitute therefore a strained and unnatural interpretation, to prevent an apprehended injustice in the future on an entirely different set of facts, as counsel for the appellant most eloquently urged us to do, does not accord with the principles of good statutory interpretation. Speculation as to the possible results in a future case assists not at all in deciding what the result should be in a case such as this which, on its facts, is so easily capable of rational resolution by simply interpreting the plain words as they appear in the statute without indulging in such speculation.

7. Accordingly, the appeal will be dismissed with costs.

* * *

Chapter 4

TAXABLE UNIT AND ATTRIBUTION OF INCOME

A. THE TAXABLE UNIT

A fundamental question for any income tax system is whether the taxable unit should be the individual, the married couple, or some other family grouping. That question is important in an income tax with progressive rates because the choice of taxable unit potentially will affect the overall tax burdens of different living arrangements.[1] The definition of the taxable unit establishes when, for tax purposes, the income of different individuals will be aggregated.

To put the policy issues raised by the choice of taxable unit into perspective, compare the tax results of married couple A and B, who each earn $100,000 of taxable income, with married couple C and D, in which C earns $200,000 of taxable income and D earns no income that is taxable. Note that if income is taxed in the system at a single flat rate, the tax liability of the two couples would be the same. If, however, the system taxes income at progressive rates and the taxable unit were the individual, the CD couple will pay more tax than the AB couple because some portion of C's income would be taxed at higher rates than A's and B's income. Alternatively, if the taxable unit were the married couple, the tax burden of each couple would be the same because each couple has the same total income. The argument for adopting the married couple as the taxable unit is based, in part, on a "benefit" theory of taxation and

---

1. See generally, Hugh Ault & Brian Arnold, Comparative Income Taxation—A Structural Analysis 259–264 (2d ed. 2004); Victor Thuronyi, Comparative Taxation 243 (2003); Lee Burns & Richard Krever, "Individual Income Taxation," Ch. 14, pp. 537–541, in Victor Thuronyi, Tax Law Design and Drafting (2000).

the assumption that a couple will share income and resources to the benefit of both of its members. In this simple example, the assumption would be that D benefits from C's income because marriage is a relationship where there is economic sharing between the spouses. Because C and D share income, the argument would be that their family relationship should be recognized for tax purposes. Another argument for aggregating the income of married taxpayers for tax purposes is that it would be inequitable to tax couple CD more than couple AB simply because the CD couple has one earner and AB has two earners. On the other hand, some might argue that the CD couple likely reaps the untaxed benefits produced by D's contributions and efforts to the family (e.g., imputed income from D's services) and that justifies treating the couples differently.[2] Also, advocates for the individual as the taxable unit argue that joint filing by spouses acts as a disincentive to nonworking spouses to enter the labor market. The argument would be that because under joint filing income earned by D will be taxed at higher rates than if D were taxed individually, joint filing will discourage D from working.[3]

If a tax system selects the married couple as the taxable unit, the system will not be neutral as between married and unmarried taxpayers. If the tax rates implement income splitting for married taxpayers (i.e., they pay two times the tax of a single taxpayer with one-half the income) marriage will generally be the tax-favored status. For example, if C and D in the preceding example were single, they would cut their total tax bill by getting married because once married, C's $200,000 of income will bear tax equal to two times the tax on a single taxpayer with $100,000 of income. The tax bill of A and B would not change as a result of getting married because they each earn one-half of their total income. If the tax rates for married taxpayers do not adopt an income-splitting approach, it is possible for marriage to be favored in some instances and not in others. For example, the current tax rates for married and single taxpayers in the United States make it so that two single taxpayers with relatively equal amounts of income may increase their total tax liability if they get married. Thus, assuming that A and B in the earlier example were single, they would suffer a tax "penalty" by getting married, while C and D would reap a tax "bonus" by tying the knot.

---

2. See generally, Michael McIntyre & Oliver Oldman, "Taxation of the Family in a Comprehensive and Simplified Income Tax," 90 Harv.L.Rev. 1573, 1607–1626

3. Lawrence Zelanak, "Marriage and the Income Tax," 67 S. Cal. L. Rev. 339, 365–67 (1994); Lee Burns & Richard Krever, "Individual Income Taxation," Ch. 14, pp. 541, in Victor Thuronyi, Tax Law Design and Drafting (2000).

If the justification for aggregating the income of spouses is that they each benefit from the total income that they earn, should a tax system also aggregate the incomes of others in relationships where income is shared? How should those relationships be identified? If a tax system adopts the "family" as the taxable unit, who should be included in that definition? Should the income of minor children be aggregated with the income of the family unit? When should changes in the family (e.g., births, death, marriages, a child reaching the age of independence) be recognized for tax purposes? These are just some of the most basic questions that arise if the family is selected as the taxable unit.

Because the choice of taxable unit involves considerations of social policy and resolution of oftentimes conflicting objectives, it is not surprising that tax systems adopt a variety of approaches to the choice of taxable unit. Australia, Canada, and Japan are examples of countries where the individual is the taxable unit.[4] The United States and Switzerland recognize married couples as a taxable unit.[5] In Germany, married taxpayers living together pay taxes jointly unless they elect to be taxed separately.[6] France has one of the most extensive and complex systems for taxing the family as a unit.[7] French tax law includes the concept of a "fiscal household," which is defined as a married couple or a domestic partnership and their dependents, who may include a child under 18 years of age, a disabled child, any disabled person who lives in the taxpayer's house, a child between 18 and 21 years of age who asks to be part of the parents' household, and a child between 21 and 25 who is a student and asks to be part of the parents household. Joint filing generally is required for married taxpayers and registered partners. Parents can refuse to file jointly with children if the child works or has income that is earned independently from the parents. There is no separate rate structure that permits fiscal households to reduce the effect of high marginal tax rates; instead, a fiscal household is taxed using a "family quotient" system. Under that system, the *equation* total household income is first divided by the number "parts" included in the family. Then, the tax on the income per part is calculated. Finally, the amount of tax calculated per part is multiplied by the number of parts to arrive at the total tax liability. In calculating "parts," each member of the couple counts as one part, the first two children each count as half a part, and each additional child counts as a full part. For example, a couple with two children would have three parts and would pay tax equal to the total tax paid by three individuals, each having income equal to one-third of

---

4. IBDF, Global Individual Tax Handbook 2007 29 (Australia); 87 (Canada); 297 (Japan) (2007).

5. Id. at 511 (Switzerland).

6. Id. at 195 (Germany).

7. Id. at 186 (France).

the household's total income. Because the family quotient system is regressive (it helps high-income households more than low-income households), its effects are limited by a rule that caps the amount of tax that can be saved per half part.

B. FAMILY ALLOWANCES

Tax systems have a variety of ways of taking into account family circumstances in determining tax liability. A deduction, exemption, credit or other type of allowance may be granted in recognition of the fact that family circumstances may affect a taxpayer's ability to pay tax. This type of allowance may be phased out or limited in order to preserve the progressive nature of the income tax. For example, in the United States, a personal exemption is allowed in calculating taxable income for the taxpayer, the taxpayer's spouse, and each individual who qualifies as a dependent.[1] Before 2010, the amount of a personal exemption is reduced once the taxpayer's adjusted gross income exceeds a threshold amount.[2] In Canada, a taxpayer is allowed a personal credit for a spouse, a common-law partner, and an eligible dependent. The amount of the credit is offset once the spouse's, partner's or dependent's income exceeds certain minimal amounts.[3] In Slovenia, allowances are permitted for dependents, disabled taxpayers, taxpayers over 65 years old, certain students, and, subject to various conditions, journalists.[4]

C. INCOME SPLITTING RULES

Depending on the principles adopted for defining the taxable unit in the system, related taxpayers will have more or less incentive to engage in transactions designed to shift income. Again, avoidance of progressive tax rates will be the goal of the taxpayers. For example, assume E and F are a married couple, E earns $200,000, and F earns no income that is taxable. If the tax system defines the taxable unit as including married couples, there is no incentive for E to shift income to F since their income is aggregated in any event. Alternatively, if the tax system defines the taxable unit as the individual, there is an incentive for E to shift income to F to take advantage of F's lower marginal tax rates. Even in systems that tax married couples jointly, there is a tax incentive to shift income to children to reduce the family's overall tax liability. Thus, the rules for attributing and assigning income must complement the tax system's choice for the taxable unit.

---

1. I.R.C. §§ 151(a)-(c), 152.

2. I.R.C. § 151(d)(3).

3. S. 118 (1)(a) & (b) (Canadian Revenue Act).

4. IBDF, Global Individual Tax Handbook 2007 478 (Slovenia).

Students of United States taxation will recall the assignment of income principles derived from cases such as *Lucas v. Earl*[1] and *Helvering v. Horst*.[2] Other tax systems apply different principles. For example, in Belgium married taxpayers are taxed separately on earned income (e.g., wages and salary), but other items of income are aggregated and taxed to the spouse with the higher income.[3] In Denmark, spouses are also taxed separately but special rules (1) let one spouse transfer losses to the other, and (2) permit a spouse to use the unused personal credits and certain other tax benefits of the other spouse.[4] In Italy, spouses are taxed separately on earned income plus half of the income from community property and half the income of minor children.[5] In Greece, spouses file a joint return but each spouse is personally liable for his or her share of the joint tax. In calculating tax, personal deductions (e.g., mortgage interest) and credits are apportioned according to the income of each spouse. Losses of one spouse may not reduce the income of the other spouse and income earned by one spouse in a business owned by the other spouse is taxed to the owner of the business. The income of children under 18 is taxed to the parent with the highest income. Income of a child is taxed to the child if it is (1) earned by the child personally, (2) earned from property acquired by the child through a gift from anyone other than parents, or (3) pension income paid on the death of a parent.[6]

D.   INCOME ATTRIBUTION IN CANADA

In Canada, each individual is a separate taxpayer. Consequently, there is a strong incentive to shift income among family members in order to ameliorate the effects of progressive tax rates. Thus, it should not be surprising to learn that Canada has an array of statutes designed to check taxpayer strategies to shift income. The rules divide into two categories. The first category relates to assignments that do not involve a transfer of property by the taxpayer. The second set of provisions is directed at situations where the taxpayer does make a transfer of property. In cases where property is transferred by a taxpayer to another person, the relevant questions are: (1) who will be taxed on the income from the property, and (2) who will be taxed on any gain or loss from a subsequent sale of the property. As you go through the materials on attribution of income in Canada, consider whether the statutory rules in Canada are more or less effective in deterring attempts by

1.   281 U.S. 111, 50 S.Ct. 241 (1930).

2.   311 U.S. 112, 61 S.Ct. 144 (1940).

3.   IBDF, Global Individual Tax Handbook 2007 59 (Belgium).

4.   Id. at 144 (Denmark).

5.   Id. at 289 (Italy).

6.   Id. at 216 (Greece).

taxpayers to shift income and save taxes than the judicially created rules in the United States.

1. Assignments Without the Transfer of Property

The Canadian tax statutes include two provisions that deal with attempted shifting of income:[1]

S. 56(2) Indirect payments

A payment or transfer of property made pursuant to the direction of, or with the concurrence of, a taxpayer to some other person for the benefit of the taxpayer or as a benefit that the taxpayer desired to have conferred on the other person * * * shall be included in computing the taxpayer's income to the extent that it would be if the payment or transfer had been made to the taxpayer.

S. 56(4) Transfer of rights to income

Where a taxpayer has, at any time before the end of a taxation year, transferred or assigned to a person with whom the taxpayer was not dealing at arm's length the right to an amount * * * that would, if the right had not been so transferred or assigned, be included in computing the taxpayer's income for the taxation year, the part of the amount that relates to the period in the year throughout which the taxpayer is resident in Canada shall be included in computing the taxpayer's income for the year unless the income is from property and the taxpayer has also transferred or assigned the property.

Section 56(4) provides that transfers and assignments of income to a person "with whom the taxpayer was not dealing at arm's length" (defined to include individuals connected by blood relationship,[2] marriage, common-law partnership, or adoption) will not be effective for tax purposes to shift the income from the transferor. Thus, Mr. Earl would not be able to shift the incidence of taxation on one-half of his salary and fees by assigning them to his wife if he had lived in Canada. Also, Mr. Horst's gift of his interest coupons to his son would not be respected for tax purposes under Section 56(4).

Section 56(2) is directed at more sophisticated income-shifting strategies than outright assignments of income. The following

---

1. A third provision deals with income shifting through interest free or low interest loans. S. 56(4.1) (Canada).

2. "Blood relationship" includes children and other lineal descendants, brothers and sisters, spouses, common-law partners, and spouses and common-law partners of others connected by blood relationship (e.g., a daughter- or son-in-law). S. 251(6) (Canada).

excerpt from an interpretation by the Canadian Revenue Agency explains the operation of that provision.

IT–335R2

Canada Revenue Agency, July 12, 2004.

* * *

Summary

This bulletin discusses a rule directed against tax avoidance which might result when amounts which would constitute income when received by a particular taxpayer are paid to another person.

Discussion and Interpretation

Conditions for the application of subsection 56(2)

¶ **1.** Subsection 56(2) will cause an amount not received by a taxpayer to be added to the taxpayer's income if the following conditions are met:

(**a**) there is a payment or transfer of property to a person other than the taxpayer;

(**b**) the payment or transfer is pursuant to the direction of, or with the concurrence of, the taxpayer (this may be implicit— see ¶ 3);

(**c**) there is a benefit to the taxpayer or a benefit the taxpayer wishes to confer on the other person;

(**d**) the taxpayer would have been taxable on the amount under some other section of the Act :f the payment or transfer had been made directly to the taxpayer.

¶ **2.** Subsection 56(2) will not generally be applicable in a situation involving a *bona fide* loan between persons because such a loan does not constitute a "payment or transfer of property" within the meaning of that subsection. Whether a *bona fide* loan has been made in a particular situation is a mixed question of law and fact that will normally require, among other things, a review of the terms and conditions of the loan agreement. Factors to be considered would include whether the loan bears interest, the repayment terms, whether security is provided to the creditor, etc. However, if a loan is forgiven in a particular situation, the advance of funds may become a "payment or transfer" of property subject to subsection 56(2) at the time of the forgiveness of the said loan.

¶ **3.** The concurrence or participation of the taxpayer in the conferring of the benefit need not be active. It may be passive or implicit and can be inferred from all the circumstances of a particular situation (for example, the degree of control which the taxpayer is entitled to exercise over the corporation conferring the benefit).

¶ 4. Except as indicated in ¶ 9 with respect to dividend income, a taxpayer to whom subsection 56(2) applies need not be legally entitled to the property paid or transferred but must have some degree of control over its payment or transfer. Thus a shareholder who does not specifically direct a payment that falls under subsection 56(2) to be made but acquiesces in its payment will be taxable on the portion of the payment equal to the proportion of the number of shares owned by the shareholder to the total number of shares. Whether or not a shareholder will be viewed as having acquiesced in the payment will depend on the facts of the particular case.

* * *

Exception—Split Income

¶ 6. Pursuant to subsection 56(5), subsection 56(2) does not apply to any amount that is included in computing a specified individual's split income for a taxation year under section 120.4. Subsection 56(5) ensures that amounts taxed as split income in the hands of a minor child are not also attributed to another person.

Examples of the application of subsection 56(2)

Gifts to Shareholders' Relatives

¶ 7. Pursuant to the direction of, or with the concurrence of, its shareholders, a particular corporation makes gifts to relatives of the shareholders. These relatives are not shareholders or employees of the particular corporation. In such a situation, subsection 56(2) would apply to include in the shareholders' income the fair market value of the gifts made by the particular corporation. These gifts would constitute payments or transfers of property pursuant to the direction of, or with the concurrence of, the shareholders to some other persons (i.e. their relatives) as a benefit that the shareholders desired to have conferred on their relatives. Furthermore, an amount corresponding to the fair market value of the gifts would have been included in the shareholders' income under subsection 15(1) if the payments or transfers had been made by the particular corporation to the said shareholders. In this situation, each shareholder that directed or acquiesced in the payments or transfers would be taxable under subsection 56(2) on a portion of the payments or transfers made by the particular corporation that is equal to the proportion of the number of issued and outstanding shares of the corporation owned by the shareholder to the total number of shares that are in fact issued and outstanding.

Property Sold to Shareholder's Child below Fair Market Value

¶ **8.** X owns all of the issued and outstanding shares of Xco. At the direction of X, Xco sells a piece of land for consideration that is less than fair market value in favour of Y, the child of X. These transactions would have the following tax consequences. First, subsection 56(2) would apply to include in X's income an amount corresponding to the difference between the fair market value of the property transferred and the consideration paid by Y. The transfer of the piece of land by Xco to some other person (i.e. Y) is made pursuant to the direction of X as a benefit that X desired to have conferred on Y and an amount corresponding to the difference between the fair market value of the property transferred and the consideration paid by X would have been included in X's income under subsection 15(1) if the transfer had been made by Xco to X. Furthermore, under paragraph 69(1)(*b*), Xco would be deemed to have received proceeds of disposition equal to the fair market value of the piece of land at the time of the transfer. Finally, the adjusted cost base of the piece of land to Y would, technically, be equal to the consideration he or she paid to Xco. See the current version of IT–405, *Inadequate Considerations—Acquisitions and Dispositions*, for additional discussions on the application of subsection 69(1).

Dividends

¶ **9.** Absent a sham, subterfuge or an artificial transaction and provided that proper consideration was given for the shares when issued, subsection 56(2) does not generally apply to dividend income since, until a dividend is declared, the profits belong to the corporation as retained earnings. However, subsection 56(2) may be applicable where dividends are paid to shareholders of a corporation who, having regard to the dividend entitlements of their shares as set out in the articles of incorporation, receive dividends to which they are not entitled and/or where another taxpayer has a pre-existing entitlement to the dividend income paid to shareholders of a corporation.

Other comments

Income or capital treatment

¶ **10.** The amount to be included in the taxpayer's income is the amount that would have been included in the taxpayer's income if the payment or transfer had been made directly to the taxpayer. The amount is considered to be income or capital to the taxpayer in the same way it would have been if the taxpayer had received the amount directly.

Application to arm's length or non-arm's length transactions

¶ **11.** Subsection 56(2) applies to both arm's-length and non-arm's length transactions if the conditions listed in ¶ 1 are met.

Inclusion of an amount in the income of a taxpayer and in the income of the recipient of the property

* * *

¶ **13.** An amount to which subsection 56(2) applies could be included in the income of both the taxpayer and the person who receives the payment or the property. However, it is normally the Canada Revenue Agency's (CRA) practice not to assess the same income twice. Accordingly, where the taxpayer agrees to the reallocation, the recipient's income will be reduced. Where the taxpayer does not agree, the CRA will also reduce the recipient's income, without requiring a waiver, provided that at the time of the assessing action, the recipient's return was not about to become statute-barred; in those cases, the CRA will seek a waiver.

Note

Introduction. The principles underlying Section 56(2) should be familiar to students of the Internal Revenue Code. Recall *Old Colony Trust v. Commissioner*,[3] where the American Woolen Company adopted resolutions agreeing to pay over $1 million of Mr. Wood's federal tax liability for 1919 and 1920. The Supreme Court characterized the issue in the case as "whether a taxpayer, having induced a third person to pay his income tax or having acquiesced in such payment as made in discharge of an obligation to him, may avoid the making of a return thereof and the payment of the corresponding tax." How would Mr. Wood have fared under Section 56(2)? Section 83 of the Internal Revenue Code also embodies principles similar to those in Section 56(2). That section taxes a taxpayer on the value of property transferred to any other person if the transfer is made in connection with the taxpayer's performance of services.

Dividends. Interpretation 335R2 states that dividends will not be attributed under Section 56(2) when they are paid in accordance with the shareholder's rights to corporate distributions. That conclusion is based on two decisions of the Canadian Supreme Court,[4] one of which is reproduced below.

3. 279 U.S. 716, 49 S.Ct. 499 (1929).

4. Neuman v. Minister of National Revenue, 98 D.T.C. 6297, 3 C.T.C. 177, 1 S.C.R. 770 (S.C.C. 1998); McClurg v. Minister of National Revenue, 91 D.T.C. 5001, 1 C.T.C.169, 3 S.C.R. 1020 (S.C.C. 1991).

NEUMAN v. MINISTER OF NATIONAL REVENUE

Supreme Court of Canada, 1998.
98 D.T.C. 6297, 3 C.T.C. 177, 1 S.C.R. 770.

IACOBUCCI, J.:

1. The principal question raised by this appeal is whether dividend income, paid by a closely held family corporation to a non-arm's length shareholder who has not contributed to or participated in the business of the corporation, in this case Ruby Neuman, should be attributed to the shareholder's spouse, the appellant Melville Neuman, for income tax purposes in accordance with s. 56(2) of the Income Tax Act, * * *. I conclude that s. 56(2) does not apply to dividend income such that the dividend income received by Ruby Neuman cannot be attributed to the appellant for income tax purposes.

1. FACTS

2. The appellant was at all material times a lawyer with the Firm of Neuman, MacLean in Winnipeg. The appellant and his partners at the law firm each owned 1,285.714 common shares in Newmac Services (1973) Ltd. ("Newmac"), which owned commercial property in downtown Winnipeg, including the offices of Neuman, MacLean. The appellant acted as secretary of Newmac. The appellant's wife. Ruby Neuman, had no involvement in the business of Newmac.

3. On April 29, 1981, the appellant incorporated Melru Ventures Inc. ("Melru") as a family holding company. Rothstein, J. of the Federal Court, Trial Division found that Melru was incorporated for tax planning and income splitting purposes and that it had no other independent business purpose * * *.

4. The capital structure of Melru provided for different classes of shares with different rights and privileges. The dividends were to be declared at the sole discretion of the directors; distributions could be done selectively among the various classes of shares. The rights and conditions of the Class "G" and "F" shares are as follows:

> (a) the holders of Class "G" shares shall in each year, in the discretion of the directors, be entitled out of any or all profits or surplus available for dividend to non-cumulative dividends at such rate as may from time to time be declared on any such shares but not exceeding the equivalent of 1% per annum en "redemption price" above the maximum prime bank rates ...

> * * *

> (e) all dividends paid or declared and set aside for payment in any fiscal year, after making payments on Class "G" shares

and preference shares of dividends declared shall be paid firstly on Class "F" shares until dividends aggregating 1¢ per share on the Class "F" shares then outstanding have been paid and then any additional dividends shall be set aside for payment on common shares until the common shares then outstanding shall have received 1¢ per share and any additional dividends shall be paid on Class "F" shares until they receive that fraction of profits properly available for payment of dividends as the number of Class "F" shares then outstanding bear to the total number of Class "F" shares and common shares then outstanding and the balance shall in the discretion of the directors be paid on common shares or set aside for future payment on common shares at the discretion of the board of directors.

5.   Pursuant to an agreement dated April 29, 1981, the appellant sold his shares in Newmac to Melru for 1,285.714 Class "G" shares of Melru. The shares were sold on a tax-deferred basis pursuant to s. 85(1) of the ITA and they were described as having a fair market value of $120,000. On May 1, 1981, a meeting of the first director was held at which the appellant was appointed president and Ruby Neuman was appointed secretary. One voting common share of Melru was issued to the appellant for $1. A special general meeting of the shareholders was held that same day at which the appellant resigned as first director and was elected director of Melru until the first annual meeting of the corporation. Ruby Neuman acted as secretary at this meeting. That same day there was a meeting of the board of directors which the appellant chaired. A resolution was passed authorizing the issue of 1,285.714 Class "G" shares to the appellant in accordance with the agreement of sale. A second resolution was passed authorizing the issue of 99 non-voting Class "F" shares to Ruby Neuman at $1.00 per share.

6.   The first annual meeting of shareholders was held on August 12, 1982. Ruby Neuman was elected sole director of Melru and the appellant and Ruby Neuman were appointed as officers.

7.   In 1982, Melru received $20,000 in dividends on the Newmac shares. These were the first dividends paid on the Newmac shares. A board of directors meeting was held on September 8, 1982 at which time Ruby Neuman declared a dividend in the amount of $5,000 to be paid on the Class "G" shares and another dividend of $14,800 to be paid on the Class "F" shares. The minutes indicate that the holder of the common shares (i.e., the appellant) was prepared to have money set aside for future payment on his shares.

8.   Ruby Neuman immediately loaned $14,800 to the appellant and she received in return a demand promissory note as security. Ruby Neuman died in 1988. The loan was not repaid.

9.   Rothstein J. made the following relevant findings of fact * * *:

1.   The dividends declared by Ruby Neuman on her own Class "F" shares and the appellant's Class "G" shares were declared pursuant to a discretionary dividend clause in the Articles of Incorporation of Melru. The dividends of $14,800 on the "F" shares and $5,000 on the "G" shares were arbitrary numbers.

2.   Ruby Neuman made no contribution to Melru, nor did she assume any risks for the company.

3.   The appellant's evidence was that when his wife was elected director of Melru, he explained to her the duties of a director, that directors manage the corporation, that they have a duty to the corporation, and that they make the decisions. The appellant said that he made recommendations to his wife which she accepted but that the decision as to the declaration of dividends was hers.

10.   The dividend income paid to Ruby Neuman in 1982 was attributed to the appellant as being a payment or transfer of property made pursuant to the direction of or with the concurrence of the appellant as described in s. 56(2) of the ITA and he was assessed tax on this income.

11.   The appellant appealed his 1982 assessment to the Tax Court of Canada and in 1992 the assessment was vacated * * *. The respondent appealed to the Federal Court, Trial Division without success, but a further appeal to the Federal Court of Appeal was successful * * *.

* * *

3.   Issues

31.   The central question raised by this appeal is whether the dividend income received by Ruby Neuman should be attributed to the appellant for tax purposes under s. 56(2) of the ITA. * * *

32.   In order for s. 56(2) to apply, four preconditions, each of which is detailed in the language of the s. 56(2) itself, must be present:

(1) the payment must be to a person other than the reassessed taxpayer;

(2) the allocation must be at the direction or with the concurrence of the reassessed taxpayer;

(3) the payment must be for the benefit of the reassessed taxpayer or for the benefit of another person whom the reassessed taxpayer wished to benefit; and

(4) the payment would have been included in the reassessed taxpayer's income if it had been received by him or her.

* * *

33.   Because I conclude that s. 56(2) does not apply to dividend income since dividend income, by its very nature, cannot satisfy the fourth precondition absent a sham or other subterfuge, it is not necessary to discuss the other three prerequisites to the application of s. 56(2).

4.   ANALYSIS

A.   Introduction

34.   As the judicial history of this appeal reveals, the interpretation of this Court's majority decision in McClurg lies at the heart of the present case. This Court held in McClurg that generally s. 56(2) will not apply to dividend income. However, Dickson C.J. suggested in obiter in McClurg that s. 56(2) may apply where dividend income is distributed through the exercise of a discretionary power to a non-arm's length shareholder who has made no legitimate contribution to the company * * *. The Federal Court of Appeal felt bound by the potential exception articulated by Dickson C.J. in obiter since the facts in the present case were similar to the facts in McClurg with the only material difference being that Ruby Neuman, unlike Wilma McClurg, had not made any contribution to the corporation.

35.   A large part of my analysis will involve a review of the holdings in McClurg. Before I turn to McClurg, however, I wish to make some observations to place the present debate into its proper perspective. First, s. 56(2) strives to prevent tax avoidance through income splitting; however, it is a specific tax avoidance provision and not a general provision against income splitting. In fact, "there is no general scheme to prevent income splitting" in the ITA (V. Krishna and J. A. VanDuzer, "Corporate Share Capital Structures and Income Splitting: McClurg v. Canada" (1992–93), 21 Can. Bus. L.J. 335, at p. 367). Section 56(2) can only operate to prevent income splitting where the four preconditions to its application are specifically met.

36.   Second, this case concerns income received by Ruby Neuman during the 1982 taxation year at which time the ITA did not provide specific guidelines to deal with corporate structures designed for the purposes of income splitting and tax minimization. Professor V. Krishna, in an article entitled "Share Capital Structure of Closely–Held Private Corporations" (1996), 7 Can. Curr. Tax. 7, at p. 9, made the following comment with respect to income splitting in the corporate context:

Except when specifically curtailed by the Income Tax Act (for example, by the attribution rules), income splitting per se is not a sanctioned arrangement. Thus, corporate structures that facilitate income splitting in private companies should not be penalized without clear statutory language and intent. * * *

Parliament has since fashioned legislation to regulate corporate income splitting (s. 74.4 of the ITA, introduced in 1985), but this legislation does not apply to the present appeal.

37.   Third, this appeal is limited to the interpretation and application of s. 56(2) of the ITA; the appeal is not based on the general anti-avoidance rule set out in s. 245 of the ITA ("GAAR"). GAAR came into force on September 13, 1988 and it applies only to transactions entered into on or after that date.

38.   Fourth, the respondent has not argued that the appellant was involved in a sham or an artificial transaction and this was acknowledged by counsel for the respondent during the hearing.

39.   Finally, it is important to remember that this Court held unanimously in Stubart, supra, at p. 575, that a transaction should not be disregarded for tax purposes because it has no independent or bona fide business purpose (Estey, J. wrote for himself and Beetz and McIntyre, JJ.; Wilson, J. wrote concurring reasons for herself and Ritchie, J.). Thus, taxpayers can arrange their affairs in a particular way for the sole purpose of deliberately availing themselves of tax reduction devices in the ITA. Estey, J. rejected the suggestion that a distinction must be drawn between non-arm's length and arm's length transactions in the application of this principle (at pp. 570–72). According to Stubart, therefore, non-arm's length arrangements can also be created for the sole purpose of taking advantage of tax reduction devices.

40.   With these points in mind, I now turn to the decision of the Court in McClurg.

B.   McClurg

41.   McClurg involved a taxpayer and business associate who were the sole directors of a corporation which they had set up and in which they and their wives were shareholders. The corporation operated an International Harvester truck dealership. The capital structure of the corporation provided for three classes of shares with different rights and privileges: Class A shares were common, voting and participating shares; Class B shares were common, non-voting and participating where so authorized by the directors; and Class C shares were preferred non-voting shares. The dividends were to be declared at the sole discretion of the directors; distributions could be done selectively among the three classes of shares.

Essentially, the capital structure was designed to permit income splitting.

42.   Jim McClurg and his associate held class A and C shares whereas their wives held class B shares. In 1978, 1979, and 1980 the wives of the directors each received $100/share on their Class B shares: $10,000/year. These were the only dividends declared in those years.

43.   Wilma McClurg made legitimate contributions to the business. She exposed herself to extensive liability by assisting in the financing of the business. She also worked as an administrative assistant, drove a truck when necessary, and generally fulfilled needs as they arose.

44.   The Minister reassessed Jim McClurg's income for 1978 to 1980 on the basis that $8000 of the $10,000 in dividends paid to his wife each year was attributable to him through the operation of s. 56(2). The Minister also challenged the validity of the discretionary dividend provision.

(i) The ratio in McClurg.

45.   Dickson, C.J., writing for himself and Sopinka, Gonthier and Cory, JJ. (Wilson, La Forest and L'Heureux–Dube, JJ. in dissent) first: dealt with the issue of whether the discretionary dividend provision was valid as a matter of corporate law; he concluded that it was. He then turned to the tax issue and he held that the dividend income paid to Wilma McClurg was not attributable to her husband for income tax purposes through the operation of s. 56(2).

46.   This Court concluded that, as a general rule. s. 56(2) does not apply to dividend income since, until a dividend is declared, the profits belong to the corporation as retained earnings. The declaration of a dividend cannot be said, therefore, to be a diversion of a benefit which the taxpayer would have otherwise received (at p. 1052). Dickson, C.J. explained the ruling as follows (at p. 1052):

> While it is always open to the courts to "pierce the corporate veil" in order to prevent parties from benefitting from increasingly complex and intricate tax avoidance techniques, in my view a dividend payment does not fall within the scope of s. 56(2). The purpose of s. 56(2) is to ensure that payments which otherwise would have been received by the taxpayer are not diverted to a third party as an anti-avoidance technique. This purpose is not frustrated because, in the corporate law context, until a dividend is declared, the profits belong to a corporation as a juridical person: [B. Welling, Corporate Law in Canada (1984), at pp. 609–10]. Had a dividend not been declared and paid to a third party, it would not otherwise have been received

by the taxpayer. Rather, the amount simply would have been retained as earnings by the company. Consequently, as a general rule, a dividend payment cannot reasonably be considered a benefit diverted from a taxpayer to a third party within the contemplation of s. 56(2).

47. Although not explicitly stated, Dickson, C.J.'s preceding comments concern the fourth precondition to the application of s. 56(2): that the payment would have been included in the reassessed taxpayer's income if it had been received by him or her. In essence, dividend income does not satisfy this prerequisite to attribution since the reassessed taxpayer would not have received the income had it not been paid to the shareholder. In effect, this Court implicitly interpreted the fourth precondition to include an entitlement requirement; entitlement is used in the sense that the reassessed taxpayer would have otherwise received the payments in dispute. * * *

48. An entitlement requirement in the sense I have described is consistent with the stated purpose of s. 56(2), which is to capture and attribute to the reassessed taxpayer "receipts which he or she otherwise would have obtained" (McClurg, at p. 1051). Dividend income cannot pass the fourth test because the dividend, if not paid to a shareholder, remains with the corporation as retained earnings; the reassessed taxpayer, as either director or shareholder of the corporation, has no entitlement to the money.

49. This is the only interpretation which makes sense and which avoids absurdity in the application of s. 56(2), as noted by Dickson, C.J. * * *:

> ... but for the declaration (and allocation), the dividend would remain part of the retained earnings of the company. That cannot legitimately be considered as within the parameters of the legislative intent of s. 56(2). If this Court were to find otherwise, corporate directors potentially could be found liable for the tax consequences of any declaration of dividends made to a third party ... this would be an unrealistic interpretation of the subsection consistent with neither its object nor its spirit. It would violate fundamental principles of corporate law and the realities of commercial practice and would "overshoot" the legislative purpose of the section.

50. I note that the decision in Outerbridge Estate, supra, which was rendered shortly before this Court's ruling in McClurg, appears to challenge the view that where a taxpayer is not entitled to a payment that payment cannot be attributed to him or her under s. 56(2). Outerbridge Estate, however, did not involve the attribution of dividend income.

51.   In Outerbridge Estate, the majority shareholder in an investment company caused the corporation to sell some of its shares to his son-in-law, who was also a shareholder in the corporation, for a price of $100 per share. The Minister calculated the fair market value of the shares at approximately $1,000 per share and reassessed the majority shareholder under s. 56(2) by adding as income the difference between what the son-in-law paid for the shares and their market value.

52.   Marceau, J.A., writing for the court, held that the fact that the taxpayer had no direct entitlement to the shares did not preclude attribution since there was no indication that s. 56(2) was intended to be so confined. Marceau, J.A. concluded * * * that:

> [w]hen the doctrine of "constructive receipt" is not clearly involved, because the taxpayer had no entitlement to the payment being made or the property being transferred, it is fair to infer that subsection 56(2) may receive application only if the benefit conferred is not directly taxable in the hands of the transferee.

Marceau, J.A. distinguished the Federal Court of Appeal's ruling in McClurg where Urie J. held that s. 56(2) does not apply to dividend income, which holding was affirmed by this Court, as follows * * *:

> [t]he McClurg decision was concerned with a declaration of dividend in accordance (in the views of the majority) with the powers conferred by the share structure of the corporation and I do not see it as having authority beyond the particular type of situation with which it was dealing.

53.   I agree with Marceau, J.A.: Outerbridge Estate concerned the conferral of a benefit which was not in the form of dividend income. The application of s. 56(2) to non-dividend income was not before this Court in McClurg and it is not before this Court in the present case. But the entitlement requirement implicitly read into the fourth precondition of s. 56(2) in McClurg clearly applies to dividend income.

54.   I conclude that, unless a reassessed taxpayer had a preexisting entitlement to the dividend income paid to the shareholder of a corporation, the fourth precondition cannot be satisfied and consequently s. 56(2) cannot operate to attribute the dividend income to that taxpayer for income tax purposes.

(ii) The obiter dicta in McClurg and the exception to the general rule.

55.   The finding that dividend income cannot satisfy the fourth precondition to the application of s. 56(2), as modified by the implicit entitlement requirement, was dispositive of the McClurg case. La Forest, J. agreed with the majority's conclusion that bona

fide dividend income does not fall within the scope of s. 56(2). However, he dissented on the finding under corporate law that the discretionary dividend clause was valid; therefore the dividend income at issue in McClurg was not, in his view, bona fide and s. 56(2) applied * * *.

56. Despite these conclusions, Dickson, C.J. went on to consider the third precondition, that the payment must be for the benefit of the reassessed taxpayer or for the benefit of another person whom the reassessed taxpayer wished to benefit, and in so doing, he qualified his earlier interpretation of the fourth precondition. In his view, Wilma McClurg's receipt of the funds was not a "benefit" as required by s. 56(2) (the third precondition) since her contributions to the corporate enterprise could be described as a "legitimate quid pro quo and were not simply an attempt to avoid the payment of taxes" (p. 1054). Since Wilma McClurg had made legitimate contributions to the corporation, the application of s. 56(2) "would be contrary to the commercial reality of this particular transaction" * * *.

57. Dickson, C.J. seemed to be of the view that the character of a shareholder's dividend income is to be determined by that shareholder's level of contribution to the corporation. This approach ignores the fundamental nature of dividends; a dividend is a payment which is related by way of entitlement to one's capital or share interest in the corporation and not to any other consideration. Thus, the quantum of one's contribution to a company, and any dividends received from that corporation, are mutually independent of one another. La Forest, J. made the same observation in his dissenting reasons in McClurg * * *:

> With respect, this fact is irrelevant to the issue before us. To relate dividend receipts to the amount of effort expended by the recipient on behalf of the payor corporation is to misconstrue the nature of a dividend. As discussed earlier, a dividend is received by virtue of ownership of the capital stock of a corporation. It is a fundamental principle of corporate law that a dividend is a return on capital which attaches to a share, and is in no way dependent on the conduct of a particular shareholder.

58. Dickson, C.J.'s finding that Wilma McClurg's contributions to the corporation resulted in the dividend being consideration for her efforts rather than a" benefit" as required by s. 56(2) opened the door to his obiter comments which have led to some confusion * * *:

> In my opinion, if a distinction is to be drawn in the application of s. 56(2) between arm's length and non-arm's length transactions, it should be made between the exercise of a discretionary

power to distribute dividends when the non-arm's length shareholder has made no contribution to the company (in which case s. 56(2) may be applicable), and those cases in which a legitimate contribution has been made.

59.   Dickson, C.J. is suggesting, it would seem, that where a non-arm's length shareholder receives a dividend from a corporation to which he or she has made no contribution (the dividend income therefore constituting a "benefit" for the purposes of s. 56(2) in Dickson, C.J.'s view), precondition four, interpreted by him to include an entitlement requirement, is automatically considered satisfied, or need not be satisfied, with the result that s. 56(2) applies.

60.   In my view, it is wrong to suggest that there may be an exception to the rule that s. 56(2) does not apply to dividend income where the recipient of the dividend income in a non-arm's length transaction has not made a "legitimate contribution" to the corporation. In so stating, I assume, of course, that proper consideration was given for the shares when issued. I am not aware of any principle of corporate law that requires in addition that a so-called "legitimate contribution" be made by a shareholder to entitle him or her to dividend income and it is well accepted that tax law embraces corporate law principles unless such principles are specifically set aside by the taxing statute.

61.   Furthermore, there is no principled basis upon which this distinction can be drawn; the fact that a company is closely held or that no contribution is made to the company by a shareholder benefiting from a dividend in no way changes the underlying nature of a dividend. Neither the fact that the transaction is non-arm's length nor the fact that the shareholder has not contributed to the corporation serves to overcome the conclusion that dividend income cannot satisfy the fourth precondition to attribution under s. 56(2).

62.   Moreover, the obiter comments raise the difficult task of determining what constitutes a legitimate contribution. What will be the criteria upon which one can ascertain with any degree of precision or certainty that a contribution is legitimate?

63.   Finally, the requirement of a legitimate contribution is in some ways an attempt to invite a review of the transactions in issue in accordance with the doctrines of sham or artificiality. Implicit in the distinction between non-arm's length and arm's length transactions is the assumption that non-arm's length transactions lend themselves to the creation of corporate structures which exist for the sole purpose of avoiding tax and therefore should be caught by s. 56(2). However, as mentioned above, taxpayers are entitled to arrange their affairs for the sole purpose of achieving a favourable position regarding taxation and no distinction is to be made in the

application of this principle between arm's length and non-arm's length transactions (see Stubart, supra). The ITA has many specific anti-avoidance provisions and rules governing the treatment of non-arm's length transactions. We should not be quick to embellish the provision at issue here when it is open for the legislator to be precise and specific with respect to any mischief to be avoided.

64. To summarize, it is inappropriate to consider the contributions of a shareholder to a corporation when determining whether s. 56(2) applies. Dividends are paid to shareholders as a return on their investment in the corporation. Since the distribution of the dividend is not determined by the quantum of a shareholder's contribution to the corporation, it would be illogical to use contribution as the criterion that determines when dividend income will be subject to s. 56(2). The same principles apply in the context of both non-arm's length relationships such as often exist between small closely held corporations and their shareholders, and arm's length relationships such as exist between publicly held corporations and their shareholders.

5. CONCLUSION

65. For the foregoing reasons, s. 56(2) does not apply to the dividend income received by Ruby Neuman. The appeal is therefore allowed, the decision of the Federal Court of Appeal is reversed, and that portion of the respondent's assessment which attributes the dividend income received by Ruby Neuman to the appellant is set aside with costs throughout.

Appeal allowed.

Note

Note that the trial court in *Neuman* "found that Melru was incorporated for tax planning and income splitting purposes and that it had no other independent business purpose * * *." If there was no business reason for the existence of Melru, how could its creation have been respected as part of a plan to avoid paying tax? Does the Supreme Court's analysis in paragraphs 35–39 help to answer that question? And note the Court's statement in paragraph 63 about the proper roles of the legislature and the courts in combating tax avoidance.

Subsequent to *Neuman,* the Canadian Parliament enacted an additional income-attribution rule. Section 74.4 of the Canadian income tax attributes interest income (calculated at designated rates) to an individual who transfers or lends property to a trust or corporation where "one of the main purposes of the transfer or loan may reasonably be considered to be to reduce the income of the individual and to benefit, either directly or indirectly," a related person including a spouse, common-law partner, or minor child. Section 74.4, however, does not apply in the case of a "small business corporation," which is defined as including a Canadian-controlled private corporation all or substantially all of the assets of which are used principally in an active business carried on primarily in Canada.[5] How effective do you think Section 74.4 will be in deterring income-splitting plans like the one in *Neuman*?

The *Overton* case, which follows, is a case decided under the Internal Revenue Code at a time when the individual was the taxable unit in the United States. Joint returns by married taxpayers were not permitted. Consider how the analysis in *Overton* might be applied to tax Mr. Neuman.

OVERTON v. COMMISSIONER
United States Court of Appeals, Second Circuit, 1947.
162 F.2d 155.

SWAN, CIRCUIT JUDGE.

These appeals involve gift tax liability of petitioner Overton for the years 1936 and 1937 and income tax liability of petitioner Oliphant for the year 1941. Each petitioner was held liable on the theory that dividends received by his wife in the year in question on stock registered in her name on the books of Castle & Overton, Inc., a New York corporation, were income of the husband for tax purposes. No gift tax return with respect to such dividends was filed by Mr. Overton in 1936 or 1937, and the dividends received by Mrs. Oliphant in 1941 were not included in her husband's return for that year.

There is no dispute as to the evidentiary facts. They are stated in detail in the opinion of the Tax Court, 6 T.C. 304, and will be here repeated only so far as may be necessary to render intelligible the discussion which follows. On May 26, 1936 the corporation had outstanding 1,000 shares of common stock without par value but having a liquidating value of at least $120 per share. On that date, pursuant to a plan devised to lessen taxes, the certificate of incorporation was amended to provide for changing the outstanding common stock into 2,000 shares without par value, of which 1,000 were denominated Class A and 1,000 Class B. The old stock was exchanged for the new, the shareholders then gave the B stock to their respective wives, and new certificates therefor were issued to the wives. The B stock had a liquidating value of one dollar per share; everything else on liquidation was to belong to the holders of the A stock, who had also the sole voting rights for directors and all ordinary matters.[1] By virtue of an agreement made in April 1937

---

5. S. 248 (1) (Canada).

1. Whether the amendment of the certificate of incorporation excluded B shareholders from voting on extraordinary matters specified in section 51 of the Stock Corporation Law of New York,

restricting alienation of their stock, the wives were precluded from realizing more than one dollar a share by selling their shares. The A stock was to receive noncumulative dividends at the rate of $10 a share per year before payment of any dividend on the B stock; if dividends in excess of $10 per share were paid on the A stock in any year, such excess dividends were to be shared by both classes of stock in the ratio of one-fifth thereof for the A stock and four-fifths for the B stock. During the six year period ending in December 1941, the dividends paid on B stock totaled $150.40 a share as against $77.60 a share paid on A stock. In 1941 the A stock had a book value of $155 per share.

The Tax Court was of opinion that the 1936 arrangement, though made in the form of a gift of stock, was in reality an assignment of part of the taxpayers' future dividends. Unless form is to be exalted above substance this conclusion is inescapable. Since the total issue of B stock represented only $1,000 of the corporate assets, it is plain that the property which earned the large dividends received by the B shareholders was the property represented by the A stock held by the husbands. In transferring the B shares to their wives they parted with no substantial part of their interest in the corporate property. Had they been content to transfer some of the original common stock they could have accomplished their purpose of lessening taxes on the family group,[2] but they would then have made substantial gifts of capital. The arrangement they put into effect gave the wives nothing, or substantially nothing, but the right to future earnings flowing from property retained by the husbands. That anticipatory assignments of income, whatever their formal cloak, are ineffective taxwise is a principle too firmly established to be subject to question. See Lucas v. Earl, 281 U.S. 111, 50 S.Ct. 241 74 L.Ed. 731; Helvering v. Horst, 311 U.S. 112, 61 S.Ct. 144, 85 L.Ed. 75, 131 A.L.R. 655; * * *. We think the Tax Court correctly applied this principle to the facts of the case at bar.

Orders affirmed.

Note

Income Splitting Via Deductible Payments. Making deductible payments to a related taxpayer is another income-splitting strategy. For example, assume that Mom is a lawyer who conducts an active litigation practice. If Mom hires her minor Son to do copying, filing, and other routine office work and pays Son an hourly wage, she will be entitled to a deduction for the expenditure and Son will have gross

---

McK. Consol. Laws, c. 59, in effect on May 26,1937, the Tax Court did not find it necessary to determine, nor do we.

2. See Blair v. Commissioner, 300 U.S. 5, 57 S.Ct. 330.

income. The net effect of the deduction to Mom and the income to Son is that the payments to Son will be taxed at his marginal tax rate rather than at Mom's presumably higher rate. There are, of course, requirements that have to be satisfied for this strategy to work. Basically, the transaction must be "real." Son must actually perform the services and his compensation must be "reasonable;" that is, paid at an arm's length rate. These safeguards are needed to prevent Mom from turning what is in reality a gift into a deductible expenditure.

The strategy employed by Mom and Son in the preceding example can be used in a variety of situations. Following is a case that involves a more intricate variation of the scheme employed in Canada.

FERREL v. HER MAJESTY THE QUEEN
Tax Court of Canada, 1997.
97 D.T.C. 1565, 1 C.T.C. 2269 (1998), aff'd 99 D.T.C.
5111, 2 C.T.C. 101 (Fed.Ct.App. 1999).

MOGAN, T.C.J.:

1.   The Appellant was the settlor of the Ferrel Family Trust ("the Trust") established in May 1983. Since December 1984, the Appellant has been the sole trustee of the Trust. Neotric Enterprises Inc. ("Neotric") is a family holding company with four subsidiary corporations. The equity shares of Neotric are held by the Trust and the non-participating voting shares are held by the Appellant. In its fiscal periods ending September 30, 1989 and 1990, Neotric accrued management fees of $152,000 and $150,000 respectively, payable to the Trust. In the 1989 calendar year, Neotric actually paid management fees of $124,000 to the Trust. In 1990, Neotric paid management fees of $128,000 to the Trust. The remaining $50,000 of the accrued management fees was paid by Neotric to the Trust in 1991. By notices of reassessment the Minister of National Revenue added to the Appellant's reported income $152,000 for 1989 and $150,000 for 1990 applying subsections 56(2) and 56(4) of the Income Tax Act. The Appellant has appealed from those reassessments. The primary issue in these appeals for the 1989 and 1990 taxation years is whether the Appellant is required to include in his income the management fees paid or payable by Neotric to the Trust.

* * *

3.   The Appellant is a chartered accountant who identified himself in the witness stand as a businessman. He explained that the Trust was established in 1983 for a variety of purposes: to set up a fund for the education of his children; to protect family assets from creditors; to permit a transfer of family assets to the children at a low cost upon the death of the parents; and to permit preferred beneficiary elections with respect to the income of the Trust. The

income beneficiaries of the Trust are the Appellant's two children, Conrad and Erin, born in 1978 and 1980, respectively.

4.   [T]he income of the Trust in each year was in fact allocated between the two income beneficiaries on an equal basis and preferred beneficiary elections were filed with respect to that income. Most of the cash was left in the Trust and loaned back to Neotric for use within the family group of corporations.

5.   The two critical documents are Exhibits A–4 and A–5 which are the agreements under which the Appellant claims that the Trust provided management services to Neotric and, in turn, earned management fees. Because these documents are important, I shall set out their relevant parts. Exhibit A–4 is an agreement made January 1, 1986 between the Trust (identified as "FFT") and the Appellant in his personal capacity (identified as "KEF"). Set out below are the recitals and the first three clauses of Exhibit A–4. The corporation described in the first recital as 299377 Alberta Limited later changed its name to Neotric Enterprises Inc. and so I have changed the nomenclature in the remaining quoted parts of Exhibit A–4 from "299377" to "Neotric".

> WHEREAS FFT has agreed that FFT shall provide management services to 299377 Alberta Ltd. ("299377")
>
> WHEREAS KEF is the only trustee of FFT
>
> WHEREAS KEF has agreed as trustee of FFT to be the manager of FFT management services offered by FFT to Neotric
>
> NOW THEREFORE THIS AGREEMENT WITNESSETH THAT for and in consideration of the mutual covenants herein contained and other good and valuable consideration, the receipt and sufficiency whereof is hereby acknowledged, the KEF as trustee of FFT and FFT agree as follows:
>
> 1.   KEF shall, subject as herein provided, be the President and Secretary/Treasurer of the Neotric and its associated companies and shall act on behalf of FFT in various other management positions. KEF may appoint and engage any other parties to represent FFT or Neotric on various boards and to perform any work necessary or needed.
>
> 2.   The trustee(s) of FFT and KEF shall agree at various times as to the remuneration to be paid to KEF, if any.
>
> 3.   In addition to the fee provided for in clause 2 hereof, KEF shall be entitled to be reimbursed for all expenses properly incurred by KEF in the performance of his duties hereunder.

Exhibit A–5 is an agreement made January 1, 1989 between Neotric (identified as the "Corporation"), the Trust (identified as

"FFT") and the Appellant (identified as "KEF"). Set out below are the relevant provisions of Exhibit A–5:

> WHEREAS the Corporation and FFT have agreed that FFT shall provide the services of KEF who shall be appointed President and Secretary of the Corporation.
>
> NOW THEREFORE THIS AGREEMENT WITNESSETH THAT for and in consideration of the mutual covenants herein contained and other good and valuable consideration, the receipt and sufficiency whereof is hereby acknowledged, the Corporation and FFT agree as follows:
>
> 1. KEF shall, subject as herein provided, be the President and Secretary of the Corporation.
>
> 2. For services rendered by KEF the Corporation shall pay FFT management fees to be agreed upon from time to time.
>
> 3. In addition to the fee provided for in clause 2 hereof, KEF shall be entitled to be reimbursed for all expenses properly incurred by KEF in the performance of his duties hereunder.

6. * * * According to the unchallenged evidence of the Appellant, Conrad and Erin together paid aggregate income taxes in excess of $95,000 in the years 1989, 1990 and 1991 with respect to the amounts $124,000 plus $128,000 plus $50,000 which were allocated to them in those respective years. None of the money paid by Neotric to the Trust as management fees ever came into the hands of the Appellant or his wife directly or indirectly.

7. The Appellant argues that the Trust is a business trust in the sense that it is a trust carrying on a business (i.e. providing management services). In accordance with Exhibit A–5, the management services were provided to Neotric not by the Appellant but by the Trust through the medium of the Appellant. Counsel for the Appellant compared the three-way relationship between the Trust, Neotric and the Appellant with professional corporations which are common in the province of Alberta where a professional corporation will agree to provide professional services to a client but the professional services will in fact be performed by a particular professionally qualified individual who owns the shares of the professional corporation. In those circumstances, the services and the compensation flow between the professional corporation and the client even though the actual services are performed by the professionally qualified individual who stands behind the corporation.

8. To support the integrity of the agreement which is Exhibit A–5, the Appellant relies on the decision of the Supreme Court of Canada in Minister of National Revenue v. Cameron (1972), 72 D.T.C. 6325 (S.C.C.). In that case, Mr. Cameron and two associates

had been employed by a company referred to as "Campbell Limited". Mr. Cameron and his two associates resigned from their employment with Campbell Limited and formed a new management company of which they became equal shareholders as well as employees. The new management company agreed to provide the services of Mr. Cameron and his two associates to Campbell Limited. The former employer paid amounts to the new management company which were approximately equal to the salaries which had previously been paid to Mr. Cameron and his two associates; but the new management company did not disburse to Mr. Cameron and his associates the full amounts received from Campbell Limited. The Minister of National Revenue looked at the whole transaction as a sham and assessed Mr. Cameron for what appeared to be his share of the amounts paid by Campbell Limited to the new management company. Mr. Cameron successfully appealed to the Exchequer Court from the assessment. The Minister's appeal to the Supreme Court of Canada was dismissed. The Supreme Court concluded that the agreement between Campbell Limited and the new management company was not a sham. At page 6328, Martland, J. delivering judgment for the Court stated:

> Those payments were made pursuant to an agreement. The receipts were reported by Independent as income, and income tax was paid by Independent and received by the Appellant. Payment of those moneys by Campbell Limited could not be legally enforced by the Respondent, Steele or Symon, or all three together, but only by Independent. The Respondent could not legally compel Independent to pay the moneys to him.

Although the Cameron decision was not based on the application of section 56 of the Income Tax Act, the Appellant argues that the same principle should apply in this appeal because the Respondent has not alleged that the arrangement between the Appellant, the Trust and Neotric was a sham. In the absence of any sham, the Appellant states that the three-party agreement in Exhibit A–5 should be given the same validity as the Supreme Court gave to the management agreement in Cameron. The Supreme Court of Canada reached a similar conclusion on different facts in R. v. Campbell (1980), 80 D.T.C. 6239 (S.C.C.).

9. Counsel for the Appellant relied on the decision of the Supreme Court of Canada in McClurg v. Minister of National Revenue (1990), 91 D.T.C. 5001 (S.C.C.). In dismissing an appeal by the Minister of National Revenue, Dickson, C.J. delivering judgment for the majority stated at page 5012:

> ... The purpose of subsection 56(2) is to ensure that payments which otherwise would have been received by the taxpayer are not diverted to a third party as an anti-avoidance technique.

This purpose is not frustrated because, in the corporate law context, until a dividend is declared, the profits belong to a corporation as a juridical person: Welling, supra, at pp. 609–10. Had a dividend not been declared and paid to a third party, it would not otherwise have been received by the taxpayer. Rather, the amount simply would have been retained as earnings by the company. Consequently, as a general rule, a dividend payment cannot reasonably be considered a benefit diverted from a taxpayer to a third party within the contemplation of subsection 56(2).

In my opinion, the last sentence in the passage quoted above distinguishes the decision in McClurg from this appeal because the payments from Neotric to the Trust were not payments of dividends. Counsel for the Respondent also relied on the decision in McClurg because La Forest, J. delivering judgment for the minority set out the ingredients for the application of subsection 56(2) at page 5021:

> Turning to the application of subsection 56(2) to the instant case, I find it useful as a starting point to break the provision down into its constituent parts. such an analytical framework was adopted by Cattanach, J. in Murphy v. The Queen (1980), 80 D.T.C. 6314 (F.C.T.D.), where he stated at pp. 6317–18:

> To fall within subsection 56(2) each essential ingredient to taxability in the hands of the taxpayer therein specified must be present.

> Those four ingredients are:

>> (1) that there must be a payment or transfer of property to a person other than the taxpayer;

>> (2) that the payment or transfer is pursuant to the direction of or with the concurrence of the taxpayer;

>> (3) that the payment or transfer be for the taxpayer's own benefit or for the benefit of some other person on whom the taxpayer wished to have the benefit conferred; and

>> (4) that the payment or transfer would have been included in computing the taxpayer's income if it had been received by him instead of the other person.

It must be determined, then, whether these four elements of prerequisites to the application of subsection 56(2) are present in the transaction at hand.

Counsel for the Respondent argued that the above four ingredients are met in the circumstances of this appeal and, therefore, subsection 56(2) should be applied. With respect to the fourth ingredient, there seems to be an assumption that the payment or transfer would have been made to the person assessed by the Minister if it had not been made to the actual recipient. In this appeal, if the management fees had not been paid by Neotric to the Trust, there is no evidence that they would have been paid to the Appellant. I am satisfied that they would not have been paid at all. There would have been nothing to include in the Appellant's income.

10. The Respondent relies on a very technical interpretation of Exhibit A–5 to argue that the Appellant was entitled to the management fees paid by Neotric. The Appellant acknowledged that he had drafted Exhibit A–5 himself without the benefit of legal assistance and so the Respondent argues that it must reflect precisely what the Appellant intended. Paragraph 2 of Exhibit A–5 states:

> For services rendered by KEF the Corporation shall pay FFT management fees to be agreed upon from time to time.

The Respondent emphasized that in the above paragraph, the services are to be rendered by KEF (Keith E. Ferrel—the Appellant herein) in his personal capacity and yet Neotric is required to pay management fees to the Trust for those services. In other words, the paragraph does not state that the services will be rendered by KEF "on behalf of the Trust". In my view, this is too narrow an interpretation to be placed upon paragraph 2 in isolation from the rest of Exhibit A–5. The first recital states:

> WHEREAS the Corporation and FFT have agreed that FFT shall provide the services of KEF who shall be appointed President and Secretary of the Corporation.

Exhibit A–5 is a three-party agreement among Neotric, the Trust and the Appellant. To me, it is clear from the wording of the first recital and paragraph 2 that the Appellant is agreeing that the Trust may provide his services to Neotric. The management fees in issue would not have been paid at all if they had not been paid to the Trust.

11. Relying on the decisions of the Supreme Court in Minister of National Revenue v. Cameron and R. v. Campbell, I find that there was a bona fide agreement between and among the Trust and Neotric and the Appellant in effect from January 1, 1989 as evidenced by Exhibit A–5. On the strength of that three-party agreement, the Appellant did not have a right to receive any management fees which may have been payable by Neotric to the Trust. Whether the Appellant received any personal compensation from the Trust for the management services which he was providing on behalf of the Trust to Neotric was a matter between only the Appellant and the Trust.

12.   In the absence of sham, there is nothing in law to prevent an individual from agreeing to provide his professional or management services to a client through the medium of a corporation or some other third party entity like a trust. Assuming that the Trust has agreed by lawful contract to provide the Appellant's services to Neotric, the question arises whether the Appellant may still be trapped by the provisions of section 56 of the Act. Specifically, the Minister relies on subsections 56(2) and 56(4) which are set out below with the irrelevant words omitted:

> 56(2) A payment or transfer of property made pursuant to the direction of, or with the concurrence of, a taxpayer to some other person for the benefit of the taxpayer or as a benefit that the taxpayer desired to have conferred on the other person ... shall be included in computing the taxpayer's income to the extent that it would be if the payment or transfer had been made.

* * *

> 56(4) Where a taxpayer has, at any time before the end of a taxation year ... transferred or assigned to a person with whom he was not dealing at arm's length the right to an amount ... that would, if the right thereto had not been so transferred or assigned, be included in computing his income for the taxation year because the amount would have been received or receivable by him in or in respect of the year, the amount shall be included in computing the taxpayer's income for the year unless the income is from property and the taxpayer has also transferred or assigned the property.

13.   The application of subsection 56(2) was considered by the Federal Court of Appeal in Outerbridge Estate v. Canada (1990), 90 D.T.C. 6681 (Fed. C.A.). The facts in that case are not important but Marceau, J.A. (delivering judgment for the Court) made the following statement at page 6684:

> It is generally accepted that the provision of subsection 56(2) is rooted in the doctrine of "constructive receipt" and was meant to cover principally cases where a taxpayer seeks to avoid receipt of what in his hands would be income by arranging to have the amount paid to some other person either for his own benefit (for example the extinction of a liability) or for the benefit of that other person (see the reasons of Thurlow, J. in Miller, supra and of Cattanach, J. in Murphy, supra). ... the language of the provision does not require, for its application, that the taxpayer be initially entitled to the payment or transfer of property made to the third party, only that he would have been subject to tax had the payment or transfer been made to him. It seems to me, however, that when the doctrine

of "constructive receipt" is not clearly involved, because the taxpayer had no entitlement to the payment being made or the property being transferred, it is fair to infer that subsection 56(2) may receive application only if the benefit conferred is not directly taxable in the hands of the transferee. Indeed, as I see it, a tax-avoidance provision is subsidiary in nature; it exists to prevent the avoidance of a tax payable on a particular transaction, not simply to double the tax normally due nor to give the taxing authorities an administrative discretion to choose between possible taxpayers.

So, I agree that the validity of an assessment under subsection 56(2) of the Act when the taxpayer had himself no entitlement to the payment made or the property transferred is subject to an implied condition, namely that the payee or transferee not be subject to tax on the benefit he received . . .

14.   As I understand the above passage, when the Minister relies on subsection 56(2) to assess a particular person concerning a payment to some third party, it is not necessary that the particular person be entitled to receive the payment. It is necessary, however, that the person would be subject to tax if he had in fact received the payment. Also, if the particular person was not entitled to receive the payment, then subsection 56(2) will apply only if the payment is not taxable in the hands of the third party.

15.   I accept the unchallenged evidence of the Appellant that all of the management fees were channelled through the Trust to the income beneficiaries of the Trust and that preferred beneficiary elections were filed on behalf of the income beneficiaries. The Respondent made no attempt to contradict the Appellant's statement that the two income beneficiaries of the Trust paid aggregate income taxes in excess of $95,000 on the management fees which were allocated to them by the Trustee. In other words, all of the management fees paid by Neotric to the Trust were in fact taxed in the hands of the income beneficiaries.

16.   Applying the decision in Outerbridge Estate to the facts of this appeal, the Appellant was not entitled to receive the management fees from Neotric but he would have been subject to tax on those fees if they had been received by him. Therefore, the first condition for the application of subsection 56(2) was satisfied. The management fees actually received by the Trust were allocated to the income beneficiaries; preferred beneficiary elections were filed with Revenue Canada; and the beneficiaries paid aggregate income taxes exceeding $95,000 on the management fees received by the Trust. Therefore, the second condition for the application of subsection 56(2) was not satisfied because the beneficiaries paid tax on

the amounts in issue. I will repeat one sentence of Marceau, J.A. quoted above from Outerbridge Estate:

> Indeed, as I see it, a tax-avoidance provision is subsidiary in nature; it exists to prevent the avoidance of a tax payable on a particular transaction, not simply to double the tax normally due nor to give the taxing authorities an administrative discretion to choose between possible taxpayers.

If the assessments under appeal are upheld, the amounts of $152,000 and $150,000 will be taxed twice.

17. Having found that the Appellant did not have any right in law to receive the management fees paid by Neotric to the Trust, I conclude that subsection 56(4) of the Income Tax Act does not assist the Respondent in supporting the assessments under appeal. Also, the Appellant was not required to include any part of the amounts of $152,000 and $150,000 in computing his income for 1989 and 1990. Therefore, the penalty assessed under subsection 163(1) for 1990 must be cancelled. The appeals are allowed, with costs.

Appeal allowed.

Note

The Tax Court's decision in *Ferrel* was affirmed by the Federal Court of Appeal,[6] relying, in part, on the Supreme Court's decision in *Neuman*. The Court of Appeal reasoned that if, under *Neuman,* a corporation may be used to avoid tax, "[i]t follows that other structures, including trusts, may also be used to save tax, as long as proper legal documentation is prepared to accomplish the purpose desired."

How would the plan in *Ferrel* be attacked under the Internal Revenue Code? Section 482 of the Code provides:

> In any case of two or more organizations, trades, or businesses (whether or not incorporated, whether or not organized in the United States, and whether or not affiliated) owned or controlled directly or indirectly by the same interests, the Secretary may distribute, apportion, or allocate gross income, deductions, credits, or allowances between or among such organizations, trades, or businesses, if he determines that such distribution, apportionment, or allocation is necessary in order to prevent evasion of taxes or clearly to reflect the income of any of such organizations, trades, or businesses. * * *

Section 482 is designed to ensure that taxpayers clearly reflect

6. Her Majesty the Queen v. Ferrel,   1999).
99 D.T.C. 5111, 2 C.T.C. 101 (Fed.C.A.

income attributable to transactions involving controlled parties.[7] The standard that is applied under Section 482 is the "arm's length standard," under which the "true" taxable income of a controlled taxpayer is determined as if the taxpayer were dealing at arm's length with an uncontrolled taxpayer.[8] Under Section 482, *Ferrel* would be a relatively straightforward case. Mr. Ferrel had control of the trust, Neotric, and his own business of providing management services, and under Section 482 he would be allocated arm's length compensation for the management services that he provided to Neotric. A deduction for Mr. Ferrel's services would be allowed to either Neotric or the trust to prevent double taxation of the income. Taxing the proper amount of compensation income to Mr. Ferrel would eliminate the tax avoidance potential from the plan.

2. *Attribution of Income, Gain, or Loss in Connection With the Transfer of Property*

Earlier, the Canadian tax rules relating to *inter vivos* gifts of property were outlined.[9] In general, if a taxpayer makes a gift of property, (1) the taxpayer is deemed to have disposed of the property for its fair market value, and (2) the donee is deemed to have acquired the property for its fair market value.[10] A special rule provides that in the case of a transfer of property to a taxpayer's spouse or common-law partner, the property is deemed to be disposed of, and acquired for, proceeds equal to the property's cost base.[11] The special rule thereby provides for nonrecognition in the case of transfers (by gift or otherwise) of property between spouses or common-law partners unless the transferor elects to be taxed under the deemed-disposition rule.[12]

Attribution of Income from the Property to the Transferor. Canadian tax law has two provisions that potentially will attribute the income from property that is transferred to another person:[13]

S. 74.1(1) Transfers and loans to spouse

Where an individual has transferred or lent property * * *, either directly or indirectly, by means of a trust or by any other means whatever, to or for the benefit of a person who is the individual's spouse or common-law partner or who has since become the individual's spouse or common-law partner, any income or loss, as the case may be, of that person for a

---

7. Reg. § 1.482–1T(a).

8. Reg. § 1.482–1(b).

9. See Chapter 3, supra.

10. S. 69(1) (Canada). Losses on dispositions between certain related persons are denied. S. 54 (superficial loss) (Canada).

11. S. 73(1) (Canada).

12. The election is provided in S. 73(1) (Canada).

13. Additional attribution rules and anti-avoidance rules apply to prevent income-splitting strategies employing trusts and corporations.

taxation year from the property or from property substituted therefor, that relates to the period in the year throughout which the individual is resident in Canada and that person is the individual's spouse or common-law partner, shall be deemed to be income or a loss, as the case may be, of the individual for the year and not of that person.

S. 74.1(2) Transfers and loans to minors

If an individual has transferred or lent property, either directly or indirectly, by means of a trust or by any other means whatever, to or for the benefit of a person who was under 18 years of age * * * and who

(a) does not deal with the individual at arm's length, or

(b) is the niece or nephew of the individual,

any income or loss, as the case may be, of that person for a taxation year from the property or from property substituted for that property, that relates to the period in the taxation year throughout which the individual is resident in Canada, is deemed to be income or a loss, as the case may be, of the individual and not of that person unless that person has, before the end of the taxation year, attained the age of 18 years.

In the case of a gift to a spouse, common-law partner, or minor child, these provisions will attribute any income from the gifted property back to the donor. Thus, if High Tax Bracket Spouse gives income-producing property to Low Tax Bracket Spouse, the income produced by the property will continue to be taxed to High Tax Bracket Spouse under Section 74.1(1). Note also that the rules are broad and apply to (1) loans of property (including money),[14] (2) contrived transactions attempting to circumvent the rules ("indirect" transfers),[15] and (3) property substituted for the transferred property. The substituted-property provision will apply to situations where the donee sells the transferred property and purchases a new property. Income from the new property also will be attributed to the donor of the first property.

While Sections 74.1(1) and 74.1(2) apply to "transfers," they do not apply in the case of property sold for fair market value, including adequate and timely interest on any indebtedness.[16] The theory of this exception is that if the property is sold for fair market value, the transferor receives property (the sales proceeds) with income-producing potential so the transaction will not shift

---

14. S. 248(1) (Canada).

15. Another section prevents "back-to-back" loans or transfers involving intermediaries. S. 74.5(6) (Canada).

16. S. 74.5(1) (Canada). Loans for value are similarly protected. S. 74.5(2) (Canada).

income from the transferor to the transferee.[17] Also, once income received by the transferee has been attributed to and taxed to the transferor, that income is not considered transferred property subject to the rules. For example, if interest earned on transferred property is taxed back to the transferor, future income earned on that interest will be taxed to the transferee.[18] Income or loss from a business transferred to another taxpayer also is not attributed to the transferor, even if the business operates with property received from the transferor.[19]

Attribution to the Transferor of Gain or Loss from Transferred Property. Section 74.2(1) provides for attribution of gain or loss in the case of transfers to a spouse or common-law partner:

S. 74.2(1) Gain or loss deemed that of lender or transferor

Where an individual has lent or transferred property (in this section referred to as "lent or transferred property"), either directly or indirectly, by means of a trust or by any other means whatever, to or for the benefit of a person (in this subsection referred to as the "recipient") who is the individual's spouse or common-law partner or who has since become the individual's spouse or common-law partner, the following rules apply for the purposes of computing the income of the individual and the recipient for a taxation year:

(a) the amount, if any, by which

(i) the total of the recipient's taxable capital gains for the year from dispositions of property (other than listed personal property) that is lent or transferred property or property substituted therefor occurring in the period (in this subsection referred to as the "attribution period") throughout which the individual is resident in Canada and the recipient is the individual's spouse or common-law partner

exceeds

(ii) the total of the recipient's allowable capital losses for the year from dispositions occurring in the attribution period of property (other than listed personal property)

---

17. Peter W. Hogg, Joanne E. Magee, & Jinyan Li, Principles of Canadian Tax Law 407 (5th ed. 2005). In the case of transfers to or for the benefit of a spouse or common-law partner, an election must be made so the transaction is taxable. S. 74.5(1)(c) (Canada).

18. IT–511R, ¶ 6 (Feb. 21, 1994) (Canada Revenue Agency).

19. Id. at ¶ 5. This exception may be based on the idea that business income comes from a combination of property and labor so attribution of the income from transferred property is not required. See Peter W. Hogg, Joanne E. Magee, & Jinyan Li, Principles of Canadian Tax Law 410 (5th ed. 2005).

that is lent or transferred property or property substituted therefor shall be deemed to be a taxable capital gain of the individual for the year from the disposition of property other than listed personal property;

(b) the amount, if any, by which the total determined under subparagraph (a)(ii) exceeds the total determined under subparagraph (a)(i) shall be deemed to be an allowable capital loss of the individual for the year from the disposition of property other than listed personal property;

(c) the amount, if any, by which

(i) the amount that the total of the recipient's gains for the year from dispositions occurring in the attribution period of listed personal property that is lent or transferred property or property substituted therefor would be if the recipient had at no time owned listed personal property other than listed personal property that was lent or transferred property or property substituted therefor

exceeds

(ii) the amount that the total of the recipient's losses for the year from dispositions of listed personal property that is lent or transferred property or property substituted therefor would be if the recipient had at no time owned listed personal property other than listed personal property that was lent or transferred property or property substituted therefor,

shall be deemed to be a gain of the individual for the year from the disposition of listed personal property;

(d) the amount, if any, by which the total determined under subparagraph (c)(ii) exceeds the total determined under subparagraph (c)(i) shall be deemed to be a loss of the individual for the year from the disposition of listed personal property; and

(e) any taxable capital gain or allowable capital loss or any gain or loss taken into account in computing an amount described in paragraph (a), (b), (c) or (d) shall, except for the purposes of those paragraphs and to the extent that the amount so described is deemed by virtue of this subsection to be a taxable capital gain or an allowable capital loss or a gain or loss of the individual, be deemed not to be a taxable capital gain or an allowable capital loss or a gain or loss, as the case may be, of the recipient.

The operation of Section 74.2(1) can be illustrated with the following example. Assume W purchased property for $100,000 and she gives the property to her husband, H, when it is worth

$125,000. H later sells the property for $175,000. On the transfer of the property, W will be deemed to dispose of it (and H acquires it) for an amount equal to W's cost basis; i.e., $100,000. Thus, the transfer will not be taxable to W. During the time that H holds the property any income that it produces will be attributed to W under Section 74.1(1). On the sale of the property by H, W will be taxed on the full $75,000 of gain under Section 74.2(1). Note that W will be taxed on the appreciation inherent in the property at the time of transfer ($25,000) as well as the appreciation in the property's value while it was held by H ($50,000). Contrast the results if the taxpayers were in the United States and the Internal Revenue Code applied. The gift of the property will be tax-free to both H and W and H will take the property with a $100,000 basis.[20] H, as owner of the property, will be taxable on the future income produced by the property, and, in the case of a sale, H will be taxable on the full $75,000 gain. The appreciation after the gift was made, as well as the $25,000 increase in the value of the property while it was held by W, will be shifted for tax purposes to H. But it is important to remember that in the United States H and W will most likely file a joint return in which they aggregate all of their income for tax purposes. Individual tax filing in Canada, at least in part, creates the need for elaborate and rigorous attribution rules.

The rule in Section 74.2(1) also does not apply in the case of property that is transferred for consideration equal to its fair market value in a taxable transaction.[21]

Kiddie taxes. Note that there is no rule corresponding to Section 74.2(1) in the case of a transfer of property to a minor child. Thus, there generally is no attribution of later gain or loss from property given to a minor child.[22] There are undoubtedly at least a couple of reasons that the rules are different for transfers to a spouse or common-law partner and minor children. First, recall that the transfer of property to a minor generally will be taxable to the donor. The special nonrecognition rule only applies in the case of transfers to a spouse or common-law partner. So a donor will not escape taxation on the appreciation in property that is given to a minor child. Also, remember that the provision taxing the transferor on income from property transferred to a minor ceases to apply when the minor attains the age of 18. It has been suggested that if a similar rule applied to gains and losses, a minor could simply defer a sale of the property until the rule no longer applies.[23] A comparison to the United States' rules again is illuminating. If a

---

20. I.R.C. §§ 102, 1041.

21. S. 74.5(1). An election must be made so the transaction is taxable. S. 74.5(1)(c) (Canada).

22. An exception exists in the case of transfers of farmland to a minor.

23. See Peter W. Hogg, Joanne E. Magee, & Jinyan Li, Principles of Canadian Tax Law 411 (5th ed. 2005).

parent makes a gift of appreciated property to a child, the gift generally is tax free to both the parent and the child.[24] The child will take the parent's basis in the property under Section 1015 and would recognize any gain or loss on a sale of the property. One obstacle that would have to be navigated is the "kiddie tax" in Section 1(g), which could effectively tax the gain at the parents' tax rates. But with patience, the child could wait out application of the kiddie tax and the gain would be taxable at the child's tax rates.

The Canadian "kiddie tax" applies in limited circumstances to backstop the income-attribution rules.[25] The kiddie tax applies at the highest marginal rates on the "split income" of a person who is a Canadian resident, has not reached the age of 17 before the year, and has a parent who is a Canadian resident. Split income generally is defined to include dividends, other than dividends from publicly traded corporations, and income derived from providing goods and services by a partnership or trust to or for the support of a business carried on by a related individual. Thus, the kiddie tax seeks, in part, to restrict the strategies employed in *Neuman* and *Ferrel*.

---

24. I.R.C. § 102.

25. S. 120.4–120.4(3) (Canada).

Chapter 5

DEForeDUCTIONS

A. INTRODUCTION

"Income" for purposes of an income tax is generally thought to be "net" income; that is, the taxpayer's total gross receipts reduced by the related costs of producing those gross receipts. For example, if during the year a dentist receives $150,000 in fees from patients and pays $90,000 for office space, utilities, supplies, and support staff, the dentist's "income" from operating the dental practice is $60,000. In calculating income, the dentist is allowed to reduce the tax base by the expenditures that are incurred to produce the taxable receipts.[1] As a corollary to that principle, when we calculate the dentist's income we should not reduce the tax base for expenditures made by the dentist that are not incurred to produce income. For example, if the dentist decides to play golf or tennis every Wednesday instead of seeing patients, the costs of the golf and tennis outings are not incurred to generate patient fees and should not reduce the dentist's income. Expenditures that are not related to the production of taxable income, like the golf and tennis outings, are "personal" in nature. Those costs represent the taxpayer's discretionary decisions about how to expend or consume resources. Because personal expenditures are not related to the measurement of a taxpayer's income, they should not be deductible in an income tax.[2]

The division of a taxpayer's expenditures between those that are deductible because they are incurred in income-producing activities and those that are not deductible because they are derived from personal consumption, sets the stage for a series of additional questions. The first is: how closely connected to an income-producing activity must an expenditure be in order to qualify as deductible? Must the expenditure be directly related to the production of

---

1. See I.R.C. §§ 162, 212.

2. See I.R.C. § 262.

income or is some looser connection sufficient to make the payment deductible? Thinking again about the dentist, suppose the annual professional dental association's convention is in Hawaii this year. If the dentist attends the convention and pays for the air fare to Hawaii, registration fees for the convention, hotel and meal expenses, and rounds of golf during free time, should all of those expenses be deductible because they are incurred to assist the dentist's practice? Or, are the expenses of attending the convention akin to paying for a vacation and therefore nondeductible? Another approach is to sort out the mixture of income-producing and personal elements of the trip, examine them in detail, and determine which ones should be deductible in calculating the dentist's income. How much of a burden should the dentist bear in proving the connection between the trip and the dental practice? How much administrative energy should an income tax system devote to maintaining the prohibition against deducting personal expenditures?

Income tax systems also commonly characterize income-producing expenditures as either currently deductible or "capital expenditures" that may not be deducted in the year in which they are made.[3] The prohibition against deducting capital expenditures is based, in part, on questions of timing and calculation of income. Suppose that our dentist decides to purchase a new chair for patients at a cost of $7,500. The cost of the chair is sufficiently related to the dentist's practice to be deductible, but should the full cost of the chair be deducted in the year the chair is purchased? The answer to that question is typically "no." The thought is that the chair is an asset that the dentist will use to produce income over a period of time extending into the future, and deducting its cost against the income that it produces will better reflect the dentist's income from the practice. The cost of the chair would normally be recovered via depreciation or cost recovery deductions.[4] The capital expenditure concept also applies to intangible assets, as well as prepayments of future expenses. Thus, if the dentist prepays three years of rent for the office, the prepayment will be deemed a capital expenditure that may not be fully deducted when made.

Sorting out and denying a deduction for personal and capital expenditures are essential elements of a levy that seeks to measure and tax "income." Income taxes, however, are the products of legislative compromise and often reflect decisions about social and economic policy. Consequently, an income tax may depart substantially from the ideal of measuring and taxing "income." Legitimate expenses to produce income may not be deductible because they

---

3. See I.R.C. § 263.   **4.** See I.R.C. § 168.

violate some social policy,[5] and specific capital expenditures may be currently deductible in order to promote certain forms of investment.[6] More importantly, the prohibition against deducting personal expenditures is often compromised by a wide array of specific deduction sections that promote different social policies or that are simply politically popular. For example, in the United States a taxpayer is permitted a deduction for home mortgage interest,[7] state and local taxes,[8] and medical expenses.[9]

The point of this brief introduction is to set out some common themes that run through the deduction provisions of many income tax systems. What follows is an examination of how some of these themes are addressed in the Australian income tax. Your base of comparison is the Internal Revenue Code. Consider how Australia and the United States address issues that are common to all individual income taxes.

B.   GENERAL RULES FOR AUSTRALIAN TAX DEDUCTIONS

Introduction. The general deduction provision in the Australian income tax, Section 8–1, provides:

s. 8–1(1) You can deduct from your assessable income any loss or outgoing to the extent that:

    (a) it is incurred in gaining or producing your assessable income; or

    (b) it is necessarily incurred in carrying on a business for the purpose of gaining or producing your assessable income.

s. 8–1(2) However, you cannot deduct a loss or outgoing under this section to the extent that:

    (a) it is a loss or outgoing of capital, or of a capital nature; or

    (b) it is a loss or outgoing of a private or domestic nature; or

    (c) it is incurred in relation to gaining or producing your exempt income or your non-assessable non-exempt income; or

    (d) a provision of this Act prevents you from deducting it.

---

5. See e.g., I.R.C. §§ 162(c)(2) (denial of a deduction for illegal bribes and kickbacks); 280E (denial of deductions in connection with the illegal sale of drugs).

6. See I.R.C. §§ 174 (expensing of research and experimentation expenditures); 179 (expensing of the cost of limited amounts of tangible property and certain computer software).

7. I.R.C. §§ 163(h)(2)(D), 163(h)(3).

8. I.R.C. § 164.

9. I.R.C. § 213.

Note the structure of Section 8–1. It begins with a grant of a deduction if the taxpayer is able to satisfy the requirements of either Sections 8–1(1)(a) or (b). Thus, a loss or "outgoing" incurred to produce income or in carrying on a business is generally deductible. Section 8–1(2) follows with limitations that deny a deduction even if one of the two earlier provisions granting a deduction is satisfied. Consistent with the earlier discussion about deductions in an income tax, Sections 8–1(2)(a) and (b) contain prohibitions against deducting a loss or outgoing that is "capital," "private," or "domestic" in nature. The following authorities explore the parameters and limitations of Section 8–1. As you read these materials consider how the expenditures would be treated under the Internal Revenue Code.

FEDERAL COMMISSIONER OF TAXATION v. SNOWDEN & WILLSON PROPRIETARY LTD.*

High Court of Australia, 1958.
32 ALJR 167, 11 ATD 463.

Dixon, C.J.

The question for decision is whether the taxpayer is entitled to a deduction from its assessable income for the year of income ended 30th June 1953 of an amount expended by the company in an attempt to meet by advertisements certain attacks made in the Legislative Assembly of Western Australia upon the conduct of its business and in its appearance by counsel before a Royal Commission subsequently appointed to inquire into the charges and any further complaints or allegations made to the commissioner by persons who had dealt with the company.

The company carried on a business which included the speculative building of houses for customers on terms. The business covered the work of an estate agent, insurance agent and the kind of things associated with such enterprises. What, perhaps, is more material for present purposes is its business in building for its customers. The company would build for a customer owning the site or it would contract to sell him the site and to build the house. The transaction would in each case be upon terms [credit sales Ed.]. It is unnecessary to enter upon the details of the complaints made in the Legislative Assembly, or elsewhere, of the company's methods. It is enough to say that they reflected on the integrity of those conducting the company's business and upon the fairness of the transactions to the customers and the sufficiency of the disclosure to them of the operation of the terms.

* Footnotes omitted.

The company's methods were attacked in the Western Australian Assembly in September 1952, the Royal Commission was appointed in December 1952 and it sat for some thirty days in January, February and March 1953, and made its report (which was by no means favourable to the taxpayer company) on 27th April 1953. The taxpayer began by expending a sum on advertising to counter the effect produced by the reports in the press concerning the charges made. The cost of this was about £637. Then the taxpayer company proceeded to defend itself and its officers before the Royal Commission. This involved fees for counsel, solicitors, valuers, surveyor and accountants. The total cost, including the advertising, was £4,252. That amount the taxpayer sought to deduct from the assessable income in the assessment for the year in question. The deduction was disallowed by the commissioner but an appeal by the taxpayer was upheld by the majority of a board of review. An appeal was instituted to the High Court * * *.

This is the proceeding now before us.

[The Court began by discussing the structure of an earlier version of Section 8–1 and then it began to analyze the taxpayer's expenditure under Section 8–1(1)(b). Ed.]

If it were not for the word "necessarily" there would be no difficulty, in my opinion, in treating the expenditure in the present case as coming within the conception expressed by this part * * *. In saying this I am pronouncing upon a question of fact rather than of law. But, as it appears to me, the carrying on of the business of the nature described brought with it the attacks against which the taxpayer company sought to defend itself. The attacks touched its business nearly; they disparaged the methods by which it was conducted; they were calculated to deter intending or likely customers from dealing with it and to destroy the faith of existing customers in their current relations with the company. No doubt it would be instinctive in the business man or, perhaps, in any man, to defend himself and those associated with him in business against an attack of such a description on the manner in which they were pursuing their business activities. But the instinct is founded upon sound if intuitive conceptions of what must be done if they are not to suffer in their pursuit of custom and profit. Whether on the merits they were in a position to defend themselves successfully or whether, on the other hand, the attacks upon them lacked adequate foundation alike seem to me to be matters not to the point.

The case does not appear so far as the element now under consideration goes to depend upon case law or upon anything but an understanding of what in fact and according to the ordinary conduct of affairs is incidental to the conduct of a business. The word "necessarily" does, however, seem to me to require consideration. Clearly its operation is to place a qualification upon the degree of connexion between the expenditure and the carrying on of the business which might suffice in the absence of such a qualification. In The Commonwealth and The Post–Master–General v. Progress Advertising & Press Agency Co. Pty. Ltd., Higgins, J. supplied an interpretation of "necessary" as not meaning essentially necessary but as meaning appropriate, plainly adapted to the needs of a department carrying out an Act. That was in another connexion but the phrase was availed of by the Court in the Ronpibon Tin Case as throwing light on the use of the word "necessarily" * * *. Clearly the expression is used in relation to business. Logical necessity is not a thing to be predicated of business expenditure. What is meant by the qualification is that the expenditure must be dictated by the business ends to which it is directed, those ends forming part of or being truly incidental to the business.

In the present case it appears to me that the taxpayer company could do nothing else but defend itself, if it was to sustain its business and continue carrying it on in anything like the same volume or according to the same plan. That seems to me to be enough.

There is no analogy here to cases in which fines or penalties are incurred. There the character of the expenditure and the reasons why the law imposes a fine or penalty separate the expenditure from the conduct of the business. It is not to the point that the conduct penalised found its motive in business considerations. Nothing of the kind can be said of the expenditure now under consideration nor is any principle of public policy affected by allowing the deduction.

There remains, however, the question whether the expenditure may not be considered to be of a capital nature and so subject to the express prohibition contained in s. [8–1] (1) against allowing losses and outgoings of a capital nature.

An examination of the facts does not support the view that the proceedings in Parliament and before the Royal Commission imperilled the existence of the business or the capital assets of the company. The proceedings were not necessarily directed at a winding-up of the company or a stoppage of the business. Precise definition or distinctions are difficult in such an affair. But what the company had most to fear was the embarrassments in the present and future conduct of its business and, no doubt, a decline in its custom.

There is no satisfactory ground for saying that the expenditure was an affair of capital.

The appeal from the decision of the board of review should be dismissed. * * *

* * *

FULLAGAR, J.

    * * *

Concur

In the present case the company was carrying on a business for the purpose of gaining or producing assessable income. Attacks were made in Parliament and before the commission upon its conduct of that business—attacks which were capable of seriously affecting that business both directly and indirectly. It would naturally seem essential to the company's directors that a vigorous effort should be made to repel those attacks, and no defence could have any prospect of being effective which did not involve the expenditure of substantial sums of money. The relation between the expenditure and the carrying on of the business is clear. The expenditure was incidental to the carrying on of the business. It was incurred in carrying on the business, and it was necessarily incurred because the exigencies of the business imperatively demanded that it should be incurred.

The question remains whether the expenditure in question was *issue* an outgoing of a capital nature. This is a question which has given rise to difficulty in a large number of cases. * * * There is an article in the Australian Law Journal by Mr. R. E. O'Neill, who observes that the English courts have been disposed to draw * * * a decisive distinction between (to put it very shortly) expenditure which adds to capital and expenditure which merely protects or preserves capital. Here the distinction has not been regarded as irrelevant, but it has not been treated generally as decisive. It is to be noted on the one hand that, although the relevant statutes differ in terms, the English courts, taking the view that capital expenditure is never deductible, have in many cases in substance addressed themselves to the question of what constitutes an outgoing of a capital nature, though often * * * subsuming it under the general question of what constitutes expenditure "wholly and exclusively" laid out in producing income. * * *

For present purposes I do not think that the general question need be pursued further. * * * I am quite unable to regard the expenditure now in question as being of a capital nature. It is true that the allegations against which the company was defending itself were calculated to affect adversely the goodwill of the company, and that fact was doubtless present to the minds of the directors. But that is very far from being the whole of the truth. The allegations were made in specific cases, and were capable of directly affecting the past present and future revenue of the company as such. They were made by persons who stood in an existing legal relationship to the company, either as contractors or as mortgagors. The object of those who made them can only have been to obtain ultimately some reduction in their obligations to the company—either by way of repayment of moneys paid or by way of partial cancellation of future indebtedness. If they had pursued this object in the courts, there could have been no doubt about the position. Expenditure incurred by the company in an action or suit to enforce a contract or a mortgage, or in resisting a claim for relief by a contractor or mortgagor, must have been deductible from the company's assessable income in the year in which it was incurred. It can surely make no difference that contractors or mortgagors chose a less direct (and perhaps in the long run less satisfactory) means of achieving the object they had in view. * * *

For the above reasons I find myself in agreement with the majority of the board of review. I do not agree with the dissenting member of the board that the present case bears any analogy to cases in which penalties and costs have been incurred in connexion with prosecutions for infringements of the law. * * *

The appeal should, in my opinion, be dismissed.

* * *

SOFTWOOD PULP & PAPER LTD v. COMMISSIONER OF TAXATION*
Supreme Court of Victoria, 1976.
76 ATC 4439.

MENHENNITT, J.

This is an appeal from a decision of the Board of Review * * *. The appellant is Softwood Pulp and Paper Ltd * * * (to which I shall refer as "the taxpayer" or "the appellant"). The assessments against which appeals were taken to the Board of Review and from the Board of Review to this court were in respect of income derived by the taxpayer during the years ended 30 June 1966, 1967 and 1969.

The taxpayer in respect of those years made claims for deductions * * * claiming that there were allowable deductions in respect of the preceding 7 years. The deductions which were disallowed by the Commissioner were held by the Board of Review to be not proper deductions from income and accordingly the appeals to the Board of Review failed and the Commissioner's assessments were upheld. I shall describe in much greater detail the nature of the deductions claimed and the basis upon which they were

* Footnotes omitted.

claimed, but they were all claimed as being deductions pursuant to [the predecessor to § 8–1 Ed.] of the Income Tax Assessment Act.

* * *

Based upon those findings and all the evidence and all the *steps taken* matters I referred to, I form the following conclusions and make the following findings. I find * * * these things, and these are not necessarily in any order of importance.

One was that investigations took place to see whether the proposed paper mill would be economically feasible.

Secondly, investigations were made to endeavour to determine what products could be produced from the mill with the local wood supplies available with a view to forming conclusions as to what products could be produced to compete economically * * *.

Thirdly, investigations were conducted aimed at reaching ultimate conclusions, although they were never in fact reached, as to what plant and equipment should be procured if the project went ahead.

Fourthly, the investigations, I conclude on all the evidence, were partly and to a significant extent designed to determine whether or not [an investor Ed.] at least would put capital into the project and whether it would go on with the project.

Fifthly, I conclude that what was done was aimed to and did in fact obtain certain technical information which would be of value to the taxpayer if the project became a real one and actually took place.

The next matter was that steps were taken to secure supplies of timber, produced locally, which would be necessary to enable the company to function if it were established.

Those appear to me to be the prime matters which were basic to and involved in the steps that were taken.

* * *

I read the relevant portion of [the predecessor to s. 8–1. Ed.]:   *statute*

"All losses and outgoings to the extent to which they are incurred in gaining or producing the assessable income, or are necessarily incurred in carrying on a business for the purpose of gaining or producing such income, shall be allowable deductions except to the extent to which they are losses or outgoings of capital, or of a capital, private or domestic nature, or are incurred in relation to the gaining or production of exempt income."

For any losses or outgoings to be deductible, they must either be incurred in gaining or producing the assessable income, or must be necessarily incurred in carrying on a business for the purpose of gaining or producing such income.

As to the first limb as to what is meant by losses or outgoings to the extent to which they are incurred in gaining or producing the assessable income, the High Court has authoritatively defined the meaning of those words in decided cases, * * *. What their Honours there decided can be conveniently referred to by the next judgment to which I will refer in which the Full Court of the High Court in a joint judgment of five judges adopted and applied what their Honours had said, that was in Ronpibon Tin NL and Tongkah Compound NL v. FC of T (1949) 78 CLR 47 at 56–7; 4 AITR 236 at 245 where Latham, C.J., Rich, Dixon, McTiernan and Webb, JJ. said this in joint judgment: "For expenditure to form an allowable deduction as an outgoing incurred in gaining or producing the assessable income it must be incidental and relevant to that end. The words 'incurred in gaining or producing the assessable income' mean in the course of gaining or producing such income. Their operation has been explained in cases decided under the provisions of the previous enactments * * *."

The critical words which were used by Latham, C.J., and Dixon, J. in the earlier case and are adopted by the court in the joint judgment are that the words "incurred in gaining or producing the assessable income" mean "in the course of gaining or producing such income".

In my opinion, none of the amounts claimed in this case, assuming that all or any of them were incurred by the taxpayer and some of them undoubtedly were, were incurred in the course of gaining or producing assessable income.

Everything that was done in this case, up till the time when the project ceased, was in my view entirely preliminary and directed to deciding whether or not an undertaking would be established to produce assessable income.

The project had not reached anything like the stage of doing anything in the course of gaining or producing assessable income. All that had happened was that certain tests had been made to ascertain whether or not the project would be feasible. Certain technical information had been acquired and certain steps had been taken to ensure that if the project did go ahead, supplies of timber, electricity, water and the like would be available. But that is as far as the project got. I reiterate that no one was committed, at all, to go on with the project, * * *. Nothing was done even to prepare plans or specifications for a mill, on the part of the taxpayer. * * * In other words, the project did not approach in any way a situation which could be described as being the course of gaining or producing income. It was all completely anterior thereto and in those circumstances, it appears to me that any losses or outgoings which were in fact incurred by the taxpayer were in the course of investigations to see whether the project would be feasible, and the course of steps to ensure that if it did start there would be available supplies, * * *. But they certainly were not, in my view, incurred in the course of gaining or producing assessable income.

Accordingly, I conclude that the taxpayer has not established that any of the losses or outgoings incurred, or claimed to be incurred, fall within the first limb of [the predecessor of § 8–1].

As to the second limb of [the predecessor of § 8–1], the expression is "losses or outgoings to the extent to which they are necessarily incurred in carrying on a business for the purpose of gaining or producing assessable income".

The meaning of this expression was made clear by Menzies, J. in John Fairfax & Sons Pty. Ltd. v. FC of T (1959) 101 CLR 30 at 49; 7 AITR 346 at 363, where his Honour said:

> "Disregarding the application of the section to losses and considering the alternative head solely in its application to outgoings, there must, if an outgoing is to fall within its terms, be found (i) that it was necessarily incurred in carrying on a business; and (ii) that the carrying on of the business was for the purpose of gaining assessable income. The element that I think it necessary to emphasise here is that the outlay must have been incurred in the carrying on of a business, that is, it must be part of the cost of trading operations."

His Honour italicized and emphasized the words "carrying on".

It is unnecessary to decide at what point of time it can be said that a business is carried on. I am not to be taken as making any pronouncement on the submission for the Commissioner that until the actual business has commenced the second limb of [the predecessor of § 8–1] has no application.

As the Chairman of the Board of Review pointed out, it is of no consequence so far as the second limb is concerned that no income was produced, and it is unnecessary for me to make any pronouncement on the question of whether or not a mill or factory must have actually started operating in the sense of the mill starting to turn before any outlay can be said to have been necessarily incurred in carrying on a business for the purpose of gaining or producing such income. It is unnecessary for me to decide that for the purposes of this case.

However, as far as this case is concerned, it appears to me to be clear that for all the reasons I have given in relation to the first limb, the losses or outgoings here claimed by the taxpayer were not necessarily incurred in carrying on a business for the purpose of gaining or producing such income.

The critical point is that the company had not reached a stage remotely near the carrying on of a business. Even assuming that at some stage prior to the mill turning, the company could be said to be carrying on a business, in this case the company had not even approached the stage of making a decision about carrying on a business. All that had happened had been that certain investigations had been made to decide whether or not the business was feasible, and whether or not it was economically viable on a competitive basis, but nothing had been done which could be said to be carrying on a business or anything associated with or incidental to the actual carrying on of a business. Everything which was done was concerned with making a decision whether or not steps should be taken to set up a business, but no decision on even that matter had been reached.

concl.

Accordingly, for those reasons I conclude that the taxpayer has not established that any part of the losses or outgoings claimed was necessarily incurred in carrying on a business for the purpose of gaining or producing assessable income.

* * *

Note

The *Snowden & Willson* and *Softwood Pulp* cases explore issues that should be familiar to a student in an introductory course on the United States' federal income tax. Sections 162 and 212 of the Internal Revenue Code allow deductions for expenditures incurred in a trade or business or income-producing activity and each of those sections includes limitations on the amounts that may be deducted. Both of those sections require that expenditures must be "ordinary and necessary" in order to be deductible. The *Snowden & Willson* case examines the requirements in Section 8–1 that to be deductible an outgoing must be "necessarily" incurred in carrying on a trade or business and cannot be "of a capital nature." Is the court's analysis of those limitations consistent with the Supreme Court's interpretation of the "ordinary and necessary" requirement in Welch v. Helvering?[1] Section 162 also requires that to be deductible an expense must be paid or incurred "in carrying on" a trade or business. The *Softwood Pulp* decision interprets nearly identical language in Section 8–1 to preclude a deduction for amounts incurred prior to carrying on a business. *Softwood Pulp* is consistent with interpretations of the "carrying on" requirement in Section 162.[2] Note, however, that the Internal Revenue Code now

---

1. 290 U.S. 111, 54 S.Ct. 8 (1933).

2. See e.g., Frank v. Commissioner, 20 T.C. 511 (1953).

provides a limited deduction in Section 195 for "start-up expenditures."

The next two decisions examine the Section 8–1(2)(a) limitation on capital expenditures and the nexus that must be established between an expenditure and a business or income-producing activity in order to be entitled to a deduction under Section 8–1.

INTERPRETIVE DECISION 2006/614

Australian Taxation Office, 2004.

Issue

Is the taxpayer entitled to a deduction, under section 8–1 of the Income Tax Assessment Act 1997 (ITAA 1997) for the expenses they incurred in installing a portable global positioning system (GPS) in their employer provided motor vehicle?

Decision

No. The taxpayer is not entitled to a deduction, under section 8–1 of the ITAA 1997 for the expenses they incurred in installing a portable GPS in their employer provided motor vehicle as the expenditure on the GPS is of a capital nature.

Facts

The taxpayer is employed as a sales representative.

The taxpayer's employment duties include travelling to new and existing clients located within their assigned area.

The taxpayer purchased and installed a portable GPS in their employer provided motor vehicle.

The GPS unit that the taxpayer installed in their employer provided motor vehicle enables them to more easily locate client addresses within their assigned area. The GPS is used only for work purposes.

Reasons for Decision

Section 8–1 of the ITAA 1997 allows a deduction for all losses and outgoings to the extent to which they are incurred in gaining or producing assessable income except where the outgoings are of a capital, private or domestic nature, or relate to the earning of exempt income.

The courts have established that, for an expense to be an allowable deduction, there must be a sufficient connection between the outgoing and the assessable income such that the expenditure is incidental and relevant to the taxpayer's income producing activities (Ronpibon Tin NL and Tongkah Compound NL v. Federal

Commissioner of Taxation (1949) 78 CLR 47; (1949) 4 AITR 236; (1949) 8 ATD 431, and it must have the essential character of an outgoing incurred in gaining assessable income (Lunney & Hayley v. Federal Commissioner of Taxation (1958) 100 CLR 478; (1958) 7 AITR 166); (1958) 11 ATD 404).

The travel requirements of the taxpayer's employment provide a sufficient connection between the expenses they incurred on the GPS and their salary, such that the expenditure is incidental and relevant to the derivation of the assessable income from their employment.

The taxpayer only uses the GPS to locate client addresses (for work purposes). In these circumstances the essential character of the expenditure is not private or domestic in nature.

However, the expenditure the taxpayer incurred on the GPS is a one-off expense without any element of being a recurrent expenditure. It brought into existence an enduring asset used in the derivation of the taxpayer's assessable income. The GPS is to provide the taxpayer with a long-term benefit in their income earning activities. In these circumstances the taxpayer's expenditure on the GPS is of a capital nature rather than of a revenue nature.

As the expenditure the taxpayer incurred on the GPS is capital in nature, they are precluded from claiming a deduction for the GPS by paragraph 8–1(2)(a) of the ITAA 1997.

MORRIS v. COMMISSIONER OF TAXATION
Federal Court of Australia, 2002.
2002 ATC 4404.

GOLDBERG, J.

INTRODUCTION AND BACKGROUND

The issues to be determined in this proceeding are whether 10 taxpayers are entitled to a deduction from their assessable income in respect of expenditure each of them has incurred in the purchase of items of sun protection being variously sunglasses, sunhats and sunscreen during the financial years ended 30 June 1998 and 30 June 1999. The applicants claim that the expenditure by each of them in respect of these items was work related expenditure, that is to say, it was an expenditure or outgoing incurred in gaining or producing their assessable income and was not an expenditure or outgoing of a private or domestic nature. The respondent (the Commissioner) contends that the expenditure by each of the applicants in respect of these sun protection items was not a deductible expenditure because it was not incurred in gaining or producing their assessable income, that is to say it was not incidental or relevant to their income-producing activities and was of an essentially private nature.

2.   Each of the applicants carries on a different occupation but a feature common to all the applicants is that the nature of their work requires each of them to work in the open air for varying periods during the day. * * *

The first applicant, Rodney James Morris

3.   Mr. Morris is 39 years of age and has been employed by the Hadley Farming Company since 1986, his present position being a farm manager. The property he manages covers 11,156 hectares and is used for cotton growing, dry land farming and cattle farming. During the summer period his working day is from 7.00 am to 7.00 pm and in the winter period it is from 7.30 am until 5.00 pm or 5.30 pm. Mr. Morris has no skin conditions caused by ultraviolet radiation, but his doctor has told him that he is in the high risk age group because the highest cause of death in Australia in the 30–40 years age group is skin cancer. His doctor recommended that he wear sunglasses because of the glare from the bonnet of the vehicle which he uses to travel around the property. Mr. Morris wears sunglasses for the whole year when driving the four-wheel drive vehicle and for 6 months each year when carrying on other activities on the property. He did not purchase a pair of sunglasses in the 1998 year of income.

4.   Mr. Morris has used and applied sunscreen at work since 1981 and always keeps a sunscreen container in his vehicle. In the 1998 year of income he purchased one big bottle of sunscreen from the New South Wales Cancer Council for $40 and he has estimated that during the 1998 year of income sunscreen to the value of $15 was used by him solely at work. The balance was used by his family and himself for recreation. When Mr. Morris is working, the sunscreen he uses protects his ears and hands and provides long-term protection from ultraviolet rays. Mr. Morris could not carry out his work without the use of sunscreen because he must work in the sun.

5.   Mr. Morris wears a hat when working, but he did not purchase a hat in the 1998 year of income. Mr. Morris wears a hat because it makes his work more comfortable, it prevents sunstroke and bad headaches, it prevents the possibility of overheating and protects him from sunburn on his face and head. If he did not wear a hat, he would not be as productive as he is when he wears a hat.

6.   In his income tax return for the 1998 year of income, Mr. Morris claimed a deduction for the expenditure of $15 in respect of his purchase of sunscreen. In the notice of assessment, the Commissioner disallowed the deduction claimed. On 7 October 1999, Mr. Morris lodged a notice of objection against the assessment and on

30 December 1999 the Deputy Commissioner of Taxation notified Mr. Morris of the decision disallowing his objection. It is in respect of that disallowance that Mr. Morris appeals to the court.

* * *

The fifth applicant, Mr. Charles Peter Giffard

26. Mr. Giffard is 38 years of age and has been the Site Construction Supervisor at the Concord Golf Club in Sydney since July 1997. He has been wearing sunglasses at work for 15 years. He works outdoors for about 85–90% of his working time from September to April and he wears sunglasses during this time. Mr. Giffard estimates that during the period from May to August each year he wears sunglasses about 40% of the time. Mr. Giffard wears sunglasses:

- to reduce glare and protect himself against ultraviolet radiation;

- to enable him to pick out objects more clearly on the golf course;

- to protect him against grass and sand coming into his eyes while mowing;

- to protect him against the need to squint, to see properly and to focus upon objects on the golf course;

- to protect him from insects when moving around in a golf cart;

- to protect him from sunburn around his eyes and the bridge of his nose.

27. During the 1998 year of income, Mr. Giffard spent $25 on a pair of sunglasses. Mr. Giffard replaces his sunglasses approximately every 12 months because of damage or loss. Mr. Giffard uses his sunglasses 80% of the time while at work and 20% of the time outside of work.

28. Mr. Giffard wears a wide brimmed canvas hat provided by his employer 100% of the time whilst working during the summer months and 50–60% of the time whilst working in winter. He wears another hat when he is not at work. Mr. Giffard wears a sunhat to protect him against sunstroke, to protect him against tree branches scratching his head while he moves around the course, and to make him cooler, less tired and more productive.

29. Mr. Giffard uses sunscreen about 40% of the time whilst working in summer and 20% of his working time in winter. During the 1998 year of income, he spent about $14 on purchasing sunscreen which he used 50% of his time at work and 50% of his time

outside work. He uses sunscreen to protect against sunburn and the consequences of having more time off work.

30.   Mr. Giffard has used both sunscreen and a hat through-out his working life. Mr. Giffard considers that the sunscreen, hat and sunglasses are necessary for him to carry out his work and that a failure to have these items may cause a misjudgment in the performance of his work duties.

31.   In his income tax return for the 1998 year of income, Mr. Giffard claimed a deduction of $25 in respect of his acquisition of a pair of sunglasses and $7 in respect of his acquisition of a quantity of sunscreen. In the notice of assessment, the Commissioner disal-lowed the deductions claimed. On 7 October 1999, Mr. Giffard lodged a notice of objection against the assessment and on 30 December 1999 the Deputy Commissioner of Taxation notified Mr. Giffard of the decision disallowing the objection. It is in respect of that disallowance that Mr. Giffard appeals to the court.

* * *

Reasoning

* * *

79.   There are a number of principles and propositions which are well-established in relation to whether expenditure is deductible as being expenditure incurred in gaining or producing assessable income

- Expenditure incurred in the course of gaining or producing assessable income is expenditure incurred in gaining or producing that assessable income * * *.

- The question whether an outgoing is wholly or partly in-curred in gaining or producing assessable income is a ques-tion of characterisation * * *. The question to be asked is whether the occasion of the outgoing operates to give it the essential character of a working expense, that is, whether the occasion of the outgoing is to be found in the income-earning activity itself * * *.

- It is not sufficient to make an expenditure deductible that it is a prerequisite to, or a sine qua non of, the derivation of assessable income * * *.

- An outgoing, in order to be deductible, must be incidental and relevant to the activities directed at gaining or producing the assessable income * * *.

- It is sufficient and necessary that the occasion of the outgo-ing be found in whatever is productive of the assessable

income, or would be expected to produce the assessable
income * * *.

● The taxpayer must show a real connection between the
expenditure and the taxpayer's employment activities as an
employee in order for the expenditure to be deductible * * *.

● The words "to the extent to which" in § 8–1 indicate that
the provision contemplates apportionment * * *.

● The fact that an employer requires an employee to expend
money on the purchase of a particular item is relevant in
considering deductibility, but it is not determinative of deductibility under § 8–1. It is still necessary to demonstrate
that the relevant expenditure is occasioned by the work
income-producing activity * * *.

82.   It should be emphasised that the relevant inquiry to be
made is whether the outgoing was incurred in the course of
deriving assessable income and not whether it was incurred for the
purpose of deriving assessable income. * * *

* * *

84.   What is common to all the applicants is that the nature
and content of their work requires them to be outdoors exposed to
the sunlight for extended periods. They do not have an option as to
the environment in which they can work. Mr. Morris, the farm
manager must work in the open on the farm; * * * Mr. Giffard, the
site construction supervisor, must work on the golf course. They
are compelled by the nature of the work they are required to
undertake in order to carry out their income producing activities to
work in an environment of exposure to sunlight.

85.   This aspect of their work gives rise to an issue of characterisation and the extent to which there is a sufficient connection
between the expenditure on the sun protection items and the
manner in which the applicants derive their respective assessable
incomes. The Commissioner contended that the fact that the applicants were required to undertake work activities in the open air did
not provide the necessary connection and that, rather, the expenditures incurred were simply incurred as a consequence of living and
working in sunlight. It is true, as the Commissioner submitted, that
none of the work activities or tasks performed by the applicants
required the wearing of a hat or sunglasses, or the application of
sunscreen as part of the work process, but that proposition fails to
have sufficient regard to the environment in which, or the place at
which, the work activity is to be undertaken. It is also important to
take into account the fact that the wearing of a hat and sunglasses
and the application of sunscreen enables the applicants to be more
productive in their work output. This aspect of assisting or enhanc-

ing productivity is not the determiner of deductibility, but it assists in demonstrating that there is a connection between the expenditure on those items and the derivation of assessable income, and that the expenditure is incidental and relevant to that derivation.

86.   The relevant consideration is not simply that the applicants work outside in the open air but, rather, that they are obliged to do so in order to carry out the work as a result of which their assessable income is derived.

87.   The Commissioner contrasted the position of a person working in a solarium in which artificial ultraviolet light was provided to enable indoor tanning. In such a case, the Commissioner said that the worker confronted an occupation-specific exposure to ultraviolet rays produced by equipment in the workplace. Thus, according to the Commissioner, it was the particular income-earning activity engaged in by the worker which provided the occasion for the expenditure incurred by the worker in limiting the worker's exposure to artificial light. This position may be accepted, but it is reached by considering the place at which and the environment under which the particular income-earning activity is undertaken.

88.   The Commissioner placed considerable emphasis on the distinction between persons working in an artificial environment and persons working in a natural environment. However, this distinction fails to pay sufficient regard to the fact that it is the nature of the particular employment of the present applicants which dictates whether they work in an artificial environment or in the natural environment.

89.   When one contrasts the worker in the solarium with, for example, the surveyor working in the open air, it is seen that it is the particular income-earning activity engaged in by each person which provides the occasion for the expenditure incurred by each person in limiting that person's exposure to harmful light rays. The fact that in one case the light source is artificial, whereas in the other case the light source is natural, is a distinction without a difference. What is common to both workers is that each must carry out his or her income-producing activities in an environment which exposes them to harmful light rays in respect of which they need protection.

90.   It is not to the point, as the Commissioner submitted, that sunglasses and hats are conventional clothing and have no intrinsic occupation-specific function in relation to the work of any of the applicants. * * * When the proposition is put by the Commissioner in these terms, it focuses on the nature of the item, the subject of the expenditure, rather than upon the activity and the environment in which the activity is undertaken which gives rise to the occasion for the expenditure. It is the nature of the use of the sunglasses,

the hat and the sunscreen in relation to the income-producing activities of the applicants which identifies the occasion of the outgoing, rather than simply the nature of the item itself.

91. The Commissioner put the distinction another way when he submitted that in some circumstances the working environment is intrinsic to the duties undertaken by a worker, and that it is of the nature of the duties that they are carried out in a particular workplace which is an artificial working environment. It was said that it is of the nature of the duties of a solarium worker that the worker is exposed to ultraviolet radiation in providing the solarium service to the customers. It was also said that it is in the nature of working in a blast furnace that a worker approaches the furnace door and needs protection against heat, molten metal and sparks. The Commissioner then drew a contrast by submitting that it is not in the nature of building or carpentry that a builder or carpenter wears a hat, and that it is not in the nature of designing golf courses that the designer puts on sunglasses. The contrasting position, put this way, concentrates on the item used instead of focusing on the income-producing activity undertaken in the partic-ular environment, which is the relevant issue to consider for the purpose of deductibility under § 8–1. The underlying factor which is common to the solarium worker, the steelworker, the builder and the carpenter is that in order to derive their assessable income they are required (by the nature of their work) to work in a particular environment, in respect of which they have no choice, in which they are exposed to harmful light and heat rays which necessitate the use of protective equipment or products.

* * *

93. The Commissioner submitted that the applicants' use of sun protection items to protect them from the sun's rays was no different from the situation of a short-sighted person who needed glasses at his or her desk to read documents and who could not undertake the work without glasses, or an employee who wore warm clothes to work because there was no heating in the office. It was said that, in these cases, expenditure on the glasses and the warm clothes was not deductible. That may be so, but the examples used are different from the situation, such as in the present circumstances, where the applicants are required to work in an environment in which they are exposed to conditions which require them to take protective steps in order to avoid harm in the course of carrying out their income-producing activities.

95. * * * It is the nature of the activity which enables a worker to derive assessable income which is relevant to consider in this context, rather than the nature of the item for which a deduction is claimed.

96. A number of cases have demonstrated that the nature of the work place and the work environment in which the income-producing activities of the taxpayer are required to be undertaken is a critical consideration in determining the deductibility of expenditure by the taxpayer which is claimed to have been incurred in the course of gaining or producing assessable income.

97. The situation most analogous to the claims of the applicants is found in Mansfield v. FCT (1995) 31 ATR 367; 96 ATC 4001. A flight attendant employed by Australian Airlines claimed deductions for expenditure on cosmetics (including moisturiser), hair care items (including conditioner), pantyhose and shoes which were disallowed by the Commissioner. Hill, J. allowed the deductions for expenditure on moisturiser, hair conditioner, pantyhose and shoes but disallowed the deductions claimed in respect of other grooming and haircare items. The taxpayer supported her claim in relation to the expenditure on moisturiser by saying that the "continual working in pressurised aircraft dries the skin and requires the use of moisturisers". The airline required certain standards of grooming and it gave attendants advice on grooming and the need for moisturisers. Hill, J. found that the taxpayer had incurred expenditure on moisturisers used to combat the dehydration effects of pressurisation and lack of humidity in the cabin.

98. Hill, J. concluded that the expenditure on moisturisers was deductible under [the predecessor of § 8–1] and said at ATR 374; ATC 4007:

> "In my view, expenditure for moisturiser, the necessity for which was brought about by the harsh conditions of employment which Mrs. Mansfield was called upon to endure, is incidental and relevant to her occupation as a flight attendant. It has the necessary connection with her activities in the cabin itself. It is these activities which are directly relevant to her gaining and producing assessable income by way of salary."

Hill, J. referred to the airline's requirement that flight attendants be well-groomed and continued at ATR 374; ATC 4007–4008:

> "As the cases indicate, the mere fact that a particular expenditure may be required to be made by the employer, while relevant will not be determinative of deductibility. The additional feature present in the present case is the fact that the occasion of the expenditure is to be found in Mrs. Mansfield's working in the cabin, that is to say, in the dehydration brought about by pressurisation of the cabin at altitude."

However, his Honour did not allow the claim for expenditure on makeup, even though it was required by the airline, as it was expenditure of a personal nature.

99. The important distinction which Hill, J. drew between the expenditure on moisturisers and the expenditure on makeup was that it was the working environment in the cabin which necessitated the use of moisturisers; that working environment did not necessitate the use of makeup to any greater extent than was required by not working in the cabin.

100. The working environment in the cabin was also the feature which enabled Hill, J. to allow the deduction claimed for expenditure on shoes. His Honour accepted that "generally expenditure on ordinary articles of apparel will not be deductible, notwithstanding that such expenditure is necessary to ensure a suitable appearance in a particular job or profession", but he found a feature in the shoes which was related to the work environment in which they were worn. Hill, J. explained this feature at ATR 375; ATC 4008:

> "The shoes in the present case were required to be worn as part of the uniform. It is true that there was nothing to distinguish the shoes from shoes which a flight attendant might purchase for domestic purposes other than, on the evidence of the present case, colour. But there are other features besides the requirement that the shoes match the remaining parts of a flight attendant's uniform which assist the taxpayer here. There is the additional feature that the cabin pressure requires the shoes to be a half-size too large for ordinary use. Further, of course, there is the fact that the taxpayer's employment brings about regular scuffing of the shoes. It is these features that lead, in my view, to the conclusion that the occasion of the outgoing on shoes, that is to say cabin shoes, should be seen as being found in the duties which Mrs. Mansfield performed as a flight attendant in the year of income."

Although the cabin shoes were worn solely inside the cabin and never outside it, what loomed large in his Honour's reasoning was the fact that it was the work environment that brought about the use of the shoes in order for the taxpayer to carry out her cabin duties.

101. Hill, J. allowed the deduction for hair conditioner which was "necessitated by the lack of humidity and pressurisation of the cabin", as it fell into the same category as the moisturiser, but did not allow expenditure claimed for the remaining hairdressing items as it was of a private nature. * * *

* * *

105. But what is important for present purposes, is that the applicants are required by the nature of their work obligations and

duties to expose themselves to the rays of the sun for sustained periods of time in order to fulfil and carry out their work activities. I use the expression "required" by reference to what has to be undertaken in order to carry out their duties. I do not use that expression by reference to an expenditure which is stipulated by the employer as it is a well accepted principle that the fact that expenditure is required by an employer to be expended by an employee will not necessarily render the expenditure deductible * * *.

106.   The Commissioner relied upon Commissioner of Taxation v. Cooper in support of his submission that the income-producing activities of the applicants did not include the use or application of sun protection items with the result there was no real connection between the expenditure on the sun protection items and the applicants' employment or work activities. In Cooper a professional footballer claimed a deduction * * * in respect of expenditure on specified quantities of food and drink he was required by his employer to consume in order to maintain an optimum playing weight.

107.   A majority of the court (Lockhart and Hill, JJ.) held that there was no necessary connection or nexus between the consumption of the food and drink, and the instruction to consume it, and that the essential character of the expenditure was private.

108.   Lockhart, J. said * * *:

> "The taxpayer incurred the expenditure on additional food and drink for the purpose of increasing his weight and thus to play professional football and earn assessable income. But its character as the cost of additional food and drink is neither relevant nor incidental to the training for and playing of football matches, which is the activity by which he gained assessable income. The expenditure was not incurred in or in the course of that activity. The taxpayer was paid money to train for and play football, not to consume food and drink. His income-producing activities did not include the consumption of food and drink."

* * *

109.   This analysis does not easily translate into the applicants' circumstances in a manner which supports the Commissioner's submissions. The connection between the sun protection items and the applicants' income-producing activities is closer, more immediate and more direct than the connection between the intake of extra food and drink and the activity of playing football in Cooper. Mr. Cooper's income-producing activities may not have included the consumption of extra food and drink, but the appli-

cants' income-producing activities were such that they included carrying out employment duties whilst exposed to the harmful rays of the sun. The nexus is closer and the expenditure on sun protection items is more incidental and relevant to the applicants' work activities than was the expenditure by Mr. Cooper on extra food and drink. It is the nature of the activity which gives rise to the expenditure upon which attention must be focused in order to determine the nexus between the subject matter of the expenditure and the activity which produces assessable income.

110. Similar reasoning underlies the conclusion of Gummow, J. in FCT v. Edwards (1993) 27 ATR 293; 93 ATC 5162 * * *, where particular emphasis was placed on the essential character of the expenditure for which a deduction was claimed. The personal secretary to the wife of the Governor of Queensland claimed a deduction under [the predecessor of § 8–1] in respect of expenditure on clothing, hairdressing and dry-cleaning which she used and required in the course of carrying out her duties. On occasions, the personal secretary was required to undertake a number of changes of clothing during the day.

111. The tribunal found that the taxpayer's income-producing activities included her being suitably dressed to meet the formality of the occasion of each engagement in any one day which required her wardrobe to be more extensive. Gummow, J. accepted the submission that it was open for the tribunal to characterise the expenditure on clothing as serving a mixed business and private purpose, notwithstanding that the clothing was conventional and the taxpayer selected the items of clothing she would wear.

112. At first instance, Gummow, J. accepted that the tribunal had not erred in finding that the essential character of the expenditure on clothing was not to clothe the taxpayer in the ordinary sense as part of daily life but to enable her to perform satisfactorily the duties of her position. His Honour held that the tribunal had not considered the essential character of the expenditure on hairdressing and dry-cleaning and held that there must have been a strong likelihood that, at least as to the dry-cleaning, the essential character of the outgoing was not sufficiently relevant to the income-producing activity of the taxpayer. Apparently with the consent of the parties, Gummow, J. held that the expenditure on these items should be disallowed as a deduction.

113. An appeal against Gummow, J.'s decision was dismissed: Commissioner of Taxation v. Edwards (1994) 49 FCR 318. The full court rejected the proposition that expenditure on conventional clothing worn conventionally when working could never be an outgoing incurred in gaining or producing assessable income and was always an outgoing of a private or domestic nature. However,

the full court made it clear that its decision did not establish that expenditure on clothing acquired and worn at work would, because of that circumstance alone, be deductible as an outgoing incurred in deriving assessable income.

114. Although the decision in Edwards turned on its own special facts, it demonstrates that expenditure on items which ordinarily might be regarded as for private or domestic use will be deductible if the expenditure on the item can be characterised as having a close and relevant connection with the income-producing activity.

115. The applicants' evidence was that the sun protection items were necessary to enable them to perform their employment duties, that these items increased productivity and provided protection from exposure to the sun and ultraviolet radiation which can cause sunburn and skin cancer. This evidence was not disputed by the Commissioner. These factors, therefore, provide a substantial and close nexus between an applicant's expenditure on sun protection items and his or her income producing activities. Working outside in conditions of exposure to the sun and ultraviolet radiation forms part of the activities undertaken by each of the applicants for the production of their assessable income. Accordingly, there is a real connection between an applicant's production of assessable income and his or her expenditure on items such as sun protection items which increase productivity and provide protection while carrying out work activities. That is to say, an applicant's income producing activities include the use of the sun protection items.

116. This does not mean that expenditure on sunscreen, sunhats and sunglasses used at work will always be deductible. In each case it will be necessary to examine the facts of the case, including the nature and scope of the income-producing activities and the nature and character of the expenditure, to determine whether there is a real connection between the expenditure on such items and the activities which produce assessable income.

117. The Commissioner submitted that in any event the applicants' expenditures on sun protection items were essentially of a private character and, therefore, were not incidental and relevant to their income-producing activities. It was said that expenditure on conventional clothing, toiletries and pharmaceuticals was prima facie a private or living expense. The sunglasses and the sunhat were conventional clothing and the sunscreen was a pharmaceutical product which enabled the applicants to perform their employment duties without pain or discomfort.

118. The evidence pointed to the fact that some of the applicants used the sun protection items at work and home and the

Commissioner conceded that the fact that such items were used at home and work did not affect the allowance of the relevant proportion of the expenditure. However, the Commissioner argued that the fact the items could be used, and were used, without differentiation for private purposes pointed to their private character. According to the Commissioner neither sunglasses (with the arguable exception of the Sportsoptic sunglasses used by Mr. Flood), nor a hat, nor sunscreen had an occupation specific function or occupational character in relation to any of the occupations of the applicants.

119.   The Commissioner accepted that a workplace with conditions which peculiarly gave rise, by way of example, to situations of dehydration or glare, could transform what was ordinarily private expenditure into an expenditure which had the relevant nexus with the income-producing activities of the taxpayer. The Commissioner acknowledged, for example, that a worker in a blast furnace would be entitled to a deduction in respect of expenditure on protective clothing and that expenditure would be an allowable deduction in respect of the purchase of special glasses required to protect a person against the glare of a visual display unit as the glasses had no use outside the workplace.

120.   However, the Commissioner's argument depended on the proposition that the income-producing activities of the taxpayer must be undertaken in what he called an artificial working environment in order to convert expenditure on private items into expenditure on items which was relevant and incidental to the gaining or producing of income.

121.   I do not consider that the distinction between an artificial working environment and a working environment under naturally occurring conditions should determine whether expenditure is of a private nature. The reason why an artificial working environment may transform expenditure on what is usually regarded as a private item into expenditure relevant and incidental to the gaining or producing of assessable income is not because the working environment is artificial rather than naturally occurring. It is because the taxpayer who is working in that environment is required (because of the nature of the work to be undertaken for the purpose of undertaking the income producing activities) to work in an environment, whether it be artificial or naturally occurring, which has features about it which create the real connection between the expenditure and the taxpayer's employment activities which have to be undertaken.

122.   Thus, if the nature of the work required to be undertaken by a taxpayer in order to carry on his or her income-producing activities is such that the taxpayer must carry on those activities in

a manner which exposes him or her to harmful rays of the sun and ultraviolet radiation and the taxpayer uses sunglasses, a hat or sunscreen to protect himself or herself from such harmful rays and radiation whilst undertaking those work activities, the expenditure on such items will not be classified as expenditure of a private nature, which it would otherwise be if the taxpayer did not have to carry out his or her income-producing activities exposed to the harmful rays of the sun and ultraviolet radiation.

* * *

124.   In short, I do not accept the Commissioner's distinction between an artificial and a natural working environment. Such a distinction is itself artificial and is not supported by the wording of § 8–1 * * *.

125.   Although expenditure on sunglasses, a sunhat and sunscreen may be of a private nature in certain contexts, I am satisfied that the circumstances in which these items were used by each of the applicants and the relationship between the expenditure on these items and the income-producing activities of each of the applicants required to be undertaken in a naturally occurring environment were such that the expenditure was not of a private nature.

* * *

127.   I turn to the circumstances of each applicant and the determination of the deductibility of their individual expenditures on sun protection items.

128.   The first applicant, Rodney James Morris. I am satisfied that the expenditure of $15 claimed as a deduction in respect of his purchase of sunscreen is incidental and relevant to his occupation as a farm manager. The necessity for the expenditure was brought about by the conditions of his employment as a farm manager which requires him to work in an environment which exposes him to the harmful rays of the sun and ultraviolet radiation for long periods. There is a sufficient real connection between the expenditure and Mr. Morris' income-producing activities which results in the expenditure being deductible under § 8–1.

* * *

134.   The fifth applicant, Charles Peter Giffard. I am satisfied that a proportion of the expenditure of $25 claimed in respect of Mr. Giffard's acquisition of sunglasses and the expenditure of $14 claimed in respect of his acquisition of sunscreen is incidental and relevant to his occupation as a Site Construction Supervisor. Mr. Giffard uses the sunglasses 20% of the time for private or domestic purposes and uses 50% of the sunscreen whilst at work. I consider

that there is a real connection between Mr. Giffard's expenditure on these items and his income-producing activities as a Site Construction Supervisor at the Concord Golf Club. His work duties require him to spend 85–90% of his working time during September to April working outdoors, during which time he wears sunglasses. Mr. Giffard wears sunglasses at work about 85–90% of the time during September to April and 40% of the time during May to August. Whilst working outdoors Mr. Giffard is exposed to the harmful rays of the sun and ultraviolet radiation. The sunglasses reduce glare, provide protection against ultraviolet radiation, protect him against sunburn, assist him to focus on objects on the golf course and therefore protect him from the conditions of his employment and enable him to carry out his work duties in the outside environment. As Mr. Giffard uses the sunglasses 80% at work and 20% outside work, it will be necessary to apportion the expenditure.

135. A proportion of Mr. Giffard's expenditure of $7 on sunscreen is also deductible as it is incidental and relevant to Mr. Giffard's income-producing activities. The sunscreen protects him against sunburn and the consequences of having time away from work. Together with the sunglasses and hat, the sunscreen also assists him in the performance of his work duties and to prevent misjudgment. As Mr. Giffard uses the sunscreen 50% at work and 50% outside of work, the expenditure should be apportioned.

* * *

CASE 29/95
Administrative Appeals Tribunal, 1995.
Australian Taxation Office.

T.E. Barnett (Senior Member):

This application is for review of the respondent's objection decision dated 11 October 1994 in respect of the applicant's objection to the private ruling for the year of income ended 30 June 1994, that interest payments and borrowing expenses on money borrowed on the security of an investment property and on his residence were not allowable deductions pursuant to the Income Tax Assessment Act 1936 ("the Act"). The Tribunal has considered the applicant's oral evidence, all material documents and the submissions of both parties.

2. Basically, the applicant submitted that the interest payments and borrowing expenses incurred on his loan from Westpac Bank are deductible pursuant to §§ [8–1(1)] and 67 of the Act. The basis of his claim was that he believed that these payments were used by him to gain or produce assessable income and if the

Tribunal adopts a common-sense approach, they should be allowable deductions.

3.   The applicant claimed that when he was transferred from Bunbury by his employer, he was obliged to rent out his Bunbury property which, at that time, was mortgaged. He was unsuccessful in an attempt to sell the Bunbury property and he was unable to arrange a further bank loan to purchase a property in Perth while he still owed money on the Bunbury loan. At considerable effort, he then proceeded to pay off the Bunbury house loan and he refers to this as "withdrawing the equity from the Bunbury property".

4.   When the mortgage on the Bunbury property was paid off in October 1992, the applicant sought to purchase a property in Perth which he would use as his principal residence. He did so by obtaining a mortgage over his Bunbury and Perth properties. The applicant claimed that this mortgage was not used only to finance the Perth property but it was also used to re-finance the Bunbury property. He submitted that when he obtained a loan of $125,000 to purchase the Perth property, $90,000 of that loan was really intended to re-finance the equity in his Bunbury property which was still rented. In support of this claim, he points to early Westpac documents which show that the original intention had been to take out two separate loans for $90,000 and $35,000 respectively.

5.   The applicant said that another way he could have proceeded would have been to sell his Bunbury property, buy his Perth property with the proceeds and then obtain a mortgage to buy an investment property. He could even buy back the Bunbury property

his case. This Tribunal is bound, however, to apply the law to the factual circumstances as they exist and not what may have occurred in hypothetical situations. The facts are that the applicant did not sell the Bunbury property and he did not arrange two separate loans.

8.   In the circumstances of this case, the Tribunal accepts the reasoning of the respondent in its entirety, as it was presented at the hearing and in the objection decision. The Tribunal is of the view that the applicant's interest payments and borrowing expenses are not deductible pursuant to any section of the Act because they were not used in gaining or producing assessable income and they are of a purely private and domestic character. The expenses were incurred in respect of borrowed funds which were applied for the acquisition of a private residence. Accordingly, this Tribunal affirms the decision under review.

Decision

9.   The decision under review is affirmed.

Note

There is no deduction in Australia for home mortgage interest. In order to be deductible, interest generally must satisfy the requirements of Section 8–1. The approach in Case 29/95, which focuses on the uses of borrowed funds, serves to prevent easy avoidance of the limitation on deductible interest.

C.   CHARITABLE DEDUCTIONS IN AUSTRALIA

INTERPRETIVE DECISION 2003/727
June 26, 2003.
Australian Taxation Office.

Issue

Is the taxpayer entitled to a deduction under Division 30 of the *Income Tax Assessment Act 1997* (ITAA 1997) for contributing a percentage of the taxpayer's trailing commission to a charitable institution nominated by the taxpayer's client, where the taxpayer undertakes to make such a contribution at the time of arranging the loan?

Decision

No. The taxpayer is not entitled to a deduction under Division 30 of the ITAA 1997 for contributing a percentage of the taxpayer's trailing commission to a charitable institution nominated by the taxpayer's client, where the taxpayer undertakes to make such a contribution at the time of arranging the loan. The contribution to the organisation is not a gift. However, the taxpayer is entitled to a deduction under section 8–1 of the ITAA 1997 as the contribution is an expense incurred in gaining or producing the taxpayer's assessable income.

Facts

The taxpayer carries on a business of mortgage broking. The taxpayer receives trailing commissions from the loan originator over the life of the loan when the taxpayer successfully arranges a loan, with the loan originator, for a client.

At the time of arranging a loan for a client, the taxpayer undertakes to contribute a specified percentage of the trailing commissions from the loan originator to an eligible organisation that is nominated by this client.

The taxpayer's business charter specifies that a client can only nominate an organisation to receive the contributions if that organisation's core objectives and activities contribute to the local community or to society as a whole. An eligible organisation can be, but does not need to be, a registered charitable institution or deductible gift recipient. However, organisations that have political alliances or are involved in political activities are not eligible to receive contributions.

Provided that the organisation nominated by the client is an eligible organisation, the taxpayer does not have any discretion to refrain from contributing the specified percentage of the trailing commission to that organisation. An organisation that is nominated by a client is called a "supported organisation." In this case, the supported organisation is a charitable institution.

The taxpayer encourages supported organisations to use their list of subscribers and members to market the possibility of taking out loans using the taxpayer's mortgage broking services as the more loans that are taken out by using the taxpayer's services, the more funds the supported organisation will receive.

Reasons for Decision

Division 30 of the ITAA 1997 deals with the deductibility of gifts and certain contributions. The table in section 30–15 of the ITAA 1997 specifies a list of gifts and contributions that a taxpayer can deduct. As the taxpayer does not make contributions to organisations that have political alliances or are involved in political activities, the contribution of a percentage of the trailing commission to the charitable institution is deductible under Division 30 of the ITAA 1997 only if that contribution is a gift.

The term "gift" is not defined in the income tax legislation, and thus takes on its ordinary meaning. The meaning of the word "gift" had been considered by the High Court in Federal Commissioner of Taxation v. McPhail (1968) 117 CLR 111; (1968) 15 ATD 16; (1968) 10 AITR 552 (McPhail's Case). Owen, J. confirmed that the word "gift" was used in the sense in which it is understood "in ordinary parlance". He noted that the Shorter Oxford Dictionary defined the act of giving as "a transfer of property in a thing voluntarily and without any valuable consideration". He then went on to say:

> But it is, I think, clear that to constitute a "gift", it must appear that the property transferred was transferred voluntarily and not as the result of a contractual obligation to transfer it and that no advantage of a material character was received by the transferor by way of return.

Therefore, the contribution of specified percentage of the trailing commissions will constitute a "gift" if:

(a) the contribution was made voluntarily and not as the result of a contractual obligation; and

(b) no advantage of a material character was received by the taxpayer by way of return, either directly or indirectly.

The two tests in McPhail's Case have been applied in a long line of cases. In Case [2000] AATA 100 43 ATR 1337; Case 3/2000 200 ATC 132, a contract for the purchase of land required the purchaser to pay $8.1 million to the vendor and $2.7 million to an unrelated charity. The AAT applied McPhail's Case and upheld a private ruling that the payment to the charity was a contractual payment and not a gift.

At the time of arranging the loan for a client, the taxpayer undertakes to contribute a percentage of the trailing commissions from the loan originator to a charitable institution that is nominated by this client. The charitable institution nominated by the client is an eligible organisation and the taxpayer does not have any discretion to refrain from contributing the specified percentage of the trailing commission to that charitable institution. It is considered that the taxpayer's lack of discretion to refrain from making the contribution, once the client takes out the loan, indicates that the contribution is made as a result of a contractual obligation. Further, it is considered that the taxpayer would receive an advantage of a material character by way of return because the supported organisation would be motivated to use its mailing list of members and subscribers to promote taxpayer's mortgage broking business as the preferred mortgage broking services to its members. Accordingly, it is considered that the contribution of the specified percentage of the trailing commission does not satisfy both the requirements of a "gift".

As the contribution is not a gift, the taxpayer is not entitled to a deduction under Division 30 of the ITAA 1997.

Under section 8–1 of the ITAA 1997, an outgoing is deductible to the extent that it is incurred in gaining or producing assessable income; or necessarily incurred in carrying on a business for the purpose of gaining or producing assessable income; and the outgoing is not of a capital, private or domestic nature.

In Ronpibon Tin NL & Tongkah Compound NL v. Federal Commissioner of Taxation (1949) 78 CLR 47; (1949) 8 ATD 431; (1949) 4 AITR 236, the High Court stated, "that for an expenditure to form an allowable deduction as an outgoing incurred in gaining or producing the assessable income, it must be incidental and relevant to that end". The High Court also stated that "necessarily incurred", in the context of carrying on a business for the purpose of gaining or producing assessable income, means "clearly appropriate or adapted for" that purpose. These statements have been cited with approval in subsequent cases.

The taxpayer receives trailing commissions over the life of the loan from the loan originator when the taxpayer successfully arranges for a loan, with the loan originator, for the client. At the time of arranging the loan, the taxpayer undertakes to contribute a percentage of the trailing commissions to the charitable institution nominated by this client. The expense of making the contribution only arises when the taxpayer successfully arranges the loan, with the loan originator, for the client. Accordingly, it is considered that the contribution of a percentage of the trailing commission to the charitable institution nominated by the client is an outgoing that is incidental and relevant to the earning of the commission from the loan originator. This outgoing is not of a capital, private or domestic nature.

Therefore, the taxpayer is entitled to a deduction under section 8–1 of the ITAA 1997, for contributing a percentage of the trailing commission to a charitable institution nominated by the taxpayer's client, where the taxpayer undertakes to make such a contribution at the time of arranging the loan.

Note: The taxpayer can claim the deduction under section 8–1 of the ITAA 1997 whether the taxpayer makes the contribution to a supported organisation that is a registered deductible gift recipient, charitable institution, or any other organisation.

INTERPRETIVE DECISION 2002/577
May 31, 2002.
Australian Taxation Office.

Issue

Is the taxpayer entitled to a deduction under section 30–15 of the Income Tax Assessment Act 1997 ("ITAA 1997") for a gift of property owned for more than 12 months if it has a value of less than $5000?

Decision

No. The taxpayer is not entitled to a deduction under section 30–15 of the ITAA 1997 for a gift of property owned for more than 12 months if the property has a value of less than $5000.

Facts

The taxpayer purchased property.

The taxpayer gifted this property to a deductible gift recipient more than 12 months after purchase.

The property's market value on the day the property was gifted was less than $5000 and the Commissioner accepts that as the property's value.

Reasons for Decision

Division 30 of the ITAA 1997 provides an income tax deduction for gifts or contributions made to a deductible gift recipient.

Section 30–15 of the ITAA 1997 deals with the types of gifts or contributions that are deductible. The types of gifts or contributions include:

- property that the taxpayer purchased during the 12 months before making the gift; and
- property valued by the Commissioner of Taxation at more than $5000 if the property was purchased by the taxpayer more than 12 months before making the gift.

As the taxpayer's property was purchased more than 12 months prior to gifting and the property's value (as determined by the Commissioner) is less than $5000, the taxpayer will not be entitled to a deduction under section 30–15 of the ITAA 1997.

D. FRENCH DECISIONS

Below are two French cases dealing with taxpayer deductions. Once again, your reference point is the Internal Revenue Code. Consider how these taxpayers' arguments would be treated in a United States court.

CASE N. 35 697

Council of State, December 5th 1983.

Corporation X contests the increase of its income tax made by the administration for the 1970 and 1971 tax years. Corporation X gave money to the managing director of Company Y, one of its suppliers. There were no invoices for these payments. Subsequently, the administration qualified these transfers of money as nondeductible since they were considered to be gifts rather than part of a price paid for goods. Therefore, the administration disallowed the deductions and imposed a fine on the petitioner * * *. The facts of the case show that a secret contract was signed on May 15th 1971. In this letter, X and Y decided that the price of goods would be reduced in the invoices when compared with the price really paid by the contractors. The difference in price, two African Francs per kilogram, was credited in a bank account in the name of the general manager of Company Y.

The administration does not contest that these payments were made in the interest of Corporation X, notably, in order to strengthen the security of its supply of goods. Moreover, the administration does not contest that the real price, marked-up with the monetary compensation, was not unusual.

On account of these findings, the fact that an excess price, compared to the invoice, was paid and regularly entered on the books, on the request of the supplier, does not imply an unusual act of management.

Therefore, the administration was wrong when, on the basis of article 39 of the tax code, it qualified this payment as an unusual act of management and refused for this reason to deduct the monetary compensation paid to the manager of Company Y.

* * *

Note

Suppose Corporation X were a United States corporation. Would it be entitled to a deduction for the full amount it pays (including the funds diverted to the general manager's account) for the goods it receives from Company Y? See Section 162(c)(2).

DECISION OF FRENCH CONSTITUTIONAL COUNCIL

n. 2007–555 DC, August 16, 2007.

[The statute referred to the Constitutional Council (the statute for the improvement of labor, employment and buying power[1]) made three changes to the income tax. First, the statute excluded wages received from overtime working hours from the income tax. Next, it authorized a credit for a part of the interest paid on a

---

1. Loi en faveur du travail, de l'emploi et du pouvoir d'achat.

mortgage, if the mortgage is used to purchase the principal residence of the taxpayer. Finally, the statute changed the "tax shield," a feature of the French direct tax system. Under the previous tax shield, the total of the taxpayer's direct taxes (income tax, local taxes and wealth tax; but not the "CSG" and "CRDS," two taxes imposed to finance the French social security scheme) were limited to 60% of the taxpayer's income. If the total of the taxpayer's direct taxes exceeded that limit, the taxpayer could receive a refund of the excess. The new statute lowered the tax shield limit to 50% and added the CSG to the calculation of the tax shield. Ed.]

* * *

The Members of Parliament have referred for review by the Constitutional Council the statute for the improvement of labor, employment and buying power. They challenge in particular the conformity of [the law] * * * with the principle of equality of the tax burden for every citizen.

Article 13 of the Declaration of Human and Civil Rights[2] states that "For the maintenance of the public force, and for administrative expenses, a general tax is indispensable; it must be equally distributed among all citizens, in proportion to their ability to pay." Article 34 of the Constitution gives to the legislature the power to determine the tax burden of each citizen, subject to constitutional principles and within the characteristics of each tax. The legislature's determination, however, cannot blatantly violate the principle of tax equality.

The principle of tax equality does not prevent the legislature from creating tax rewards designed to enhance the general welfare. These rewards have to be based on objective and rational criteria linked to the goal of the measure. The provision must be consistent with the effects it is aimed to reach.

On the 1st article of the statute (overtime working hours)

The first article of the statute created a tax reward that is aimed to enhance the use of overtime working. To this end, the earnings received from overtime hours will not be taxable under the income tax. This article also creates a deduction for social security taxes paid for these hours. The petitioners argue that this provision infringes on the right to have employment and the principle of equal taxation among citizens.

2. The 1789 Declaration of Human and Civil Rights and the preamble of the 1946 Constitution are part of the French Constitution. See decision of the Constitutional Council n. 71–44 DC July 16th 1971, Liberté d'association. These texts create a charter of social and human rights for the French citizen.

For the right to employment

The petitioners argue that this provision will provide an incentive for the employers to ask their employees to work overtime instead of hiring new employees. Therefore, they argue, this statute infringes the constitutional right to employment and does not create a legal guaranty for the employee [to refuse to work overtime. Ed.].

The fifth section of the preamble of the 1946 Constitution states that "each person has the duty to work and the right to employment...." Article 34 of the Constitution states that "statutes shall lay down the basic principles of ... Employment law." Therefore, the legislature must define the right for everyone to have employment while allowing the practice of this right to the vast majority of people.

The legislative history from the Senate and the National Assembly show that this law was enacted to increase the number of working hours in order to stimulate economic growth and employment. Thus, the aim of this first article is to create the conditions needed to implement the fifth section of the preamble of the 1946 Constitution. Moreover, the Constitutional Council does not have the same general power of decision and assessment as the legislature. Therefore, the provision created by the referred law is not blatantly inconsistent with the aim pursued by the legislature.

* * *

Concerning the principle of tax equality

The petitioners argue that Article 1 of the law creates a breach of tax equality between taxpayers since an employee could have different tax results for the income from his work. Moreover, the overtime hours will be taxed differently and the part-time employees cannot benefit from this tax reward. In addition, the petitioners argue that the exoneration of CSG–CRDS [the deduction for social security taxes Ed.] does not take into account other incomes of the taxpayer, income from the other members of his household, and his dependents. Therefore, this tax relief creates a clear disparity that is contrary to Article 13 of the Declaration of Civil and Human Rights.

First, the goal of this tax reward is to increase the number of working hours in our economy in order to stimulate economic growth and employment. Therefore this law is intended to promote the general welfare.

Second, these tax rewards apply for all the overtime hours, without taking into account the organization of working time in the undertaking. In addition, the overtime hours of the part-time employees can qualify for this tax reward. The implementation of this law is therefore objectively and rationally consistent with its aim.

Third, the legislature, by creating this tax benefit for working hours exceeding the legal working time, regardless of the contract between the employee and the employer, far from creating a breach of tax equality, creates a remedy to a possible breach of this principle.

* * *

Finally, this law does not exonerate the taxpayer from the CSG but creates a reduction of this tax if the taxpayer works overtime. This measure, that has a limited effect, does not create a breach of tax equality within the meaning of the thirteenth article of the 1789 declaration.

Therefore, the first article of the law does not infringe any constitutional rules or principles.

On Article 5 of the referred law

The first paragraph of this article creates [a new article] of the tax code. This new article introduces an income tax credit for the interest paid on mortgages for the principle residence of the taxpayer. This tax credit is available only for the first five years of the mortgage and requires that the mortgage be acquired from a financial institution. The tax credit is equal to 20% of the interest paid on the mortgages. The tax credit cannot exceed 3,750 euros for a single taxpayer or 7,500 euros for a couple. Each dependent increases the limit allowed to the taxpayer by 500 euros.

The legislative history from the Parliament shows that the legislature intended to increase home ownership of residences built or bought after the enactment of the law. Hence, this article of the law is written with a purpose to improve the general welfare. Its object, its length, its nature and the conditions to grant this tax credit constitute accurate and rational criteria within the purpose of the legislature. In addition, the amount of this credit is not grossly disproportionate with that purpose.

The legislative history also shows that the tax credit that is allowed for residences built or bought before the enactment of the law is intended to promote consumption and buying power. But, by deciding to increase the buying power of the persons who built or bought a house during the last five years, the legislature created, between taxpayers, a difference in treatment that is not justified by its original intent. The tax rewards are an undue burden for the State when compared with the legislature's intended effect. Therefore, there is a clear breach of tax equality between the taxpayers.

Thus, Article 5 of this law must apply only for the mortgages that are concluded after the enactment of this statute.

On Article 11 (tax shield)

Article 11 of the statute modifies * * * the tax code rules relating to the tax shield for direct taxes. This article lowers the rates of the maximum income a household has to pay for direct taxes from 60% to 50%. Moreover, this tax shield now includes social contributions [the CSG and CRDS Ed.].

The petitioners argue that this article creates, in fact, an almost systematic exoneration of wealth and local taxes for taxpayers who are in the highest bracket of the income tax. Besides this exoneration, this article will create a breach of tax equality between taxpayers since taxpayers who had an important patrimony [a large inherited estate Ed.] will not pay the wealth or local taxes.

Article 13 of the Declaration of Human and Civic Rights will be infringed if a tax is in effect a seizure of all the taxpayers' assets or if a category of taxpayer is excessively burdened by a tax without regard to their taxpaying capacity. Hence, the tax shield, far from breaching the principle of tax equality, is purported to avoid a breach of equality.

First, the social contributions are taxes within the meaning of Article 34 of the Constitution. Therefore, the legislature appropriately included these taxes in its intent [to reduce the tax burden of taxpayers who pay particularly high taxes Ed.].

Second, the fact that all the taxes paid over 50% of the income are reimbursed is not obviously disproportionate.

Finally, it is necessary to compute all the taxes paid to determine if the taxpayer paid more than 50% of its income in direct taxation. Therefore, the tax shield does not privilege the taxpayer who paid certain taxes (like the wealth tax).

We conclude therefore that Article 11 of the referred statute is not contrary to Article 13 of the 1789 Declaration.

* * *

Decision:

Article 1: Article 5 of the law for the improvement of the law for labor, employment and buying power is unconstitutional but only for the tax reward given to the taxpayer who bought a house before the enactment of this law.

Article 2: Articles 1 [and] 11 * * * of this law and the rest of Article 5 respect the Constitution.

Article 3: This decision shall be published in the Journal officiel of the French Republic.

Note

Almost any tax provision will distinguish some taxpayers from others. If an item of income is excluded from the tax base or a deduction is created, taxpayers who meet the criteria of the statute will receive a tax benefit and others will not. When should taxpayers be able to successfully challenge tax distinctions drawn by Congress? In general, constitutional challenges to tax provisions, like challenges to other economic regulations, are subjected to "rational basis" analysis. A tax provision generally will be sustained if it promotes a legitimate governmental purpose.[1] Challenges to tax provisions based on differential treatment of taxpayers are rarely successful under that standard.[2] What is the likelihood that the distinction made by the Constitutional Council concerning the application of Article 5 to purchases of homes before the statute's enactment would be followed by a United States court?

1. See generally, Boris Bittker & Lawrence Lokken, Federal Taxation of Income, Estates and Gifts ¶ 1.2.5 (1999).

2. Id.

Chapter 6

TAXATION OF CAPITAL GAINS AND LOSSES

A. INTRODUCTION

THE CALIFORNIAN COPPER SYNDICATE
v. THE INLAND REVENUE
United Kingdom, Second Division, 1904.
12 S.L.T. 196.

[The taxpayer in this case, The Californian Copper Syndicate, *facts* is a mining company that was originally capitalized in 1901 with £30,000. The company acquired 480 acres of land for mining at a price of £24,000 and it expended £4332 to develop the property. In 1902, the company sold 80 of the acres for £105,000, and in 1903 it sold the remaining 400 acres for £195,000. The purchase price was paid in shares of stock of the purchaser, the Fresno Company. Late in 1903, the taxpayer distributed the Fresno Company stock to its shareholders. The issue in the case is whether the sales of the land were taxable to The Californian Copper Syndicate. The Commissioners held that the taxpayer had "carried on an adventure or concern in the nature of trade" and that the profits were, therefore, taxable. The taxpayer argued that it had no "income" because the sales of property were transactions that merely "substituted for its capital in the form of land a capital in the form of shares, and that any benefit which might result to the Company by the sales was a growth of capital and not income." This decision is an appeal from the Commissioners' decision. Ed.]

The Lord Justice–Clerk.

It is quite a well settled principle in dealing with questions of assessment of Income Tax, that where the owner of an ordinary investment chooses to realise it, and obtains a greater price for it than he originally acquired it at, the enhanced price is not profit in

137

the sense of Schedule D of the Income Tax Act of 1842, and therefore assessable to Income Tax. But it is equally well established that enhanced values obtained from realisation or conversion of securities may be so assessable where what is done is not merely a realisation or change of investment, but an act done in what is truly the carrying on or carrying out of a business. The simplest case is that of a person or association of persons buying and selling lands or securities speculatively in order to make gain, dealing in such investments as a business, and thereby seeking to make profits. There are many companies which in their very inception are formed for such a purpose, and in these cases it is not doubtful that where they make a gain by a realisation, the gain they make is liable to be assessed for income tax.

What is the line which separates the two classes of cases may be difficult to define, and each case must be considered according to its facts, the question to be determined being, is the sum of gain that has been made, a mere enhancement of value by realising a security, or is it a gain made by an operation of business in carrying out a scheme for profit-making?

In this particular case a syndicate was formed with a capital of £30,000, inter alia, to acquire copper and other mines, and certain mines round in particular, and to prospect and explore for the purpose of obtaining information, and to enter into treaties, contracts, and engagements with respect to mines, mining rights, and a number of other matters in the United States and elsewhere. It was also to carry on mercantile, commercial, financing and trading businesses, and to work minerals, to establish and form companies for such objects, to subscribe for purchase or otherwise acquire shares or stock of any company and accept payment in shares for property sold, or business undertaken, or services rendered, and to hold, sell, or dispose of the same, to promote companies for the purpose of acquiring the undertaking, property and liabilities of the Company, or carrying on business deemed conducive to the prosperity of the Company.

These are, shortly, some of the main purposes of this Company, and they certainly point distinctly to a highly speculative business, and the mode of their actual procedure was in the same direction. Of the £28,332 realised by shares which were subscribed for, £24,000 was invested in a copper-bearing field in the United States, and the balance was spent in development of the field and in preliminary and head office expenses.

The Company then were successful in selling the property to the Fresno Company, £300,000 in fully paid up shares being given by the Fresno Company for the property; and although that was a sale the price to be paid in shares, I feel compelled to hold that this

Company was in its inception a company endeavouring to make profit by a trade or business, and that the profitable sale of its property was not truly a substitution of one form of investment for another. It is manifest that it never did intend to work this mineral field with the capital at its disposal. Such a thing was quite impossible. Its purpose was to exploit this field, and obtain gain by inducing others to take it up on such terms as would bring substantial gain to themselves. This was that the turning of investment to account was not to be merely incidental, but was, as the Lord President put it in the case of the Scottish Investment Company, the essential feature of the business, speculation being among the appointed means of the Company's gains.

In these circumstances I am of opinion that the finding of the Commissioners was right.

LORD TRAYNER. (concurrence)

I agree with your lordship that the determination of the Commissioners is right. This is not, in my opinion, the case of a company selling part of its property for a higher price than it had paid for it and keeping that price as part of its capital, nor a case of a company merely changing the investment of its capital to pecuniary advantage. My reading of the appellant Company's articles of association, along with the other statements in the case, satisfies me that the sale on which the advantage was gained in respect of which income tax is said to be payable, was a proper trading transaction—one within the Company's power under their articles, and contemplated as well as authorised by their articles. I am satisfied that the appellant Company was formed in order to acquire certain mineral fields or workings, not to work the same themselves for the profit of the Company, but solely with the view and purpose of re-selling the same at a profit. The facts before us all point to this. The properties were bought for £24,000, leaving only a share capital of less than £ 6000, a capital quite inadequate, even if all subscribed (which it was not), to enable the Company to work their minerals and bring them to market. It is said the Company commenced business shortly after its incorporation in February 1901 and continued to carry it on with the sales which were effected in April 1902 and August 1903, but it is not said that in the course of that time—and the period was short—the appellants worked any part of the minerals. The business they carried on may have been solely connected with their efforts to sell the property—and selling it was part of the business which the Company was formed, and directly authorised, to carry on. The price obtained, namely, £300,000 for a subject which cost £24,000, points in the same direction.

But it was said that the profit, if it was profit, was not realised profit, and therefore not taxable. I think the profit was realised. A profit is realised when the seller gets the price he has bargained for. No doubt here the price took the form of fully paid-up shares in another company, but if there can be no realised profit except when that is paid in cash, the shares were realisable and could have been turned into cash, if the appellants had been pleased to do so. I cannot think that Income Tax is due or not according to the manner in which the person making the profit leases to deal with it. Suppose, for example, a seller makes a profit on a trade transaction, but leaves the price (including the profits) in the hands of the buyer at so much per cent. interest. That he so deals with it, rather than take the cash into his own pocket, would not affect the claim of the Revenue for the tax payable on the profit. No more, in my opinion, does it affect the liability for the tax, that the appellants left their profit in the hands of the company they sold to and took that company's shares as their voucher.

MERCHANTS' LOAN & TRUST CO. v. SMETANKA
Supreme Court of the United States. 1921.
255 U.S. 509, 41 S.Ct. 386.

MR. JUSTICE CLARKE delivered the opinion of the Court.

* * *

Arthur Ryerson died in 1912, and the plaintiff in error is trustee under his will of property the net income of which was directed to be paid to his widow during her life and after her death to be used for the benefit of his children, or their representatives, until each child should arrive at 25 years of age, when each should receive his or her share of the trust fund.

The trustee was given the fullest possible dominion over the trust estate. It was made the final judge as to what "net income" of the estate should be, and its determination in this respect was made binding upon all parties interested therein, "except that it is my will that stock dividends and accretions of selling values shall be considered principal and not income."

The widow and four children were living in 1917.

Among the assets which came to the custody of the trustee were 9,522 shares of the capital stock of Joseph T. Ryerson & Son, a corporation. It is averred that the cash value of these shares, on March 1, 1913, was $561,798, and that they were sold for $1,280,996.64, on February 2, 1917. The Commissioner of Internal Revenue treated the difference between the value of the stock on March 1, 1913, and the amount for which it was sold on February 2, 1917, as income for the year 1917, and upon that amount assessed the tax which was paid. No question is made as to the amount of the tax if the collection of it was lawful.

The ground of the protest, and the argument for the plaintiff in error here, is that the sum charged as "income" represented appreciation in the value of the capital assets of the estate which was not "income" within the meaning of the Sixteenth Amendment, and therefore could not constitutionally be taxed, without apportionment, as required by section 2, clause 3, and by section 9, clause 4, of article 1 of the Constitution of the United States.

It is first argued that the increase in value of the stock could not be lawfully taxed under the act of Congress because it was not income to the widow, for she did not receive it in 1917, and never can receive it, that it was not income in that year to the children for they did not then, and may never, receive it, and that it was not income to the trustee, not only because the will creating the trust required that "stock dividends and accretions of selling value shall be considered principal and not income," but also because in the "common understanding" the term "income" does not comprehend such a gain or profit as we have here, which it is contended is really an accretion to capital and therefore not constitutionally taxable under Eisner v. Macomber, 252 U.S. 189, 40 Sup.Ct. 189, 64 L.Ed. 521, 9 A. L. R. 1570.

The provision of the will may be disregarded. It was not within the power of the testator to render the fund nontaxable.

Assuming for the present that there was constitutional power to tax such a gain or profit as is here involved, are the terms of the statute comprehensive enough to include it?

Section 2(a) of the act of September 8, 1916 (39 Stat. 757), (40 Stat. 300, 307, § 212), applicable to the case, defines the income of "a taxable person" as including "gains, profits, and income derived from * * * sales, or dealings in property, whether real or personal, growing out of the ownership or use of or interest in real or personal property * * * or gains or profits and income derived from any source whatever."

Plainly the gain we are considering was derived from the sale of personal property, and, very certainly the comprehensive last clause "gains or profits and income derived from any source whatever," must also include it, if the trustee was a "taxable person" within the meaning of the act when the assessment was made.

That the trustee was such a "taxable person" is clear from section 1204(1)(c) of the act of October 3, 1917 (40 Stat. 331), which requires that—

'Trustees, executors * * * and all persons, corporations, or associations, acting in any fiduciary capacity shall make and render a return of the income of the person, trust, or estate for whom or which they act, and be subject to all the provisions of this title which apply to individuals.'

And section 2(b) of the act of September 8, 1916, supra, specifically declares that the—

'income received by estates of deceased persons during the period of administration or settlement of the estate, * * * or any kind of property held in trust, including such income accumulated in trust for the benefit of unborn or unascertained persons, or persons with contingent interests, and income held for future distribution under the terms of the will or trust shall be likewise taxed, the tax in each instance, except when the income is returned for the purpose of the tax by the beneficiary, to be assessed to the executor, administrator, or trustee, as the case may be.'

Further, section 2(c) clearly shows that it was the purpose of Congress to tax gains, derived from such a sale as we have here, in the manner in which this fund was assessed, by providing that—

'For the purpose of ascertaining the gain derived from the sale or other disposition of property, real, personal, or mixed, acquired before March 1, 1913, the fair market price or value of such property as of March 1, 1913, shall be the basis for determining the amount of such gain derived.'

Thus, it is the plainly expressed purpose of the act of Congress to treat such a trustee as we have here as a "taxable person" and for the purposes of the act to deal with the income received for others precisely as if the beneficiaries had received it in person.

There remains the question, strenuously argued, whether this gain in four years of over $700,000 on an investment of about $500,000 is "income" within the meaning of the Sixteenth Amendment to the Constitution of the United States.

The question is one of definition, and the answer to it may be found in recent decisions of this Court.

The Corporation Excise Tax Act of August 5, 1909 (36 Stat. 11, 112), was not an income tax law, but a definition of the word "income" was so necessary in its administration that in an early case it was formulated as "A gain derived from capital, from labor, or from both combined." Stratton's Independence v. Howbert, 231 U.S. 399, 415, 34 Sup.Ct. 136, 140 (58 L.Ed. 285).

This definition, frequently approved by this court, received an addition, in its latest income tax decision, which is especially significant in its application to such a case as we have here, so that it now reads:

[handwritten marginal note: income defined]

"Income may be defined as a gain derived from capital, from labor, or from both combined, provided it be understood to include profit gained through sale or conversion of capital assets." Eisner v. Macomber, 252 U.S. 189, 207, 40 Sup.Ct. 189, 193 (64 L.Ed. 521), 9 A.L.R. 1570.

The use made of this definition of "income" in the decision of cases arising under the Corporation Excise Tax Act of August 5, 1909, and under the Income Tax Acts, is, we think, decisive of the case before us. Thus, in two cases arising under the Corporation Excise Tax Act:

In Hays v. Gauley Mountain Coal Co., 247 U.S. 189, 38 Sup.Ct. 470, 62 L.Ed. 1061, a coal company, without corporate authority to trade in stocks, purchased shares in another coal mining company in 1902, which it sold in 1911, realizing a profit of $210,000. Over the same objection made in this case, that the fund was merely converted capital, this court held that so much of the profit upon the sale of the stock as accrued subsequent to the effective date of the act was properly treated as income received during 1911, in assessing the tax for that year.

In United States v. Cleveland, Cincinnati, Chicago & St. Louis Railway Co., 247 U.S. 195, 38 Sup.Ct. 472, 62 L.Ed. 1064, a railroad company purchased shares of stock in another railroad company in 1900, which it sold in 1909, realizing a profit of $814,000. Here, again, over the same objection, this court held that the part of the profit which accrued subsequent to the effective date of the act was properly treated as income received during the year 1909 for the purposes of the act.

Thus, from the price realized from the sale of stock by two investors, as distinguished from dealers, and from a single transaction as distinguished from a course of business, the value of the stock on the effective date of the tax act was deducted, and the resulting gain was treated by this court as "income" by which the tax was measured.

It is obvious that these decisions in principle rule the case at bar if the word "income" has the same meaning in the Income Tax Act of 1913 that it had in the Corporation Excise Tax Act of 1909, and that it has the same scope of meaning was in effect decided in Southern Pacific Co. v. Lowe, 247 U.S. 330, 335, 38 Sup.Ct. 540, 62 L.Ed. 1142, where it was assumed for the purposes of decision that there was no difference in its meaning as used in the act of 1909 and in the Income Tax Act of 1913 (38 Stat. 114). There can be no doubt that the word must be given the same meaning and content in the Income Tax Acts of 1916 and 1917 that it had in the act of 1913. When to this we add that in Eisner v. Macomber, supra, a case arising under the same Income Tax Act of 1916 which is here involved, the definition of "income" which was applied was adopted from Stratton's Independence v. Howbert, supra, arising under the Corporation Excise Tax Act of 1909, with the addition that it should include "profit gained through sale or conversion of capital assets," there would seem to be no room to doubt that the word must be given the same meaning in all of the Income Tax Acts of Congress that was given to it in the Corporation Excise Tax Act, and that what that meaning is has now become definitely settled by decisions of this Court.

In determining the definition of the word "income" thus arrived at, this Court has consistently refused to enter into the refinements of lexicographers or economists, and has approved, in the definitions quoted, what it believed to be the commonly understood meaning of the term which must have been in the minds of the people when they adopted the Sixteenth Amendment to the Constitution. Doyle v. Mitchell Brothers Co., 247 U.S. 179, 185, 38 Sup.Ct. 467, 62 L.Ed. 1054; Eisner v. Macomber, 252 U.S. 189, 206, 207, 40 Sup.Ct. 189, 64 L.Ed. 521, 9 A.L.R. 1570. Notwithstanding the full argument heard in this case and in the series of cases now under consideration, we continue entirely satisfied with that definition, and, since the fund here taxed was the amount realized from the sale of the stock in 1917, less the capital investment as determined by the trustee as of March 1, 1913, it is palpable that it was a "gain or profit" "produced by" or "derived from" that investment, and that it "proceeded" and was "severed" or rendered severable from it by the sale for cash, and thereby became that "realized gain" which has been repeatedly declared to be taxable income within the meaning of the constitutional amendment and the acts of Congress. Doyle v. Mitchell Brothers Co. and Eisner v. Macomber, supra.

It is elaborately argued in this case, in No. 609, Eldorado Coal & Mining Co. v. Harry W. Mager, Collector, etc., submitted with it, and in other cases since argued, that the word "income" as used in the Sixteenth Amendment and in the Income Tax Act we are considering does not include the gain from capital realized by a single isolated sale of property, but that only the profits realized from sales by one engaged in buying and selling as a business—a merchant, a real estate agent, or broker—constitute income which may be taxed.

It is sufficient to say of this contention that no such distinction was recognized in the Civil War Income Tax Act of 1867 (14 Stat. 471, 478), or in the act of 1894 (28 Stat. 509, 553), declared unconstitutional on an unrelated ground; that it was not recognized in determining income under the Excise Tax Act of 1909, as the cases cited, supra, show; that it is not to be found, in terms, in any of the income tax provisions of the Internal Revenue Acts of 1913,

1916, 1917, or 1919 (40 Stat. 1057); that the definition of the word "income" as used in the Sixteenth Amendment, which has been developed by this Court, does not recognize any such distinction; that in departmental practice, for now seven years, such a rule has not been applied; and that there is no essential difference in the nature of the transaction or in the relation of the profit to the capital involved, whether the sale or conversion be a single, isolated transaction or one of many. The interesting and ingenious argument, which is earnestly pressed upon us, that this distinction is so fundamental and obvious that it must be assumed to be a part of the "general understanding" of the meaning of the word "income," fails to convince us that a construction should be adopted which would, in a large measure, defeat the purpose of the amendment.

The opinions of the courts in dealing with the rights of life tenants and remaindermen in gains derived from invested capital, especially in dividends paid by corporations, are of little value in determining such a question as we have here, influenced as such decisions are by the terms of the instruments creating the trusts involved and by the various rules adopted in the various jurisdictions for attaining results thought to be equitable. Here the trustee, acting within its powers, sold the stock, as it might have sold a building, and realized a profit of $700,000, which at once became assets in its possession free for any disposition within the scope of the trust, but for the purposes of taxation to be treated as if the trustee were the sole owner.

* * *

The British income tax decisions are interpretations of statutes so wholly different in their wording from the acts of Congress which we are considering that they are quite without value in arriving at the construction of the laws here involved.

* * *

The judgment of the District Court is
Affirmed.

* * *

Note

The taxation of capital gains is an area where a tax system's approach to the concept of "income" may be critical.[1] In the *California Copper Syndicate* case, the issue was whether the sale of the land was

---

1. Victor Thuronyi, Comparative Tax Law 260–261 (2003); Hugh Ault & Brian Arnold, Comparative Income Taxation— A Structural Analysis 198–199 (2d ed. 2004).

"merely a realisation or change of investment" that was not taxable, or whether it was derived from "the carrying on or carrying out of a business" and, therefore, included in the tax base. Underlying that inquiry is a concept of "income" that is based on trust law, which distinguishes between the rights of a beneficiary who is entitled to the trust's income (its return on capital) from the rights of the holder of the trust's remainder who is entitled the trust's property (the capital itself). In the *Merchants' Loan & Trust Co.* case, the court is applying a statute that adopts an accretion concept of income; this is, the statutorily established definition of income includes "gains or profits derived from any source whatever." Students who have studied the current United States regime for taxation of capital gains will recognize aspects of both approaches. In the United States, usually all gains derived from dealings in property are included in income, but certain specific types of gains are taxed at preferential rates. In general, a gain from the sale or exchange of a capital asset held for more than one year is taxed at rates that are lower than the rates that apply to ordinary income. The determination of whether property is a "capital asset" frequently rests on the distinction that was critical in *California Copper Syndicate*. Gains from property held for investment generally are entitled to a preference whereas sales of property that are made in connection with the taxpayer's regular business activity are not.[2]

The trend in most jurisdictions like the United Kingdom, where capital gains were initially determined to not be income, has been to either legislatively expand the tax base to include such gains or enact a separate capital gains tax. Often the gains are taxed at preferential rates.[3] For example, in France, capital gains are not taxed under the income tax because it was determined that "income" under the income tax is earnings that have to be periodical and come from a source.[4] The French legislature subsequently passed a law requiring capital gains to be taxed under a separate, specific regime that has its own deductions and tax rates.[5]

The justification for a capital gains preference and the form that any preference should take, continue to be key aspects of the tax policy debate regarding capital gains.

B. POLICY

In the late 1970s, the United States Treasury undertook a major, year-long, study of the United States tax system. The goal of the study was no less than to replace the tax system, and return to "basic principles" and the "cornerstones" of a sound tax struc-

2. See I.R.C. § 1221(a)(1); see also, I.R.C. § 1231.

3. Hugh Ault & Brian Arnold, Comparative Income Taxation—A Structural Analysis 198 (2d ed. 2004).

4. S. 1942. III. 23, concl. Letourneur.

5. See Jean Lamarque, Cours de Droit Fiscal General, Universite paris II Assas, pp. 143–147 (2001).

ture—equity, efficiency, and simplicity.[1] Titled "Blueprints for Basic Tax Reform," the study presented two specific model tax systems. One model was based on a consumption tax where net savings would not be taxed. The second was a plan to broaden the base of the income tax. The income-tax model addressed the taxation of capital gains and their interaction with corporate income taxation. The taxation of corporate income is closely related to capital gains taxation because many capital gains are realized from sales of corporate stock. *Blueprints* recommended elimination of the corporate income tax and adoption of rules that would integrate corporate income with the other income of shareholders by allocating all corporate income, whether distributed or not, to individual shareholders. The shareholders then would be responsible for paying tax on their individual allocations of corporate income. The corporate integration proposal thus eliminated the largest source of capital gains by taxing individual shareholders on corporate retained earnings. *Blueprints* also recommended that any capital gains realized on the sale or exchange of assets be taxed fully *after* a step-up in the basis of the asset to reflect the effects of inflation. The proposal also would have allowed capital losses (again adjusted to account for inflation) to be fully deductible against ordinary income.[2] Following is analysis from *Blueprints* on the policy issues involved in taxing capital gains in a comprehensive income tax.

BLUEPRINTS FOR BASIC TAX REFORM
Department of Treasury, pp. 75–83.
January 17, 1977.

CAPITAL GAINS AND LOSSES

Capital gains appear to be different from most other sources of income because realization of gains involves two distinct transactions—the acquisition and disposition of property—and each transaction occurs at a different time. This difference raises several issues of income measurement and taxation under an income tax.

Accrual Versus Realization

The first issue is whether income (or loss), ought to be reported annually on the basis of changes in market values of assets—the accrual concept—or only when realized. The annual change in market value of one's assets constitutes a change in net worth and, therefore, constitutes income under the "uses" definition. If tax consequences may be postponed until later disposition of an asset, there is deferral of taxes, which represents a loss to the government and a gain to the taxpayer. The value of this gain is the amount of

---

1. Department of Treasury, Blueprints for Basic Tax Reform (Forward) (1977).

2. Id. at 5–6.

the interest on the deferred taxes for the period of deferral. Distinct from, but closely related to, the issue of deferral is the issue of the appropriate marginal tax rate to be applied to capital gains. If capital gains are to be subject to the tax only when realized, there may be a substantial difference between the applicable marginal tax rate during the period of accrual and that faced by the taxpayer upon realization. Also, the extent to which adjustment should be made for general price inflation over the holding period of an asset must be considered. Finally, the desirability of simplicity in the tax system, ease of administration, and public acceptability are important considerations.

The range of possible tax treatments for capital gains can be summarized in an array that ranges from the taxation of accrued gains at ordinary rates to the complete exclusion of capital gains from income subject to taxation. Alternatives within the range may be modified to allow for (a) income averaging to minimize extra taxes resulting from the bunching of capital gains and (b) adjustments to reflect changes in the general price level.

* * *

Accrual Taxation Alternative

Accrual taxation of capital gains poses three problems that, taken together, appear to be insurmountable. These are (1) the administrative burden of annual reporting; (2) the difficulty and cost of determining asset values annually; and (3) the potential hardship of obtaining the funds to pay taxes on accrued but unrealized gains. Under accrual taxation, the taxpayer would have to compute the gain or loss on each of his assets annually. For common stock and other publicly traded securities, there would be little cost or difficulty associated with obtaining year-end relations. But for other assets, the costs and problems of evaluation would be very formidable, and the enforcement problems would be substantial. It would be very difficult and expensive to valuate assets by appraisal; valuation by concrete transactions, which taxing realizations would provide, has distinct advantages.

For taxpayers with little cash or low money incomes relative to the size of their accrued but unrealized capital gains, accrual taxation may pose cash flow problems. This circumstance is similar to that encountered with local property taxes assessed on homeowners. There is no cash income associated with the asset in the year that the tax liability is owed. However, in cases of potential hardship certain taxpayers could be allowed to pay a later tax on capital gains, with interest, at the time a gain is realized.

Realization–With–Interest Alternative

An alternative method that attempts to achieve the same economic effect as accrual taxation is taxation of capital gains at realization with an interest charge for deferral. But, in addition to the present complex rules defining realizations that would not be avoided in the model tax plan, rules would be required for the computation of interest on the deferred taxes. An appropriate rate of interest would have to be determined and some assumption made about the "typical" patterns of accruals. In order to eliminate economic inefficiency, the interest rate on the deferral should be the individual taxpayer's rate of return on his investment. However, because it is impossible to administer a program based on each investor's marginal rate of return, the government would have to charge a single interest rate. The single interest rate would itself tend to move alternatives away from neutrality. Moreover, for simplicity, it would have to be assumed that the gain occurred equally over the period or that the asset's value changed at a constant rate. This assumption would be particularly inappropriate in those cases where basis was changed frequently by inflation adjustments, depreciation allowances, capital improvements, etc. Because a simple time pattern of value change would reflect reality in very few cases, the deferral charge would introduce additional investment distortions. To the extent that gains occur early in the holding period, capital gains would be undertaxed; when gains occurred late in the period, capital gains would be overtaxed.

The Income Averaging Problem

Under a progressive income tax system, the tax rate on a marginal addition to income differs depending on the taxpayer's other income. Generally, the higher the income level, the higher the tax rate. Similarly, under a progressive tax system, people with fluctuating incomes pay tax at a higher rate over time on the same amount of total income than do those persons whose incomes are more nearly uniform over time.

Clearly, if a taxpayer's income (apart from any capital gains) is rising over time, the longer he delays realization, the higher his tax rate will be. Similarly, if he realizes gains only occasionally, his gains will tend to be larger, and the average tax rate on the gains will be increased. The bunching problem could be solved by spreading the game, via income averaging, over the holding period of the asset. This flexibility would involve great complexity, but the result could be approximated reasonably well by a fixed-period averaging system similar to the general 5–year averaging system [now repealed Ed.] or the special 10–year averaging system for lump sum distributions, both of which are in present law.

The problem of postponement of tax to periods of higher marginal rates is a more difficult one. One optional solution would be to calculate an average marginal tax rate over a fixed number of years and to modify the amount of gain included in the tax base for the year of realization to reflect the ratio of the average marginal rate over the period to the marginal rate in the current year. Thus, if the current rate were higher, some of the gain would be excluded from an income; if the current rate were lower, more than 100 percent of the gain would be included. As is the case with charges of interest for deferral, however, such systems would add significantly to the complexity of the tax law, and represent inexact adjustments besides.

Inflation Adjustment

The proper tax treatment of capital gains is further complicated by general price inflation. Capital gains that merely reflect increases in the general price level are illusory. For example, suppose an individual's capital assets increased in value, but a rate precisely equal to the rise in the cost of living. His net worth will not have increased in real terms, and neither, therefore, will his standard of living. If no basis adjustment is made to account for inflation, the reported capital gain for an asset held over a period of years of time will largely reflect the level of prices in previous years. This contrasts with other income flows, such as salaries, that are always accounted for in current dollars.

Accounting for other transactions that are affected by inflation, such as borrowing and lending, is largely corrected for anticipated inflation by market adjustments. For example, a lender will insist on a higher interest rate to compensate for taxes against the depreciating value of principal. Therefore, an adjustment of basis for inflation is desirable in the case of ownership of capital assets to avoid overtaxation of capital gains relative to other income sources, even if general indexing of income sources and/or tax rates is not prescribed.

Inflation adjustment would introduce additional complexity. The basis for each asset would have to be revised annually, whether sold or not. For this reason, it might be desirable to restrict the inflation adjustment to those years in which the inflation rate exceeds some "normal" amount, such as 2 or 3 percent.

Clearly, there are competing objectives of simplicity, equity, and economic efficiency involved in the tax treatment of capital gains. In this case, the model tax treatment would favor simplicity by forgoing accrual treatment that would require annual valuation of all assets, or interest charges for deferral. On the other hand, clear moves in the direction of accrual taxation are taken by introducing current taxation of corporate-retained earnings and more accurate measurement of depreciation. Annual adjustments of basis for general inflation also is judged to be worth the additional administration and compliance cost.

Note

Blueprints analyzes the difficulties in both measuring and properly taxing the appreciation in assets under an income tax. Inflation, the realization principle, and changes in tax rates over time, all present challenges when considering how capital gains should be taxed. *Blueprints*, however, does not address the issues of "equity" or fairness that are raised in the taxation of capital gains. Those arguments can be summarized as follows:[3]

> A tax, if it is to be imposed equitably, should satisfy two requirements. It should provide for horizontal equity, the equal tax treatment of persons in the same circumstances, that is, with similar claims on resources; and for vertical equity, a "fair" allocation of the total tax burden between those in different circumstances.
>
> The first requirement would call for the same tax treatment for the wage earner who pays for his car by working overtime and his fellow worker who uses his net gains from the stock market to acquire a car. * * *
>
> Because property gains generally become proportionately larger as income increases, vertical equity is particularly lacking under * * * [a tax system that exempts capital gains from tax. Ed.] If property gains are exempt from tax, those members of the upper income groups who derive a major part of their revenue from property gains would pay a lower average rate of tax on their comprehensive tax bases than persons in lower income groups.

Are the proposals for taxation of capital gains and losses in *Blueprints* consistent with the ideals of vertical and horizontal equity?

C. THE TAX TREATMENT OF CAPITAL GAINS IN FOREIGN JURISDICTIONS

A basic point of *Blueprints* is that tradeoffs and compromises are inevitable to achieve a system for taxing capital gains that both advances policy goals and is simple enough to be administered. Thus, the taxation of capital gains in foreign jurisdictions runs the gamut from full taxation at regular tax rates[1] to complete exemption from taxation.[2] Despite great differences in the specifics, taxation of capital gains falls into three basic patterns.[3] The first model,

3. Excerpt from the Report of the Royal Commission on Taxation, Vol. 3, 331 (1966).

1. IBDF, Global Individual Tax Handbook 2007 300 (Jersey) (2007).

2. Id at 135 (Czech Republic).

3. Hugh Ault & Brian Arnold, Comparative Income Taxation—A Structural Analysis 198 (2d ed. 2004).

generally employed in European countries, fully taxes gains recognized on dispositions of assets in a business. Gains from nonbusiness assets may not be taxed at all or may be taxed only in limited situations. For example, in the Netherlands gains derived in the course of business are fully taxed like other income and other capital gains are tax exempt. A special provision taxes gains from substantial shareholdings (at least 5%, counting ownership by certain related persons) of a corporation's stock or a particular class of stock.[4] A second approach to taxation of capital gains has evolved from systems following the United Kingdom model, such as Australia and Canada. Early on, capital gains, in contrast to business income, simply were not considered income. Later statutory changes either brought such gains within the tax base or created a separate capital gains tax, generally with preferential treatment. Specifically, in Canada capital gains first became taxable in 1972 and 50% of qualifying gains may be excluded from income.[5] In addition, a taxpayer may exclude up to $500,000 (Canadian) in gains from "qualified farm property" and "qualified small business corporation shares." Special exemptions also exist for sales of a principal residence and small amounts of personal-use assets.[6] In Australia, capital gains generally became taxable in 1985.[7] Currently, individuals generally can exclude 50% of a gain from taxation on assets held for more than one year and an inflation adjustment may be available for periods before 2000. An exemption exists for sales of a principal residence and deferral of gains is allowed on certain specific transactions.[8] A last approach to the taxation of capital gains is employed by countries like the United States, that begin with a global definition of income and generally include all gains in the tax base. Once again, preferential treatment is common. In Sweden all gains are included in income but several special rules apply. For example, only 90% of the gain on the sale of real property used in an individual's business is taxable. A taxpayer may fully exclude the gain from the sale of a principal residence meeting certain conditions and only two-thirds of the gain on sales of other dwellings is taxable. In the case of publicly listed stock and securities, a taxpayer's gain is the difference between the sale price and the purchase price. For the purchase price, the taxpayer may use the greater of the actual purchase price, an average purchase price

---

4. IBDF, Global Individual Tax Handbook 2007 385 (Netherlands) (2007).

5. See generally, Peter Hogg. Joanne Magee, Jinyan Li, Principles of Canadian Income Tax Law Chapter 10 (5th ed. 2005).

6. IBDF, Global Individual Tax Handbook 2007 89 (Canada) (2007).

7. See generally, Woellner, Barkoczy, Murphy & Evans, Australian Taxation Law Chapters 7 & 8 (17th ed. 2007).

8. IBDF, Global Individual Tax Handbook 2007 30 (Australia) (2007).

if purchases were made at different times, or 20% of the selling price after deduction of costs related to the sale.[9]

Preferential treatment for capital gains may come in a variety of forms. Exemption from taxation, lower rates, partial exclusions, and indexation for inflation are just some of the ways to lower the effective tax rate on capital gains. Another approach is to provide what is called "taper relief." Under taper relief a smaller percentage of any gain is taxable the longer the taxpayer owns the property. For example, in the United Kingdom 100% of the gain from a business asset is taxed if the asset is held less than one year, 50% of the gain if the asset is held more than one but less than two years, and 25% of the gain if the asset is held two or more years.[10] In France, on the sale of real property held for investment, the taxable gain is reduced by 10% for each year the property is held beyond five years. Thus, after 15 years the property may be sold tax free. That provision does not apply if the property is considered inventory in the hands of the seller.[11]

Note

Another of the basic points made in *Blueprints* is that income measurement is difficult in the case of sales of property because of the tax deferral that results from the realization principal. Because we generally wait for a sale or other disposition of an asset before we require a taxpayer to tally any gain and pay tax, property can appreciate in value and the taxpayer is able to defer paying the related tax until the property is sold.[12] Some tax systems depart from the realization principle in certain instances. For example, in Canada a taxpayer is deemed to dispose of property if it is converted from a personal use to an income-producing use. Consequently, a change in the use of property may trigger recognition of gain even though the taxpayer still owns the property. For example, if a taxpayer moves out of her residence and begins to rent it to a tenant, the taxpayer is deemed to have disposed of the residence for its fair market value and immediately reacquired it at a cost equal to the fair market value.[13] Canadian tax law also provides a tax exemption for a disposition of property that was the taxpayer's principal residence.[14] Thus, if a taxpayer converts her home to a rental unit, the deemed-sale-rule may operate in conjunction with the tax exemption for sales of a principal residence. The following guidance from the Canadian Revenue Agency explores the interaction between these rules and some of the more specialized provisions that can apply in Canada to this fairly common situation.

9. Id. at 505 (Sweden).
10. Id. at 554 (United Kingdom).
11. Id. at 184 (France).
12. See generally, I.R.C. § 1001.

13. Canada Federal Statutes, Income Tax Act S. 45(1).

14. Canada Federal Statutes, Income Tax Act S. 40(1)(b).

INCOME TAX INTERPRETATION 120R6
Canada Revenue Agency.
July 17, 2003.

* * *

Complete Change in Use of a Property From Principal Residence to Income–Producing

¶ 25. If a taxpayer has completely converted his or her principal residence to an income-producing use, he or she is deemed by paragraph 45(1)(a) to have disposed of the property (both land and building) at fair market value (FMV) and reacquired it immediately thereafter at the same amount. Any gain otherwise determined on this deemed disposition may be eliminated or reduced by the principal residence exemption. The taxpayer may instead, however, defer recognition of any gain to a later year by electing under subsection 45(2) to be deemed not to have made the change in use of the property. This election is made by means of a letter to that effect signed by the taxpayer and filed with the income tax return for the year in which the change in use occurred. If the taxpayer rescinds the election in a subsequent taxation year, he or she is deemed to have disposed of and reacquired the property at FMV on the first day of that subsequent year (with the above-mentioned tax consequences). If capital cost allowance (CCA) is claimed on the property, the election is considered to be rescinded on the first day of the year in which that claim is made.

* * *

¶ 26. A property can qualify as a taxpayer's principal residence for up to four taxation years during which a subsection 45(2) election remains in force, even if the housing unit is not ordinarily inhabited during those years by the taxpayer or by his or her spouse or common-law partner, former spouse or common-law partner, or child (see ¶ 5). However, the taxpayer must be resident, or deemed to be resident, in Canada during those years for the full benefit of the principal residence exemption to apply (see the numerator "B" in the formula in ¶ 8 or the years included in the statement in ¶ 22(b), as the case may be). It should also be noted that the rule described in ¶ 6 prevents the designation of more than one property as a principal residence for any particular year by the taxpayer (or, for any particular year after the 1981 taxation year, by the taxpayer or any other member of his or her family unit). Thus, for example, a taxpayer's designation for the same year of one property by virtue of a subsection 45(2) election being in force, and another property by virtue of the fact that he or she ordinarily inhabited that other property, would not be permitted.

Example

Mr. A and his family lived in a house for a number of years until September 30, 1993. From October 1, 1993 until March 31, 1998 they lived elsewhere and Mr. A rented the house to a third party. On April 1, 1998, they moved back into the house and lived in it until it was sold in 2001. When he filed his 2001 income tax return, Mr. A designated the house as his principal residence for the 1994 to 1997 taxation years inclusive (i.e., the maximum four years) by virtue of a subsection 45(2) election (which he had already filed with his 1993 income tax return) having been in force for those years. (He was able to make this designation because no other property had been designated as a principal residence by him or a member of his family unit for those years.) He designated the house as his principal residence for all the other years in which he owned it by virtue of his having ordinarily inhabited it during those years, including the 1993 and 1998 years. Having been resident in Canada at all times, Mr. A's gain otherwise determined on the disposition of the house in 2001 was, therefore, completely eliminated by the principal residence exemption.

Any income in respect of a property (e.g., the rental income in the above example), net of applicable expenses, must be reported for tax purposes. However, for taxation years covered by a subsection 45(2) election, CCA should not be claimed on the property (see ¶ 25).

¶ 27. Section 54.1 removes the above-mentioned four-year limitation for taxation years covered by a subsection 45(2) election if all of the following conditions are met:

(a) the taxpayer does not ordinarily inhabit the housing unit during the period covered by the election because the taxpayer's or his or her spouse's or common-law partner's place of employment has been relocated;

(b) the employer is not related to the taxpayer or his or her spouse or common-law partner;

(c) the housing unit is at least 40 kilometers farther from such new place of employment than is the taxpayer's subsequent place or places of residence; and

(d) either

- the taxpayer resumes ordinary habitation of the housing unit during the term of employment by that same employer or before the end of the taxation year immediately following the taxation year in which such employment terminates; or

• the taxpayer dies during the term of such employment.

With regard to condition (d), two corporations that are members of the same corporate group, or are otherwise related, are not considered to be the same employer.

Complete Change in Use of a Property From Income–Producing to Principal Residence

¶ 28. If a taxpayer has completely changed the use of a property (for which an election under subsection 45(2) is not in force) from income-producing to a principal residence, he or she is deemed by paragraph 45(1)(a) to have disposed of the property (both land and building), and immediately thereafter reacquired it, at FMV. This deemed disposition can result in a taxable capital gain. The taxpayer may instead defer recognition of the gain to a later year by electing under subsection 45(3) that the above-mentioned deemed disposition and reacquisition under paragraph 45(1)(a) does not apply. This election is made by means of a letter to that effect signed by the taxpayer and filed with the income tax return for the year in which the property is ultimately disposed of (or earlier if a formal "demand" for the election is issued by the CCRA).

* * *

Even if a subsection 45(3) election is filed in order to defer recognition of a gain from the change in use of a property from income-producing to principal residence, the net income from the property for the period before the change in use must still be reported. However, for purposes of reporting such net income, it should be noted that an election under subsection 45(3) is not possible if, for any taxation year ending after 1984 and on or before the change in use of the property from income-producing to a principal residence, CCA has been allowed in respect of the property to

• the taxpayer;

• the taxpayer's spouse or common-law partner; or

• a trust under which the taxpayer or his or her spouse or common-law partner is a beneficiary.

CCA so allowed would cause subsection 45(4) to nullify the subsection 45(3) election.

¶ 29. Similar to the treatment for a subsection 45(2) election (see ¶ 26), a property can qualify as a taxpayer's principal residence for up to four taxation years prior to a change in use covered by a subsection 45(3) election, in lieu of fulfilling the "ordinarily inhabited" rule (discussed in ¶ 5) for these years. As in the case of a subsection 45(2) election, residence or deemed residence in Canada during these years is necessary for the full benefit of the principal residence exemption to apply. Furthermore, the rule described in ¶ 6 prevents the designation of more than one property as a principal residence for any particular year by the taxpayer (or, for any particular year after the 1981 taxation year, by the taxpayer or any other member of his or her family unit).

Example

Mr. X bought a house in 1993 and rented it to a third party until mid–1999. Mr. X and his family then lived in the house until it was sold in 2001. Mr. X has been resident in Canada at all times. When he filed his 2001 income tax return, Mr. X designated the house as his principal residence for the 1999 to 2001 taxation years inclusive, by virtue of his having ordinarily inhabited it during those years. He also designated the house as his principal residence for the 1995 to 1998 years inclusive (i.e., the maximum 4 years) by virtue of a subsection 45(3) election, which he filed with his 2001 income tax return (he was able to make this designation because (i) no other property had been designated by him or a member of his family unit for those years, and (ii) he did not claim any CCA when reporting the net income from the property before the change in use). However, his gain otherwise determined on the disposition of the house in 2001 could not be fully eliminated by the principal residence exemption formula in ¶ 8 because he could not designate the house as his principal residence for the 1993 and 1994 years.

Partial Changes in Use

¶ 30. If a taxpayer has partially converted a principal residence to an income-producing use, paragraph 45(1)(c) provides for a deemed disposition of the portion of the property so converted (such portion is usually calculated on the basis of the area involved) for proceeds equal to its proportionate share of the property's FMV. Paragraph 45(1)(c) also provides for a deemed reacquisition immediately thereafter of the same portion of the property at a cost equal to the very same amount. Any gain otherwise determined on the deemed disposition is usually eliminated or reduced by the principal residence exemption. If the portion of the property so changed is later converted back to use as part of the principal residence, there is a second deemed disposition (and reacquisition) thereof at FMV. A taxable capital gain attributable to the period of use of such portion of the property for income-producing purposes can arise from such a second deemed disposition or from an actual sale of the whole property subsequent to the original partial change in use. An election under subsection 45(2) or (3) cannot be made where there is a partial change in use of a property as described above.

¶ 31. The above-mentioned deemed disposition rule applies where the partial change in use of the property is substantial and of a more permanent nature, i.e., where there is a structural change. Examples where this occurs are the conversion of the front half of a house into a store, the conversion of a portion of a house into a self-contained domestic establishment for earning rental income (a duplex, triplex, etc.), and alterations to a house to accommodate separate business premises. In these and similar cases, the taxpayer reports the income and may claim the expenses pertaining to the altered portion of the property (i.e., a reasonable portion of the expenses relating to the whole property) as well as CCA on such altered portion of the property.

¶ 32. It is our practice not to apply the deemed disposition rule, but rather to consider that the entire property retains its nature as a principal residence, where all of the following conditions are met:

(a) the income-producing use is ancillary to the main use of the property as a residence,

(b) there is no structural change to the property, and

(c) no CCA is claimed on the property.

These conditions can be met, for example, where a taxpayer carries on a business of caring for children in his or her home, rents one or more rooms in the home, or has an office or other work space in the home which is used in connection with his or her business or employment. In these and similar cases, the taxpayer reports the income and may claim the expenses (other than CCA) pertaining to the portion of the property used for income-producing purposes. Certain conditions and restrictions are placed on the deductibility of expenses relating to an office or other work space in an individual's home—see the current version of IT–514, Work Space in Home Expenses (if the income is income from a business) or the current version of IT–352, Employee's Expenses, Including Work Space in Home Expenses. In the event that the taxpayer commences to claim CCA on the portion of the property used for producing income, the deemed disposition rule is applied as of the time at which the income-producing use commenced.

Note

The sale of a taxpayer's principal residence often is eligible for special tax treatment. For example, in the United States a single taxpayer generally may exclude $250,000 of gain and a married couple generally may exclude $500,000 of gain from the sale of a property if the property has been owned and used by the taxpayer for two or more years out of the prior five years as a principal residence.[15] In France the sale of a principal residence is tax-exempt without limit.[16] For purposes of this rule, the question of whether a residence is the taxpayer's principal residence is a question of fact.[17] Occupation of the residence must not be "temporary," a requirement that is considered met by living in the house for two years. Another approach to the taxation of sales of principal residences is to permit the taxpayer to defer recognition of some or all of the gain recognized on the sale if the taxpayer acquires a new principal residence within a set period of time.[18]

D. RESTRICTIONS ON CAPITAL LOSSES

When capital gains are provided a tax preference, it is common to restrict the deductibility of capital losses in order to create some "balance" in the system of taxing capital gains and losses. Without restrictions on the deductibility of capital losses, a taxpayer would be able to pay lower taxes on capital gains and deduct capital losses against more highly taxed income. Timing of gains and losses through strategic sales of property also could be used to exploit differences in taxation of capital gains and losses. The "win-win" opportunity for taxpayers normally is restricted by limits on the use of capital losses in order to protect the government's treasury.

Restrictions on capital losses, like preferences for capital gains, come in a variety of forms. For example, in the United States, capital losses may be deducted against capital gains. Excess capital losses can be deducted against ordinary income in an amount up to $3,000.[1] Capital losses that remain after these rules are carried over to future years.[2] In Australia, net capital losses may be carried forward indefinitely but may only be deducted against capital gains.[3] In Luxembourg, "speculative" capital losses (from personal property held six months or less and real property held two years or less) only may be deducted against speculative capital gains from the same year.[4] In India, long-term gains and losses are from assets

---

15. I.R.C. § 121.

16. Article 150 U–II 1 (France).

17. Regulation BOI 8–M–1–04.

18. IBDF, Global Individual Tax Handbook 2007 505 (Sweden) (2007).

1. I.R.C. § 1211(b).

2. I.R.C. § 1212(b).

3. IBDF, Global Individual Tax Handbook 2007 31 (Australia) (2007).

4. Id. at 329 (Luxembourg).

held at least three years (one year for shares of stock and certain other investments). Short-term capital losses may be deducted against both short-term and long-term capital gains but long-term capital losses are only deductible against long-term capital gains. Excess losses carry over for eight years and carryovers of long-term capital losses may only be deducted against long-term capital gains.[5]

In some tax systems, loss limitations are applied to different categories of property. For example, in Denmark, capital losses from immovable property (real estate) may be deducted only against gains from similar property and capital losses on publicly traded stock may only be deducted against capital gains from traded stock. Losses on shares that are not traded may be deducted against income from such shares and excess losses carry forward.[6] In Russia, gains and losses from sales of publicly traded and non-marketable securities are separated, and losses from one category only may be deducted against gains from that same category.[7]

5. Id. at 259 (India).

6. Id. at 143 (Denmark).

7. Id. at 453 (Russia).

Chapter 7

INTERNATIONAL INCOME TAXATION

A. INTRODUCTION

International trade is an increasingly important component of economic growth. In 2006, the United States exported nearly $2.1 trillion and imported $2.8 trillion of goods and services.[1] The taxation of international trade raises a host of issues, in large part, because international trade transactions are multi-jurisdictional. For example, consider the simple case where a United States citizen owns income-producing property located in Mexico. Should the income that is produced by the property be taxed by Mexico, the United States, or both? Much of international taxation is devoted to sorting out the answer to this seemingly straightforward and simple question. It is understood that Mexico has a right to tax the income from the property because Mexico is the "source" of the income. The United States's view of our hypothetical taxpayer's situation is explained in the following case.

COOK v. TAIT*
Supreme Court of the United States, 1924.
265 U.S. 47, 44 S.Ct. 444.

MR. JUSTICE MCKENNA delivered the opinion of the Court.

* * *

Plaintiff is a native citizen of the United States, and was such when he took up his residence and became domiciled in the city of Mexico. A demand was made upon him by defendant in error,

---

1. Bureau of Economic Analysis, U.S. Department of Commerce, "News Release: U.S. International Transactions," (Sept. 14, 2007), *at* http://www. bea.gov/newsreleases/international/trans actions/transnewsrelease.htm.

* Footnotes omitted.

161

designated defendant, to make a return of his income for the purpose of taxation under the revenue laws of the United States. Plaintiff complied with the demand, but under protest; the income having been derived from property situated in the city of Mexico. A tax was assessed against him in the sum of $1,193.38, the first installment of which he paid, and for it, as we have said this action was brought.

The question in the case, and which was presented by the demurrer to the declaration is, as expressed by plaintiff, whether Congress has power to impose a tax upon income received by a native citizen of the United States who, at the time the income was received, was permanently resident and domiciled in the city of Mexico, the income being from real and personal property located in Mexico.

Plaintiff assigns against the power, not only his rights under the Constitution of the United States, but under international law, and in support of the assignments cites many cases. It will be observed that the foundation of the assignments is the fact that the citizen receiving the income and the property of which it is the product are outside of the territorial limits of the United States. These two facts, the contention is, exclude the existence of the power to tax. Or to put the contention another way, to the existence of the power and its exercise, the person receiving the income and the property from which he receives it must both be within the territorial limits of the United States to be within the taxing power of the United States. The contention is not justified, and that it is not justified is the necessary deduction of recent cases. In United States v. Bennett, 232 U.S. 299, 34 Sup.Ct. 433, 58 L.Ed. 612, the power of the United States to tax a foreign-built yacht owned and used during the taxing period outside of the United States by a citizen domiciled in the United States was sustained. The tax passed on was imposed by a tariff act, but necessarily the power does not depend upon the form by which it is exerted.

It will be observed that the case contained only one of the conditions of the present case, the *property* taxed was outside of the United States. In United States v. Goelet, 232 U.S. 293, 34 Sup.Ct. 431, 58 L.Ed. 610, the yacht taxed was outside of the United States, but owned by a citizen of the United States who was "permanently resident and domiciled in a foreign country." It was decided that the yacht was not subject to the tax—but this was a matter of construction. Pains were taken to say that the question of power was determined "wholly irrespective" of the owner's "permanent domicile in a foreign country," and the court put out of view the situs of the yacht. That the court had no doubt of the power to tax was illustrated by reference to the income tax laws of prior years and their express extension to those domiciled abroad. The illustration has pertinence to the case at bar, for the case at bar is concerned with an income tax, and the power to impose it.

We may make further exposition of the national power as the case depends upon it. It was illustrated at once in United States v. Bennett by a contrast with the power of a state. It was pointed out that there were limitations upon the latter that were not on the national power. The taxing power of a state, it was decided, encountered at its borders the taxing power of other states and was limited by them. There was no such limitation, it was pointed out, upon the national power, and that the limitation upon the states affords, it was said, no ground for constructing a barrier around the United States, "shutting that government off from the exertion of powers which inherently belong to it by virtue of its sovereignty."

The contention was rejected that a citizen's property without the limits of the United States derives no benefit from the United States. The contention, it was said, came from the confusion of thought in "mistaking the scope and extent of the sovereign power of the United States as a nation and its relations to its citizens and their relation to it." And that power in its scope and extent, it was decided, is based on the presumption that government by its very nature benefits the citizen and his property wherever found, and that opposition to it holds on to citizenship while it "belittles and destroys its advantages and blessings by denying the possession by government of an essential power required to make citizenship completely beneficial." In other words, the principle was declared that the government, by its very nature, benefits the citizen and his property wherever found, and therefore has the power to make the benefit complete. Or, to express it another way, the basis of the power to tax was not and cannot be made dependent upon the situs of the property in all cases, it being in or out of the United States, nor was not and cannot be made dependent upon the domicile of the citizen, that being in or out of the United States, but upon his relation as citizen to the United States and the relation of the latter to him as citizen. The consequence of the relations is that the native citizen who is taxed may have domicile, and the property from which his income is derived may have situs, in a foreign country and the tax be legal—the government having power to impose the tax.

Judgment affirmed.

MR. JUSTICE McREYNOLDS took no part in the consideration or decision of this case.

Note

Mr. Cook, like our hypothetical taxpayer described above, had income-producing property in Mexico and the Supreme Court makes it clear that his U.S. citizenship is a sufficient contact to support the United States exercising its full taxing power over his income. International tax systems generally adopt one of two jurisdictional principles. The first approach, which is taken by the United States, is to base the jurisdiction to tax on citizenship or residency. Thus, in the United States, all citizens and residents are taxable on their worldwide income.[2] Alternatively, many tax systems base the jurisdiction to tax on the source of income. Under this territorial approach, income is taxable if it is derived from sources within the country. Like many areas of tax law, no system is based purely on a single approach. Typically, a tax system is predominantly of one variety or the other and will also include certain aspects of the other jurisdictional principle. For example, while United States citizens are taxable on their worldwide income, individuals who are neither citizens nor residents generally are taxed by the United States on the income they earn from sources within the country.[3]

Consider one other aspect of Mr. Cook's situation. Assuming that Mexico taxes him on the income from his property within the country, that income is going to be subject to tax in both the United States and Mexico. Another basic international tax principle is that "double taxation" of income earned in international transactions should be avoided. It is also understood that in Mr. Cook's situation, the country of source (Mexico) should have the first claim on taxing the income and that the country of citizenship (United States) should forgo revenue and provide him with tax relief. Typically, Mr. Cook will be allowed to credit his Mexican taxes against the United States tax levied on his Mexican source income.[4] A foreign tax credit is a common response to the double-taxation problem. Alternatively, a taxpayer may be allowed a deduction for foreign taxes[5] or an exclusion for certain foreign source income.[6] A tax treaty between the United States and Mexico could also provide Mr. Cook with some tax relief.

Theorists dispute whether citizenship/residency-based taxation or source-based taxation better promotes economic efficiency, equity, and simplification of the tax laws.[7] The full extent of that debate is beyond the scope of this text but a few simple questions will give you a flavor of the controversy. Consider the taxation of someone who is exporting inventory from the United States to Europe. In terms of efficiency and

---

2. Reg. § 1.1–1(b). Domestic corporations are also subject to taxation on their worldwide income. Reg. § 1.11–1(a).

3. See I.R.C. § 871.

4. See I.R.C. §§ 901, 904.

5. See I.R.C. § 164(a)(3).

6. I.R.C. § 911.

7. See generally, Michael Graetz, Foundations of International Income Taxation Ch.1 (2003).

equity, should the tax system treat the United States exporter like domestic sellers within the United States? Alternatively, is the relevant comparison between the United States exporter and other sellers in the European market (e.g., European manufacturers and exporters from other parts of the world)? Does your analysis depend at all on the relative tax rates in the U.S. and Europe? Will one approach or another promote domestic business over foreign trade, and is that an important consideration in designing the tax system for international transactions?

B.   AN OVERVIEW OF UNITED STATES INTERNATIONAL TAXATION

Introduction. The United States generally taxes its citizens, residents, and domestic corporations on their worldwide income. An individual's residency in the U.S. typically is determined either under the immigration laws of the U.S. or a largely objective test that determines whether the individual has a "substantial presence" in the United States.[1] Nonresidents and foreign corporations generally are only taxable on income earned from U.S. sources.[2]

The Section 911 exclusion for citizens and residents living abroad is an exception to the general principle that those individuals are taxed on their worldwide income. Under Section 911, (1) a citizen who is a bona fide resident of a foreign country for an uninterrupted period which includes an entire taxable year, or (2) a citizen or resident who is present in a foreign country on at least 330 full days during a period of twelve consecutive months, may elect to take advantage of the exclusion.[3] Under Section 911, a qualifying taxpayer may exclude (1) up to $80,000 of earned income (the $80,000 limit is adjusted for inflation beginning in 2006), and (2) reimbursement of housing expenses in excess of a statutorily calculated amount.[4] If a taxpayer's housing expenses are not reimbursed by an employer, the taxpayer is allowed a limited deduction for those expenditures.[5]

Foreign tax credit. A United States taxpayer generally is entitled to a foreign tax credit for foreign income taxes paid or accrued during the year.[6] The foreign tax credit is allowed up to the amount of United States tax attributal to the taxpayer's foreign source income. For example, assume that U.S. Co., a domestic corporation, is paying U.S. tax at a 35% marginal tax rate and it earns $100,000

---

1. See I.R.C. § 7701(b).

2. See I.R.C. §§ 871, 881.

3. I.R.C. § 911(a), (d)(1). If the election is made, no foreign tax credits are allowed with respect to foreign taxes paid on the excluded income. I.R.C. § 911(d)(6).

4. I.R.C. § 911(b), (c). Housing expenses include costs such as utilities and insurance but interest and property taxes. See I.R.C. § 911(c)(3).

5. I.R.C. § 911(c)(4).

6. I.R.C. § 901.

in a foreign country where it has to pay $40,000 in income tax. On those facts, the United States will limit U.S. Co.'s foreign tax credit to $35,000, the amount of U.S. tax owed on the foreign source income. This limitation is necessary because if a $40,000 credit were allowed, the U.S. would essentially be paying its taxpayers to do business in another country. That is, the United States will relieve the foreign source income from double taxation, but it will not, in effect, subsidize the foreign jurisdiction's treasury.

A taxpayer in U.S. Co.'s situation is said to be in an "excess credit" position. U.S. Co. has paid $5,000 in foreign taxes that are not creditable and it has an incentive to improve its tax results. Suppose that U.S. Co. is able to earn an additional $100,000 of foreign source income that is taxed at a 10% rate so that its total foreign tax liability is now $50,000 ($40,000 plus $10,000). U.S. Co.'s domestic tax liability on the foreign source income is now $70,000 (35% of $200,000) and all of its foreign taxes are now creditable. It is said that U.S. Co. has "averaged" its foreign tax rates to get out of the excess credit position, or that the low-taxed income "soaked up" the excess credits. To combat, or at least limit, this type of strategy, taxpayers are required to calculate the foreign tax credit limitation with respect to different categories, or "baskets," of income.[7] Beginning in 2007, the limitation must be separately calculated with respect to passive category income and general category income. Thus, for U.S. Co.'s strategy to work, all of its $200,000 of foreign source income would all have to be in either the passive category or general category basket. If $100,000 of the income were in the passive category basket and the other $100,000 were in the general category basket, then the $10,000 of tax on the 10%-taxed foreign income would be fully creditable, but only $35,000 of the tax on the 40%-taxed foreign income would be creditable.

Indirect foreign tax credit. The foreign tax credit allowed to a taxpayer who actually pays foreign taxes is referred to as the "direct credit." In addition to the direct credit, a domestic corporation may be entitled to an "indirect" foreign tax credit for taxes paid by its foreign subsidiaries. In general, a domestic corporation is deemed to have paid, and receives a credit for, foreign income taxes paid by a 10%-or-more-owned foreign subsidiary when the subsidiary either makes, or is deemed to have made, a dividend distribution to the parent corporation.[8]

Anti-deferral rules. Recall that the United States generally only taxes nonresidents and foreign corporations on income earned from U.S. sources. That jurisdictional principle offers an opportunity for

---

7. I.R.C. § 904(d).   **8.** I.R.C. §§ 902, 960.

deferral of tax liability through the use of a foreign base company. Consider Investor, a U.S. citizen, who intends to purchase a portfolio of foreign stocks, bonds, and other investments. If Investor purchases those investments directly, he will be immediately taxable on all of the dividends, interest, and investment income produced by the portfolio. Suppose, instead, that Investor forms a foreign corporation, F Co., in a tax haven country that does not tax investment income, and F Co. purchases the portfolio. In that situation, F Co. could receive the investment income free of U.S. tax because it is not a U.S. corporation and its income is from foreign sources. Eventually, Investor will be taxed by the United States on F. Co.'s investment income when F. Co. pays him dividends, but Investor potentially will be free to defer his U.S. tax liability for a very long time. In order to prevent this type of abuse, the Internal Revenue Code has anti-deferral rules which will tax F Co.'s investment income directly to Investor as it is earned. The Code's anti-deferral rules operate to prevent taxpayers from shifting investment income and easily moved income to low-taxed jurisdictions. Income earned from the active conduct of a business generally may be deferred.

The Code's principal anti-deferral rules are the provisions dealing with "controlled foreign corporations" (CFCs) in subpart F of the Code. A CFC is a foreign corporation that is more than 50% owned (by vote or value) by "United States shareholders."[9] A United States shareholder is a United States person who owns (constructively or by way of attribution) 10% or more of the combined voting power of the stock of such foreign corporation.[10] Thus, in general, for a foreign corporation to be a CFC, 10%-or-more-U.S shareholders must own more that 50% of its stock.

If a foreign corporation is a CFC, then each U.S. shareholder is required to include in income his or her share of (1) the corporation's subpart F income and (2) the corporation's earnings invested in U.S. property.[11] Thus, the U.S. shareholders are denied tax deferral on those categories of income. Subpart F income is defined to include foreign base company income,[12] which includes investment income, foreign base company sales income, and foreign base company services income.[13]

An example will help explain the purpose of these definitions. Assume U.S. Co. forms a 100%-owned subsidiary, CFC Co., in a low-tax foreign jurisdiction. CFC Co. is a controlled foreign corporation because it is wholly owned by a U.S. shareholder (U.S. Co.). U.S. Co. handles its export sales by selling its goods first to CFC

---

9. I.R.C. § 957(a).

10. I.R.C. § 951(b).

11. I.R.C. § 951(a).

12. I.R.C. § 952(a).

13. I.R.C. §§ 952, 954.

Co., which then resells the goods to the consumer. Without subpart F, CFC Co.'s income from the resale of goods would not be taxed by the U.S. until CFC Co. pays a dividend up to U.S. Co. To prevent that tax deferral, subpart F defines foreign base company sales income to include income derived from the purchase of personal property from a related taxpayer and the sale of such property to another person where the property is neither manufactured nor sold for use in the country where the CFC is incorporated.[14] Thus, unless CFC Co. is selling the goods for use in its own country, its income will be subpart F income that will be immediately taxable to U.S. Co. The thought here is that there is no real business reason for U.S. Co.'s sales to be routed through CFC Co., other than tax deferral. But if CFC Co.'s home country has a significant connection with the goods or the sale then the separate existence of CFC Co. will be respected for tax purposes.

The earnings of a CFC that are invested in U.S. property generally includes amounts invested in both tangible and intangible property located in the United States.[15] However, significant exceptions are provided for various types of property, including obligations of the United States government, bank deposits, and property purchased for export.[16]

Additional anti-deferral rules apply to passive foreign investment companies.[17] The main purpose of those rules is to catch taxpayers who structure investments in property producing passive income so as to avoid the provisions of subpart F.

Taxation of nonresident aliens and foreign corporations. Nonresidents and foreign corporations generally are only taxed by the United States on income that is earned from U.S. activities. Specifically, income that is effectively connected with trade or business activities in the U.S. is taxed on a net basis at the graduated rates applicable to citizens and domestic corporations.[18] Income from investments in the U.S. that is not effectively connected with a trade or business (e.g., interest, dividends, rents, etc.) is taxed on a gross basis at a 30% rate.[19] Important exceptions from the 30% tax are provided for interest earned on deposits with banks and savings institutions and on portfolio investments.[20] Capital gains not connected with a trade or business and not from real estate generally are tax exempt.[21] Gains from the disposition of real estate are taxable as if the taxpayer were engaged in a trade or business

---

14. I.R.C. § 954(d).

15. I.R.C. §§ 956(a), (c)(1).

16. I.R.C. § 956(c)(2).

17. See I.R.C. § 1297.

18. I.R.C. § 871(b)(1), 882(a)(1). A foreign corporation operating in the U.S.

through a branch may also be subject to a 30% branch profits tax. See I.R.C. § 884.

19. I.R.C. §§ 871 (a)(1), 881(a)(1).

20. I.R.C. §§ 871(h), (i)(2)(A); 881(c), (d).

21. I.R.C. § 871(a)(2).

within the U.S. and such gains were effectively connected with the business.[22] Taxpayers may elect to treat real estate as a trade or business to ensure that operational income, such as rent, is taxed on a net basis with an allowance for expenses like interest and depreciation, rather than on a gross basis.[23]

Transfer pricing. Taxpayers have an incentive to shift their profits to jurisdictions with the lowest effective tax rates in order to reduce their overall tax burden. Transfer-pricing arrangements with controlled taxpayers are one strategy for achieving those results. For example, assume U.S. Co. manufactures its inventory at a cost of $3 per unit and it exports inventory to foreign buyers who pay $10 per unit. Thus, U.S. Co. will make a $7 profit on each unit of its export sales. Suppose U.S. Co.'s United States tax rate is 35% and the export jurisdiction taxes profits at a 20% rate. U.S. Co. clearly has an incentive to shift as much of its profit from the inventory sales as possible to the foreign jurisdiction to take advantage of its lower tax rate. It could accomplish that result by forming Foreign Sub Co., a sales subsidiary, in the foreign jurisdiction. U.S. Co. could then sell the inventory to Foreign Sub Co. at a price slightly above its cost, and then have Foreign Sub Co. resell the inventory to the ultimate foreign buyer for fair market value. For example, suppose U.S. Co. sells the inventory to Foreign Sub Co. for $5 per unit. If the sales price were respected for tax purposes, U.S. Co.'s profit taxable in the United States would now only be $2 ($5 selling price less $3 cost). The remaining $5 of profit from the sale of the inventory to the ultimate foreign buyer would be recognized by Foreign Sub Co. and taxed at a 20% rate in the foreign jurisdiction. Shifting the $5 of profit to the foreign jurisdiction through the pricing of the inventory between U.S. Co. and Foreign Sub Co. would save 75¢ in tax per unit (the 15% difference in tax rates multiplied by the $5 of profits that were shifted).

Section 482 of the Internal Revenue Code is the IRS's primary weapon to combat transfer pricing abuses. Section 482 grants the government authority to distribute, apportion, or allocate gross income, deductions, credits, or allowances between or among controlled or owned organizations, trades, or businesses if such action is necessary to prevent evasion of taxes or to clearly reflect income. Under Section 482, the taxpayer is supposed to realize the same amount of income from a transaction with a controlled taxpayer as would be realized in a transaction with an uncontrolled taxpayer.[24] This so-called "arm's length standard" is the core of an extensive body of regulations that govern transfer pricing. In the preceding example, U.S. Co. would be required to calculate its U.S. tax

---

22. I.R.C. § 897(a).

23. I.R.C. §§ 871(d), 882(d).

24. Reg. § 1. 482–1(b).

liability based on an arm's length price for sales of inventory to Foreign Sub Co. In addition to the general arm's length standard, the regulations contain explicit rules for a variety of specific transactions, including the pricing of loans and advances, services, the use of tangible property, transfers of tangible property, and transfers of intangible property.[25] Enforcement of the transfer pricing regime is supported by both reporting requirements[26] and penalties.[27]

When the IRS exercises its authority under Section 482 to make a transfer pricing adjustment, it will take into account "appropriate collateral adjustments."[28] For example, if an increase in income is made to one member of a group because it undercharged for some goods or services, a corresponding decrease in income may be made to another member in order to properly reflect the correct change in its income.[29] The following revenue ruling illustrates the operation of Section 482 and the types of adjustments that may be made under that section.

REVENUE RULING 69–630

1969–2 C.B. 112.

Advice has been requested as to the treatment of a "bargain sale" between two corporate entities controlled by the same shareholder(s).

A, an individual, owns all of the stock of X corporation and all of the stock of Y corporation. In 1967, A caused X to sell certain of its property to Y for less than an arm's length price. It has been determined that such sale had as one of its principal purposes the avoidance of Federal income tax and resulted in a significant understatement of X's taxable income.

Section 482 of the Internal Revenue Code of 1954 provides authority to distribute, apportion, or allocate gross income, deductions, and credits among related organizations, trades, or businesses if it is necessary in order to clearly reflect the income of such entities or to prevent the evasion of taxes.

Section 482 of the Code applies to bargain sale transactions between brother-sister corporations that result in significant shifting of income. Where an allocation is made under section 482 of the Code as a result of a bargain sale between brother-sister corporations, the amount of the allocation will be treated as a distribution to the controlling shareholder(s) with respect to the stock of the

---

25. Reg. §§ 1.482–2,–2T,–3,–4,–9T.

26. I.R.C. §§ 6038A, 6038C.

27. See I.R.C. § 6662(e).

28. Reg. § 1.482–1(g)(1).

29. Reg. § 1.482–1(g)(2).

entity whose income is increased and as a capital contribution by the controlling shareholder(s) to the other entity involved in the transaction giving rise to the section 482 allocation.

Accordingly, in the instant case, the income of X for 1967 will be increased under section 482 of the Code to reflect the arm's length price of the property sold to Y. The basis of the property in the hands of Y will also be increased to reflect the arm's length price. See section 1.482–1(d) of the Income Tax Regulations. Furthermore, the amount of such increase will be treated as a distribution to A, the controlling shareholder, with respect to his stock of X and as a capital contribution by A to Y.

* * *

Note

Tax treaties. Bilateral tax treaties operate to coordinate the tax systems of the contracting countries in a variety of ways. The primary objectives of a tax treaty are to facilitate business and commerce between the treaty partners and to reduce the likelihood of double taxation. The United States has a network of nearly 60 tax treaties.

Tax treaties have elaborate sets of rules designed to sort out the jurisdiction of the treaty partners over the taxpayers and the income that each may tax.[30] Additionally, tax treaties limit the ability of each treaty partner to tax residents of the other country by reducing the tax rates applicable to various types of income such as dividends,[31] interest,[32] and royalties.[33] The threshold level of activity for taxation of services performed by residents of one country in the other country is also raised.[34] For business profits, a tax treaty will provide that a resident of one treaty partner can be taxed by the other country only (1) if the enterprise is carried on through a "permanent establishment" located in that country, and (2) only on profits attributable to the permanent establishment.[35] A permanent establishment is defined as a fixed place of business such as a branch, office, factory or workshop.[36] Special rules determine when an agent's activities will constitute a permanent establishment.[37] The effect of these rules is to permit a resident of one treaty country to earn business profits in the other country tax free if the business is not conducted through a permanent establishment.

30. See United States Model Income Tax Convention of September 20, 1996, Articles 1, 2 & 4.

31. Id. at Article 10.

32. Id. at Article 11.

33. Id. at Article 12.

34. Id. at Articles 14–18.

35. Id. at Article 7.1.

36. Id. at Article 5.

37. Id. at Article 5.5, 5.6.

JOHANSSON v. UNITED STATES*

United States Court Of Appeals, Fifth Circuit, 1964.

336 F.2d 809.

RIVES, CIRCUIT JUDGE.

On three occasions, Ingemar Johansson, a citizen of Sweden, fought Floyd Patterson for the heavyweight boxing championship of the world. All three fights took place in the United States. Taxes in the amounts of $598,181.92 for the calendar year 1960 and $411,620 for the period January 1, 1961, through March 13, 1961, were assessed against Johansson on the income he earned from the Patterson fights and related activities. The Government brought an action against Johansson to collect the taxes assessed and against Feature Sports, Inc., Thomas Bolan, Roy Cohn, and Humbert Fugazy to foreclose tax liens against funds held by them for Johansson's benefit. The District Court for the Southern District of Florida entered judgment against Johansson for the full amount of the taxes claimed by the Government, plus interest. At the same time, it ordered the other defendants named above to render an accounting of the funds held by them for Johansson and to turn those funds over to the United States. In so ordering, the court refused to allow a setoff of $287,750.60 claimed by the lienees. All the defendants have appealed the judgment and adverse post-trial rulings of the district court.

The first question for this court is whether Johansson may be taxed by the United States on the income he earned from his activities here during the period in question. Section 871[b] of the Internal Revenue Code of 1954 provides that a nonresident alien individual engaged in trade or business within the United States shall be taxable. [T]he term ["trade or business within the United States"] includes the performance of personal services within the United States at any time within the taxable year, * * *. Since the express exceptions contained in section 871 are inapposite here, we must view that section as authorizing the assessments involved in this case unless an applicable tax convention requires a contrary result. I.R.C.1954 §§ 894, 7852(d). The Income Tax Convention with Sweden, March 23, 1939, 54 Stat. 1759, T.S. No. 958 (effective Jan. 1, 1940), does not bar the assessments. See article XI(a), (d). However, Johansson claims an exemption under the Income Tax Convention with Switzerland, May 24, 1951 (1951), 2 U.S.T. & O.I.A. 1751, T.I.A.S. No. 2316 (effective Sept. 27, 1951). Particular reliance is placed upon article X(1), which provides:

'An individual resident of Switzerland shall be exempt from United States Tax upon compensation for labor or personal services performed in the United States * * * if he is tempo-

* Footnotes omitted.

rarily present in the United States for a period or periods not exceeding a total of 183 days during the taxable year and * * *

'(a) his compensation is received for such labor or personal services performed as an employee of, or under contract with, a resident or corporation or other entity of Switzerland * * *.'

It is undisputed that Johansson was not present in the United States for more than 183 days in either of the tax years in question. But to bring himself within the purview of the treaty, Johansson had to establish (1) that he was a resident of Switzerland and (2) that he received the income in question as an employee of, or under contract with, a Swiss entity.

The term "resident" is nowhere defined in the Swiss treaty, but under article II(2) each country is authorized to apply its own definition to terms not expressly defined "unless the context otherwise requires." Johansson contends that, because of its position within the phrase "an individual resident of Switzerland," the term "resident" must be defined according to Swiss law. As conclusive proof that he comes within the Swiss definition of "resident" for tax purposes, he relies upon a determination by the Swiss tax authorities that he became a resident of Switzerland on December 1, 1959. Although the evidence on this point in ambiguous, the determination by the Swiss tax authorities may well have been based primarily upon Johansson's own declaration as to his residence in that country. See Govt. exh. 133–F, Def. exh. I, and Def. exh. J. Be this as it may, we are not bound by the determination of the Swiss tax authorities. Article II(2) does no more than to provide the standard for defining the terms used in the rest of the treaty; the application of that standard to particular facts remains, in this case, the job of the courts. There is no reason to decide whether the applicable standard for defining "resident" as used in the Swiss treaty is to be found in Swiss or American law, for under both laws the criteria are the same. Compare Locher, statement of Dec. 29, 1962, in C.C.H. 1963 Stand.Fed.Tax Rep. Paragraph 6407, p. 71286 ("sojourn * * * with the intention to remain"), with Treas.Reg. § 1.871–2(b) ("intentions with regard to the length and nature of his stay").

Applying this standard to the facts of the present case, the district court concluded that Johansson was not a resident of Switzerland during the period in question. This conclusion is fully supported by the evidence. In the year and a half between the date Johansson claims to have moved to Switzerland and March 13, 1961, the record shows that he spent only 79 days in that country as compared with 120 days in Sweden and 218 days in the United States. Except for his activities in the United States during this period, his social and economic ties remained predominantly with Sweden. Indeed, the summary of Johansson's ties with Switzerland presented in his brief to this Court cites only his maintenance of an apartment and bank account there, his self-declaration of residence, and two acts by the Swiss government that may well have been predicated entirely upon his self-declaration of residence. See Brief on Behalf of Appellants Johansson and Scanart, S.A., pp. 3–6, 9.

Even if we were to find that the district court erred in determining that Johansson was not a resident of Switzerland, the tax exemption in the Swiss treaty does not apply unless Johansson received the income in question as an employee of or under contract with a Swiss entity. A contract of employment was entered into by Johansson in December 1959 with Scanart, S.A., a Swiss corporation formed that very month. Scanart's sole employee and sole source of revenue is Johansson, who is entitled under the terms of the contract to seventy per cent of Scanart's gross income, plus a pension fund. All expenses are to be paid by Scanart. During the period in question, Johansson conducted his affairs largely independent of Scanart's sole director or its stockholders. The circumstances surrounding the formation of Scanart, the terms of the contract, and the conduct of the parties under the contract led the district court to find that:

> 'Scanart, S.A., had no legitimate business purpose, but was a device which was used by Ingemar Johansson as a controlled depositary and conduit by which he attempted to divert temporarily, his personal income, earned in the United States, so as to escape taxation thereon by the United States.' (R., pp. 197–98.)

As with the question of Johansson's residence, the record amply supports this finding.

Of course, the fact that Johansson was motivated in his actions by the desire to minimize his tax burden can in no way be taken to deprive him of an exemption to which an applicable treaty entitles him. See Gregory v. Helvering, 293 U.S. 465, 469, 55 S.Ct. 266, 79 L.Ed. 596 (1935). And in determining the applicability of a treaty, we recognize the necessity for liberal construction. Jordan v. K. Tashiro, 278 U.S. 123, 127, 49 S.Ct. 47, 73 L.Ed. 214 (1928). But "To say that we should give a broad and efficacious scope to a treaty does not mean that we must sweep within the Convention what are legally and traditionally recognized to be * * * taxpayers not clearly within its protections; * * *''. Maximov v. United States, 373 U.S. 49, 56, 83 S.Ct. 1054, 10 L.Ed.2d 184 (1963). In determining whether the taxpayer in a given case is protected by the terms of a treaty, abstract and desultory definitions of such terms as "resident" and "legitimate business purposes" are of limited, if any, assistance. "To give the specific words of a treaty a meaning consistent with the genuine shared expectations of the contracting parties, it is necessary to examine not only the language, but the entire context of agreement." Maximov v. United States, 2 Cir., 1962, 299 F.2d 565, 568, aff'd, 373 U.S. 49, 83 S.Ct. 1054, 10 L.Ed.2d 184 (1963).

The primary objective of our treaty with Switzerland, as well as of those with more than twenty other countries, is the elimination of impediments to international commerce resulting from the double taxation of international transactions. The basic mechanism of these treaty arrangements is the establishment of standards for determining the single most appropriate locus for the taxation of any given transaction. Although some treaty provisions are inevitably the results of political compromise, the dominant criterion for determining the appropriate taxing locus is economic impact. Thus, as a general rule, the income from services is taxable where the services are rendered. See Smith, The Functions of Tax Treaties, 12 Nat'l Tax J. 317, 320 (1959). Where, as here, services are performed in the United States and the compensation for them is drawn from the wealth of the United States, this is the country of primary economic impact and, consequently, the appropriate taxing locus.

There are, however, a number of prudential exceptions to the general "economic impact" rule. Among these is the view that a business enterprise engaged in international commerce ought not to be subject to taxation in every country in which it may transact some business. Although such an enterprise does draw upon the wealth of all the various countries with which it comes into contact, the over-all objective of encouraging international commerce, as well as the practical necessities of business planning, are better satisfied by a centralized regime of taxation at the enterprise's "business seat" or "permanent establishment." The "business seat" exception is found in article III of the Swiss treaty.

Elements of this exception are also found in article X. Typical of what have become known as "commercial traveler provisions" in international tax conventions, the article is designed to assure business establishments in each of the contracting states that they may freely send their agents and employees into the other contracting state without thereby subjecting those employees to the latter's taxes. Like article III, it is an exception to the "economic impact" rule carved out in the interest of facilitating international trade. Where the practical reasons for the exception do not obtain, however, the general rule must apply. Thus, while Johansson may have brought himself within the words of the Swiss treaty by his "residence" in Switzerland and his "employment" by a "Swiss corporation," he has failed to establish any substantial reasons for deviating from the treaty's basic rule that income from services is taxable where the services were rendered. International trade will not be seriously encumbered by our refusal to grant special tax treatment to one only marginally, if at all, a Swiss resident and only technically, if at all, employed by a paper Swiss corporation. Therefore we affirm the district court's judgment that Johansson is liable for the taxes assessed against him in 1960 and 1961.

* * *

SIMENON v. COMMISSIONER*
United States Tax Court, 1965.
44 T.C. 820.

Harron, Judge:

The respondent determined a deficiency in income tax for the taxable year 1955 in the amount of $22,895.57. The main question is whether petitioner had a "permanent establishment" in the United States until March 19, 1955, within the meaning of the income tax convention between the United States and France and respondent's regulations adopted thereunder, with the consequence that author's royalties from U.S. sources received while he was in France are not tax exempt.

Findings of Fact

* * *

Petitioner is, and at all times has been, a citizen of Belgium where he was born. His wife, Denyse (also known as Denise), is a citizen of Belgium. Petitioner's family consists of his wife and three children.

Petitioner is a professional writer of fiction, an eminent author. He writes in French. He is by experience and practice a European novelist. He writes psychological and mystery novels and stories. In his mystery stories, the principal character is Inspector Maigret. All of his literary works, except six, have a European background. His literary works have been published in various countries, including the United States, Canada, and Great Britain, and many have been translated into the English language.

Prior to 1946, petitioner lived in several countries in Europe and in England for varying periods of time. In 1946, he lived in Canada until September, and in the United States during September through December, under a visitor's visa. He entered the United States from Cuba under a permanent visa in February 1947, and thereafter he continued living in the United States as an alien

* Footnotes omitted.

resident through March 19, 1955, except for occasional trips of short duration to European countries.

Beginning on July 27, 1950, petitioner rented residential property, called Shadow Rock Farm, in Lakeville, Conn., where he lived with his family until March 19, 1955. On November 1, 1950, he purchased this property. The purchase price plus improvements was $55,000.

While residing in the United States, petitioner wrote 46 books, novels, and short stories, all of which were written in French and have French titles. All have European backgrounds and are based on experiences and knowledge which petitioner had acquired in Europe, except six books of novels and stories in which petitioner made use of knowledge acquired in the United States. Prior to 1955, petitioner's main publishers in the United States were Prentice–Hall, Inc., and Doubleday & Co. During 1955, Doubleday was his exclusive publisher.

In about 1955, petitioner decided to go to Europe. He believed that he could carry on his creative writing better in a European background. He departed from the United States, with his family, on March 19, 1955, and went directly to France, where he remained until June 20, 1956. He then went to Switzerland where he and his family have lived continuously ever since. He has not returned to the United States at any time.

* * *

OPINION

Royalties from sources within the United States, in the amount of $25,291.95, were paid to petitioner in 1955 after he left the United States on March 19, 1955. Petitioner did not include these royalties in his gross income on his return for 1955. He took the position that they are exempt from the U.S. income tax under the provisions of article 7 of the income tax convention, or treaty, between the United States and France. The respondent made the following determinations: (1) That article 7 of the income tax treaty does not apply because petitioner had a "permanent establishment" in the United States at some time during 1955. (2) That since the treaty exemption does not apply, the royalties are subject to the U.S. income tax under section 871(c) of the 1954 Code.

The issue for decision is whether the royalties in question, from U.S. sources, are exempt from the U.S. income tax under article 7 of the income tax treaty with France. Section 894 of the Code exempts from the Federal income tax income of any kind, "to the extent required by any treaty obligation of the United States." The tax treaty involved is the income tax convention with France which was signed on July 25, 1939, and in due course became effective on January 1, 1945. Article 7 of the convention, in title I, Double Taxation, provides as follows:

> Royalties derived from within one of the contracting States by a resident or by a corporation or other entity of the other contracting State as consideration for the right to use copyrights, patents, secret processes and formulae, trade marks and other analogous rights shall be exempt from taxation in the former State, provided such resident, corporation or other entity does not have a permanent establishment there.

* * *

Petitioner failed to prove that he was qualified for the claimed tax relief under article 7 of the convention on the basis that in 1955 he was "a resident" of France for French tax purposes. This element of failure of proof is sufficient to disqualify petitioner for the tax relief in dispute. However, because of the novelty of the question, we also give consideration to whether petitioner had a "permanent establishment" in the United States during part of 1955, from January 1 to March 19.

3.   Treaty Article 7, Permanent Establishment

Respondent determined that petitioner had a "permanent establishment" in the United States during part of 1955 where he carried on a trade or business. He contends that petitioner maintained an office in his home at Shadow Rock Farm which constituted a permanent establishment within the meaning of article 7. His contention is limited to the period January 1 to March 19, and to the office at petitioner's home. Respondent's regulation in conjunction with article 7 states that royalties derived from U.S. sources by a nonresident individual, who is a resident of France, are exempt from the U.S. Federal income tax, provided that such individual has no permanent establishment within the United States "at any time" during the taxable year in which such income is so derived. * * *

* * *

We turn now to the final question whether petitioner had a "permanent establishment" in the United States during the period January 1 through March 19, 1955. * * *

Petitioner converted part of his house at Shadow Rock Farm to the use of an office. He reported on his 1955 return that 50 percent of this property was used for his business and took depreciation on that basis; and that furniture and fixtures acquired in 1954 were devoted 100 percent to business use, and he took depreciation on that basis. Respondent has not questioned those deductions and petitioner still adheres to them. * * * Lacking evidence to the contrary, the inference and conclusion are that petitioner used part of his house for business purposes, hence as an office, for 4 years prior to 1955 and that such use continued in 1955 to March 19. * * * There is nothing in the treaty definition of "permanent establishment," insofar as it includes an "office," which would serve to exclude from the term "office" an office at the taxpayer's residence, provided it was devoted to petitioner's business. We are unable to find any merit in petitioner's contention that the office at petitioner's residence cannot be regarded as his "permanent establishment" in the United States within the treaty definition of that term and its meaning in article 7.

The treaty definition of "permanent establishment" is a fairly broad and inclusive one in which there is the catchall term "and other fixed place of business." The term "business" has a broad meaning, which has been defined as including "that which occupies the time, attention, and labor of men for the purpose of livelihood or profit." Flint v. Stone Tracy Co., 220 U.S. 107, 171. It is also true that whether an occupation constitutes a trade or business must be decided on the facts in each case, * * * and the intent of the taxpayer has a material bearing on the issue, although it is not conclusive, * * *. The determination of whether the activities of a taxpayer constitute the carrying on of a trade or business requires an examination of all of the facts in each case. Higgins v. Commissioner, 312 U.S. 212. * * * Continuous or repeated activity in the literary field, coupled with a reasonable expectation of making a profit, is convincing evidence of an intent to engage in writing as a business of profession. Cf. Kerns Wright, supra at 1267. In Fahs v. Crawford, 161 F.2d 315, it is said: "carrying on a business * * * implies an occupational undertaking to which one habitually devotes time, attention, or effort with substantial regularity." See also Doggett v. Burnet, supra, which stands for the principle that, in general, activities engaged in with the hope and expectation of making a profit constitute a trade or business.

In view of the evidence in this case, it seems unnecessary to set forth the above observations about certain general principles. In fact, petitioner took the position in his 1955 return that he was engaged in a business during part of 1955, in the United States, as an author. He reported on Schedule C, income from his business in excess of $40,000, and he took "business deduction" in excess of $12,000 for wages, depreciation, legal and accounting fees ($1,484), business entertainment, publicity photographs, auto expenses, 50 percent of the utilities at his house, 50 percent of building maintenance, stationery and printing, and postage; and he also included a U.S. self-employment tax of $126. The evidence indicates that petitioner's general occupation and business activities as a professional author had been carried on in the United States for several years before 1955, and that what he did in the period January 1 to March 19, 1955, was a continuation of the same activities which previously had been carried on with regularity and continuity for the purpose of producing a livelihood, income, and profits.

* * * In article 7, "permanent establishment" is defined broadly to include several kinds of "fixed places of business." In the United States, petitioner had an office and he engaged in a business, both, for several years up to March 19 or 20, 1955. Upon the record in this case, we are not able to conclude that petitioner's office in his house was not his fixed place of business, prior to 1955 and up to March 19 or 20, 1955, when he departed. Petitioner may have been able to, and probably did, develop plots for his stories while sitting out in a park or driving through the country, all of which is immaterial under the particular question. * * *

It is held that petitioner had a "permanent establishment" in the United States during the period January 1 through March 19, 1955. Petitioner's U.S. source royalties received during the whole calendar and taxable year of 1955 are subject to the U.S. income tax, and no part thereof is exempt from our tax under article 7 of the convention. Respondent's determination is sustained.

* * *

C. INTERNATIONAL TAXATION IN FOREIGN TAX SYSTEMS

The main themes of international income taxation were set out in the preceding sections of this chapter. They include: the jurisdictional principles that a country employs for taxing international transactions, avoidance of double taxation, deferral of tax liability, and the use of tax treaties to coordinate the tax systems of treaty partners. Following is an excerpt from a congressional study on international tax rules and the competitiveness of business. The excerpt includes brief descriptions of the international income tax rules of five countries. Note how each country addresses the common questions that arise in taxing international business transactions. Also, note the tax incentives that these countries have created to promote international business.

EXCERPT FROM THE IMPACT OF INTERNATIONAL TAX REFORM: BACKGROUND AND SELECTED ISSUES RELATING TO U.S. INTERNATIONAL TAX RULES AND THE COMPETITIVENESS OF U.S. BUSINESS PP. 32–54.

Prepared by the Staff of the Joint Committee on Taxation, 2006.
JCX–22–06.

* * *

III. BRIEF DESCRIPTIONS OF SELECTED TERRITORIAL AND OTHER SYSTEMS

A. Selected Territorial Systems

1. France[107]

In general

Individuals resident in France are taxed on their worldwide income. Corporations, wherever resident, are subject to tax only on income derived from French sources. * * *

Taxation of corporations

Domestic corporations

Income from domestic activities

France has a territorial system of corporate income taxation. Thus, corporations, wherever resident, are subject to tax only on income derived from French sources. * * *

Income from foreign activities

As a general rule, foreign income earned directly by a French company is exempt from French taxation.* Foreign subsidiary income of a French multinational is also generally exempt from French tax. Such income is not taxed when it is earned by the foreign subsidiaries and 95 percent of it is exempt on repatriation to France. The exemption applies provided the French recipient owns 5 percent of the equity capital of the paying company and provided the recipient either subscribed for the original shares or purchased the shares with the intention of holding them for at least two years.

In order to be exempt from French taxation, income generated abroad must be attributable to a foreign permanent establishment or other independent establishment that regularly conducts business activities. Where there is no applicable treaty, case law is used to provide a definition of what is a "business conducted abroad." In accordance with case law, French corporations are not subject to tax on: (1) profits realized by a foreign establishment; (2) profits

---

107. Unless otherwise noted, the following discussion is drawn from Bernard Chesnais, Francois Froment–Meurice and Sandra Hazan, Foreign Income: Business Operations in France, BNA Tax Management Portfolio 961–3rd (2005); Ernst & Young, Worldwide Corporate Tax Guide, pp. 254–264 (2005); and the National Foreign Trade Council, International Tax Policy for the 21st Century (2001).

* A French corporation can opt, after an agreement from the Ministry of Fi-

nance, to be taxed on its worldwide income, therefore including the income arising from its branches. Foreign income taxes then are creditable against the French income tax to the limit of the French income tax. A French corporation also can opt to be taxed on its worldwide income, plus the income of its branches and all subsidiaries that are at least 50% owned (some exceptions are allowed). See article 209 quinquies of the Tax Code and Instruction 4 H–4–95 [Ed.].

from transactions habitually conducted abroad involving the participation of intermediaries who are not professionally independent; or (3) profits from transactions that constitute a "complete commercial cycle" carried out abroad, distinct from the entity's other operations. A complete commercial cycle means the resale of purchased or manufactured goods. The corporate income tax applies to transactions conducted abroad by means of an independent agent or intermediary, and to profits resulting from foreign transactions if: (1) neither their nature nor their mode of execution distinguish them from the company's other business; and (2) they do not represent a commercial activity habitually conducted abroad.

The rules governing foreign source income are subject to an important exception described below.

Special rules for income from foreign activities

Under the controlled foreign company ("CFC") rules, an exemption is not allowed for specifically defined types of low-taxed, non-business income. A French company is required to pay French tax on its pro rata share of foreign source income received or deemed received from a CFC established in a low-tax jurisdiction. Only certain categories of non-business income are targeted, such as securities or royalty income and intra-group services income. The CFC rules were substantially amended in December 2004. The new legislation is effective starting January 1, 2006.

The French CFC regime is jurisdiction-based, applying to CFCs in countries with a "privileged tax system." Generally, a foreign country is considered to have a privileged tax system when the foreign tax actually borne by the CFC is at least 50 percent lower than that of France. In addition, the resident company must directly or indirectly hold a participation of more than 50 percent in the foreign company. A country is also considered to have a privileged tax system if it does not impose tax on foreign-source income of corporations established there. There is an unofficial list of the countries that are considered tax havens under the French regime.

The new CFC rules do not apply if the company is established within the European Union unless the French tax administration can demonstrate that it is part of "an artificial arrangement aimed at circumventing the French tax legislation." Outside the European Union, the rules do not apply if the foreign company is principally engaged in active commercial or industrial activities. However, even in this case, the French company must prove that the operation of the foreign company is not an artificial arrangement to circumvent French tax when: (1) more than 20 percent of its income is derived from the management of shares, participations, or assets for its own account or for the account of companies belonging to a group controlled by the French company, or more than 20 percent of its income is derived from the sale or concessions of intangible rights related to industrial or intellectual property; or (2) more than 50 percent of its income is derived from operations listed in (1) and from intra-group services.**

Foreign corporations

Nonresident corporations are generally subject to withholding taxes at the following rates, in lieu of the progressive income tax to which residents are subject: 25 percent on dividends; 16 percent on interest; and 33.33 percent on royalties from patents and know-how. Furthermore, repatriation of profits from a French branch of a foreign corporation is generally subject to a 25–percent withholding tax.

Avoidance or relief of double taxation

France does not have detailed statutory rules dealing with the allocation of expenses to exempt foreign-source income. Expenses that are directly related to exempt foreign-source income are non-deductible. Expenses that are not directly related must be apportioned between taxable and exempt income and are likewise non-deductible.

Since France fully excludes foreign income from French taxable income, foreign losses never enter into French taxable income. Thus, resourcing provisions like the U.S. overall foreign loss rules are not necessary.

France has entered into a large number of tax treaties whose main objective is the elimination of double taxation of income and capital. These tax treaties are aimed at eliminating conflict between the tax rules of two taxing jurisdictions that, if the national rules alone were applied, would result in the same items being taxed twice in the hands of the same taxpayer by two separate taxing authorities.

France has entered into a bilateral tax treaty with the United States that eliminates withholding tax on dividends paid by one corporation to another corporation that owns at least 80 percent of the stock of the dividend-paying corporation (often referred to as "direct dividends"), provided that certain conditions are met. The elimination of withholding tax under these circumstances is intended to reduce further the tax barriers to direct investment between the two treaty countries. In addition, under the European Union

** The legality of this rule in the case of countries that have a tax treaty with France may be questionable. A French court struck down a similar provision because it was inconsistent with the tax treaty between France and Switzerland. See Conseil d'etat, June 28th 2002, Schneider Electric, n 232276 and Le Dispositif Anti–Evasion Fiscale Revu, Bernard Dussert, Les Echos, February 14th 2007. [Ed.]

"Parent Subsidiary Directive," withholding taxes are eliminated on intra-group dividend payments between European Union countries in the case of shareholdings of at least twenty-five percent.[109] Under the Parent Subsidiary Directive, France generally does not impose withholding tax on such dividends paid by French companies to other European Union companies (e.g., Germany) and other European Union companies generally do not impose a withholding tax on such dividends paid to French companies.

In the absence of a treaty, France generally provides double tax relief to resident individuals by way of a deduction from taxable income. Since corporations are not generally subject to French tax on income from sources outside France, they are not provided double tax relief.

* * *

3. Netherlands[115]

In general

Individuals resident in the Netherlands are taxed on their worldwide income. * * * Corporations are subject to tax on their worldwide income, but the Netherlands employs an exemption system that is applicable to both domestic and foreign shareholdings and such exemption allows for the avoidance of double taxation when the profits of a subsidiary are distributed to its parent company.

* * *

Taxation of corporations

Domestic corporations

Entities resident in the Netherlands are subject to corporate income tax on their worldwide income. All income earned by companies is deemed to be business income. Corporate income tax is levied at a rate of 29 percent on the first 22,689 of taxable profits and at 31.5 percent on the excess. Losses may be carried forward and deducted from profits in a subsequent year. Profits distributed to shareholders are not deductible from taxable profits for purposes of the corporate income tax.

109. The European Union is in the process of decreasing this ownership threshold to 10 percent.

115. Unless otherwise noted, the following discussion is drawn from Kees van Raad, Foreign Income: Business Operations in The Netherlands, BNA Tax Management Portfolio 973–2nd (2005); Ernst & Young, Worldwide Corporate Tax Guide, pp. 625–642 (2005); and the National Foreign Trade Council, International Tax Policy for the 21st Century (2001).

The Companies Income Tax Act provides for a participation exemption, which is applicable to both domestic and foreign shareholdings. Corporate tax need not be paid on the profits generated by the participation. The exemption allows for the avoidance of double taxation when the profits of a subsidiary are distributed to its parent company. A participation exists if the taxpayer (1) holds at least five percent of the nominal paid-up capital of a company, or (2) holds less than five percent, but ownership of the shares is necessary for the conduct of normal business, or the acquisition of the shares serves a general interest. All profits gained from shareholdings are exempt from taxation unless shares in a foreign corporation are held as an investment or the foreign company in which the shares are held is not subject to tax on its profits in the foreign country (the rate of tax is unimportant). A 25 percent withholding tax is imposed on dividends from corporations resident in the Netherlands, unless the participation exemption applies. Dividends received from a qualifying subsidiary company are exempt from tax in the hands of the parent company. Similarly, capital gains realized on the disposition of shares of such a subsidiary company are exempt.

Under certain conditions a parent corporation may be taxed as a group together with one or more of its subsidiaries. Group taxation allows losses of one company to be set off against profits of another company, and fixed assets may be transferred tax-free from one company to another. Group taxation is allowed only if all the companies involved are based in the Netherlands for tax purposes and the parent company holds at least 95 percent of the shares in the subsidiary.

Special rules for income from foreign activities

As mentioned above, the Netherlands provides for a participation exemption that generally exempts all dividend income received from foreign subsidiaries from taxation in the Netherlands. Because the Netherlands exempts dividends from a foreign subsidiary from income, there is no domestic income on which to defer tax (and thus no need for an extensive anti-deferral regime). However, the Netherlands denies the benefit of the participation exemption to income derived from certain passive investments. One consideration in determining whether an investment is passive is the level of ownership associated with such investment. The greater the ownership, the less likely the investment will be considered passive. In the case of a holding company, there is a look-through to the companies that the holding company owns to determine whether ownership is passive. If the participation exemption does not apply, the annual increase in the value of the subsidiary is fully taxable at the level of the Netherlands parent company, whether or not profits were distributed.

Because multinationals that are resident in the Netherlands are not taxed on current income of a foreign subsidiary under an anti-deferral regime or on the dividends from foreign subsidiaries when remitted, they enjoy a relative advantage over other multinationals that are subject to an extensive anti-deferral regime with CFC rules.

Foreign corporations

Nonresident corporations are subject to tax in the Netherlands on business income derived through a permanent establishment in the Netherlands, real property income and gains, dividends and interest received from a resident country at least five percent of the shares of which are held by the entity as portfolio investment, and certain other categories of income.

Avoidance or relief of double taxation

The Netherlands has entered into a large number of tax treaties whose main objective is the elimination of double taxation of income and capital. These tax treaties are aimed at eliminating conflict between the tax rules of two taxing jurisdictions that, if the national rules alone were applied, would result in the same items being taxed twice in the hands of the same taxpayer by two separate taxing authorities.

Recently, the Netherlands has entered into a bilateral tax treaty with the United States that eliminates withholding tax on dividends paid by one corporation to another corporation that owns at least 80 percent of the stock of the dividend-paying corporation (often referred to as "direct dividends"), provided that certain conditions are met. The elimination of withholding tax under these circumstances is intended to reduce further the tax barriers to direct investment between the two treaty countries. In addition, under the European Union "Parent Subsidiary Directive," withholding taxes are eliminated on intra-group dividend payments between European Union countries in the case of shareholdings of at least twenty-five percent.[117] Under the Parent Subsidiary Directive, the Netherlands generally does not impose withholding tax on such dividends paid by Dutch companies to other European Union companies (e.g., Germany) and other European Union companies generally do not impose a withholding tax on such dividends paid to Dutch companies.

In the absence of a treaty, the Netherlands generally provides double tax relief under the 2001 Unilateral Decree on the Avoidance of Double Taxation ("the Decree"). The Decree relieves inter-

---

117. The European Union is in the process of decreasing this ownership threshold to 10 percent.

national double taxation either by way of a proportional tax reduction (sometimes referred to as "exemption with progression") or by way of a foreign tax credit. The major income elements to which the proportional tax reduction applies are business income, income from foreign real property, and income from employment exercised abroad. Double taxation relief by way of the foreign tax credit applies to dividends, interest and royalties received from sources in developing countries (dividends received by a corporate shareholder generally qualify for double tax relief under the participation exemption).

4. Singapore[118]

* * *

Taxation of corporations
In general

Singapore's corporate income tax regime is territorial. A corporation, whether incorporated or registered in Singapore or elsewhere, generally is subject to Singapore tax on all income derived from Singapore sources or received in Singapore. Companies resident in Singapore may be subject to tax by Singapore on non-Singapore source income only when that income is remitted to Singapore. There generally are no special rules for the taxation of nonresident companies. Like resident companies, nonresident companies are taxed in Singapore on income derived from Singapore sources or received in Singapore. In practice, under this rule nonresident companies are taxed in Singapore on income from business operations in Singapore. Certain payments to a nonresident company of Singapore-source income not connected with Singapore business operations of the nonresident may be subject to Singapore withholding tax.

Singapore maintains a variety of preferential tax rules for targeted industries and activities. These rules are briefly summarized below.

Taxation of resident companies
Income from domestic activities

As described above, under Singapore's territorial taxing regime, resident companies are subject to tax on their income derived from Singapore sources or received in Singapore. The place of residence of a company is determined by where the management and control of the company is exercised. Income from Singapore

---

118. Unless otherwise noted, the following discussion is drawn from Brij S. Soin, Foreign Income: Business Operations in Singapore, BNA Tax Management Portfolio 983–3rd (2005); Ernst & Young, Worldwide Corporate Tax Guide, pp. 811–21 (2005); and Angela Tan & Tan How Teck, Singapore Master Tax Guide Handbook 2005, 24th ed., CCH Asia Pte Ltd. (2005).

sources encompasses most sorts of profits from business activities but does not include capital gains.

The rate of corporate tax generally is 21 percent in 2006 and is scheduled to be reduced to 20 percent in 2007.

Dividends received by a resident corporation (or by an individual shareholder) from another resident corporation, whether paid out of fully-taxed corporate income or out of income exempt from tax or subject to a reduced rate of tax, are exempt from income tax.[119]

Special tax rules apply in a variety of circumstances. Examples include the following:

- Under rules intended to help small and medium size businesses, companies generally are eligible for a partial exemption from income tax for the first S$100,000 (about $63,000) of taxable income.

- New companies may be exempted from paying income tax on the first $100,000 of taxable business income—dividend income does not qualify for the exclusion—for each of their first three years of tax assessment.

- Under a headquarters program, entities incorporated or registered in Singapore that provide headquarters services to affiliated companies regionally or worldwide and that satisfy certain other conditions are subject to tax rates of zero to 15 percent for a specified period on certain qualifying income.

- Other tax incentives and preferences exist for, among other things, certain capital expenditures; payments of certain royalties, technical assistance fees, and research and development costs; payments to nonresidents for software and other technological goods and services; remittances of foreign-source royalties and interest income when used for research and development purposes; financial institutions' income from qualifying activities; and income from global trading operations involving commodities and certain other products.

Income from foreign activities

As described previously, resident companies may be subject to tax by Singapore on non-Singapore source income (earned, for example, through foreign branch operations) only when that income is remitted to Singapore. Dividends received from nonresident

---

119. Before 2003, Singapore maintained a full imputation system under which dividends paid by a resident company out of profits subject to the normal corporate tax rate generally were treated as paid net of a 20–percent tax. Shareholders then could claim a credit for this tax as an offset against their income tax liability. Any excess of the credit over the shareholder's tax liability was refundable.

companies are exempt from Singapore tax so long as the income underlying the dividends has been earned in a country with a headline tax rate of at least 15 percent.

Special rules for income from foreign activities

Singapore has no rules analogous to the U.S. controlled foreign corporation rules. Various anti-avoidance rules, however, including a general anti-avoidance provision, grant the Singapore tax authorities the power to combat tax avoidance schemes, including schemes involving elements outside Singapore.[120]

Nonresident companies

As described above, nonresident companies are subject to Singapore tax on income derived from business operations in Singapore. No additional branch profits tax is imposed when income is remitted by a Singapore branch of a nonresident company to its foreign base.[121]

Certain payments to nonresident companies of Singapore-source income not derived by the nonresident from Singapore business operations may be subject to Singapore withholding tax. These payments include interest, commissions, fees, and other payments in relation to loans or indebtedness; royalties for the use of moveable property; fees for technical assistance or management; directors remuneration; and gains from real property transactions. Royalty payments for the use of intellectual property in Singapore generally are subject to withholding at a 10–percent rate (reduced from the 15–percent rate in effect before 2005). Singapore-source interest payments generally are subject to withholding tax at a 15–percent rate. Dividend payments are not subject to withholding tax.

Avoidance or relief of double taxation

In general, because foreign-source income of Singapore resident companies is exempt from Singapore tax, no possibility of double taxation arises until income is remitted to Singapore. As described above, moreover, dividend payments to Singapore resident companies are exempt from Singapore taxation so long as the income out of which the dividends are paid is earned in a country with a headline tax rate of 15 percent. To the extent any non-Singapore-source income may be subject to tax by both Singapore and another country, a foreign tax credit generally is available to offset the foreign tax imposed on that income.

---

120. International Bureau of Fiscal Documentation, Asia–Pacific Taxation Analysis, Singapore, Country Survey, at ¶ 28.2 (2006) (accessed through RIA Checkpoint internet-based research service).

121. International Bureau of Fiscal Documentation, Asia–Pacific Taxation Analysis, Singapore, Country Survey, at ¶ 26.1 (2006) (accessed through RIA Checkpoint internet-based research service).

Singapore has a network of at least 50 bilateral tax treaties. These treaties largely are based on the OECD model income tax treaty. Singapore's tax treaties generally have three chief purposes: the avoidance of double taxation through provisions allocating taxing power between the treaty countries; the promotion of bilateral trade and investment; and, through information exchange provisions, the prevention of tax avoidance and evasion by treaty residents. Many Singapore tax treaties include tax sparing provisions under which each treaty country agrees to provide a credit for taxes forgone by the other treaty country under an incentive measure. Where tax treaties permit a Singapore resident to be taxed by Singapore on an item of income that also may be taxed by the other treaty country, the treaties typically provide a credit against Singapore tax for the foreign tax imposed on the income.

B. Selected Nonterritorial Systems

1. China[122]

* * *

Taxation of businesses

In general

Since the 1980s, China has undertaken a series of tax reform efforts. Business income taxation in China now is generally carried out through two sets of rules.

State-owned enterprises and other domestic enterprises are subject to the enterprise income tax regulations. Under these regulations, enterprises are subject to tax in China on Chinese and non-Chinese source income at a rate of 33 percent, a significantly lower rate than the 55–percent rate that was applicable to Chinese enterprises before 1994.

Chinese-foreign joint ventures and cooperative enterprises and foreign-owned businesses with Chinese business operations or Chinese-source income are subject to tax in China under the Income Tax Law of the People's Republic of China Concerning Foreign Investment Enterprises and Foreign Enterprises ("FEITL"). The FEITL generally imposes a 33–percent tax on income from foreign business activity in China.

State-owned and other domestic enterprises

As mentioned above, under the enterprise income tax regulations, state-owned enterprises and other domestic businesses are liable for tax in China on their worldwide income at a 33–percent

---

122. Unless otherwise noted, the following discussion is drawn from Owen D. Nee, Jr. and Deborah J. Goldstein, *Foreign Income: Business Operations in* *the People's Republic of China*, BNA Tax Management Portfolio 957–2d (2003), and Ernst & Young, Worldwide Corporate Tax Guide, pp. 147–56 (2005).

rate. Income under the enterprise income tax regulations includes income from business operations, income from the sale of property, and portfolio income such as interest, leases, royalties, and dividends.

Foreign income tax paid on income derived from non-Chinese sources may be offset by a credit against Chinese income tax. The credit may not exceed the amount of the Chinese income tax imposed on the foreign-source income.

Chinese tax law applicable to domestic enterprises does not included controlled foreign corporation rules or other anti-avoidance rules, other than transfer pricing rules, for income earned through foreign subsidiaries.[124]

FEITL

In general

The FEITL is, as described above, applicable to Chinese-foreign joint ventures and cooperative enterprises and to foreign-owned businesses with operations in China. Foreign investment enterprises with headquarters in China are subject to tax under the FEITL on their worldwide income; other foreign enterprises are liable for tax only on Chinese-source income.

The generally applicable FEITL net-basis tax rate on Chinese business operations is, as stated above, 33 percent. This 33–percent rate is comprised of a 30–percent central tax and a 3–percent local tax. The 33–percent rate is reduced or eliminated in certain circumstances described below. Taxable income under the net basis tax generally includes all income from business operations. Capital gains generally are treated the same as other income except that foreign investors are subject to a 10–percent withholding tax on gain from the sale of ownership interests in a foreign owned enterprise in China.

Payments to nonresidents of Chinese-source amounts that are not connected with business operations in China generally are subject to gross-basis withholding tax. The stated withholding rate on interest and royalties under the FEITL is 20 percent, but this rate has been reduced to 10 percent by a notice issued in 2000.[125]

Dividend payments to a nonresident owner of a foreign investment enterprise are not subject to Chinese withholding tax.

Preferential rules

124. International Bureau of Fiscal Documentation, Asia–Pacific Taxation Analysis, China, Country Survey, at ¶ 47 (2006) (accessed through RIA Checkpoint internet-based research service).

125. International Bureau of Fiscal Documentation, Asia–Pacific Taxation Analysis, China, Country Survey, at ¶ 23.4 (2006) (accessed through RIA Checkpoint internet-based research service).

The FEITL offers preferential net-basis tax regimes in many circumstances. A 15–percent rate is available for foreign enterprises operating in Special Economic Zones or in designated zones of various Chinese cities. The 15–percent rate also is available for enterprises in particular sectors, including manufacturing and high technology, provided the enterprises satisfy various other criteria. A 24–percent rate is available for foreign investment enterprises engaged in production and manufacturing activities in certain specified coastal and urban areas. China also grants tax holidays and significant rate reductions for certain favored activities and projects.

If profits are reinvested for at least five years in China in the same enterprise or in another foreign investment enterprise, a 40–percent refund of taxes paid on those profits may be available. A full tax refund may be available if the reinvestment is in a technologically advanced business or an export enterprise.

A foreign investment enterprise that purchases certain domestically-made equipment maybe eligible for a credit against their income tax liability under the FEITL. The maximum credit amount is, subject to additional income-based limitations, 40 percent of the amount of the purchase.

Foreign tax credit

A credit against Chinese tax liability under the FEITL generally is available for foreign taxes paid by foreign investment enterprises. The maximum foreign tax credit is the amount of Chinese tax imposed on the income.

Tax treaties[126]

China has entered into bilateral tax treaties with more than 80 countries, including the United States. These tax treaties generally follow the OECD model treaty. Treaties generally provide for reduced rates of withholding tax on cross-border payments. Most treaties also provide for tax sparing and for credits against foreign tax where double taxation otherwise is not eliminated.

2. Ireland[127]

* * *

---

126. International Bureau of Fiscal Documentation, Asia–Pacific Taxation Analysis, China, Country Survey, at ¶ 45.2 (2006) (accessed through RIA Checkpoint internet-based research service).

127. Unless otherwise noted, the following discussion is drawn from John Ryan, Foreign Income: Business Operations in Ireland, BNA Tax Management Portfolio 965–3rd (2004), and Ernst & Young, Worldwide Corporate Tax Guide, pp. 391–410 (2005).

Taxation of corporations

In general

Under the Irish corporation tax, Irish resident corporations generally are subject to tax on all profits (income and gains) regardless of source. A credit for foreign taxes imposed on foreign source income may be available under a tax treaty, and if a tax treaty does not apply, limited relief may be provided under Irish domestic law. Nonresident companies generally are taxed by Ireland only on income derived from and attributable to a trade or business carried on in Ireland.

Domestic corporations

In general

As described above, Irish resident corporations are subject to tax on their worldwide income. Gross income is determined under a comprehensive schedular system. Items that would be included in calculating income or loss from operations under generally accepted accounting principles are included in gross income for tax purposes.

Tax residence is determined under two tests. First, a corporation is considered a tax resident of Ireland if it is managed and controlled in Ireland. Second, if a company is incorporated in Ireland, it also is considered a resident unless (1) the company or a related company carries on a trade in Ireland and either (a) it is under the control of persons who are resident in a tax treaty country or another EU jurisdiction, provided those persons are not controlled by persons not resident in those countries, or (b) the principal class of shares in the company or a related company are regularly traded on an exchange in another EU country or a treaty country; or (2) the company is treated under a tax treaty country as being a resident in a treaty country and not resident in Ireland.

The general rate of corporate tax is 12.5 percent. Certain items of passive income and income from certain industries such as mining and petroleum are taxed at a rate of 25 percent. Capital gains generally are subject to tax at a 20 percent rate. Until recently, the tax rate on income from manufacturing activities in Ireland was 10 percent, but this preferential rate was considered a harmful tax measure under European Union ("EU") rules. After negotiations with the European Commission, the Irish government enacted phase-out rules for this preferential manufacturing rate. The preferential rate is due to expire completely in 2010.

Special rules for capital gains and dividends

In 2004 the Irish government enacted an exemption from capital gains taxation for gains from certain sales by a corporation of stock in another corporation (the "investee corporation"). The exemption is available if: (1) at the time of the sale, the investee corporation is a resident for tax purposes in Ireland, in another EU member state, or in a country with which Ireland has a tax treaty; (2) the Irish company has owned (directly or indirectly) for at least 12 of the 24 months preceding the sale at least five percent of the shares of the investee company; and (3) the investee company is wholly or principally engaged in a trade or, taken together, the holding company, its five-percent group, and the investee company are wholly or principally engaged in a trade.

Dividend distributions received by an Irish resident company from another Irish resident company generally are excluded from income. Consequently, the 20–percent dividend withholding tax applicable to distributions by an Irish company generally does not apply to distributions made to another Irish resident company provided the recipient owns at least a five percent interest in the paying corporation.

Special rules for income from foreign activities

In general, as described above, Irish resident corporations are subject to Irish corporate tax on their income from foreign sources, including income earned in a foreign country through a branch (but not through a nonresident subsidiary). This tax applies regardless of whether the income is remitted to Ireland.

Ireland does not have rules analogous to the U.S. controlled foreign corporation rules. Irish taxing authorities instead may argue that a nominally nonresident company in fact is managed and controlled in Ireland and thus should be taxed as an Irish resident company.[129]

Special rules for relief of double taxation with respect to dividends received from foreign subsidiaries are discussed below.

Nonresident companies

As described previously, nonresident companies (including nonresident subsidiaries of Irish resident companies) generally are taxed by Ireland on a net basis only on income derived from and attributable to a trade or business carried on in Ireland through a branch or an agency and on gains from the sale of Irish assets used or held for use by the branch or agency.

Irish-source income of nonresident companies that is not attributable to an Irish trade or business may be subject to Irish withholding tax. A 20–percent withholding tax generally applies to payments of dividends, interest, and royalties, but payments to nonresident companies may be exempt from withholding tax in the circumstances described below.

---

129. International Bureau of Fiscal Documentation, European Taxation Analysis, Ireland, Corporate Taxation (detailed) at ¶ 13.4 (2006) (accessed through RIA Checkpoint internet-based research service).

Dividend distributions to nonresident companies are exempt from the 20–percent dividend withholding tax in certain circumstances, including when the nonresident recipient of the dividend is regularly traded on a recognized stock exchange or is a resident in an EU member country or a treaty country and is not controlled by Irish residents.

Interest and royalties paid by Irish resident companies to nonresident companies also are exempt from Irish withholding tax in certain circumstances. These circumstances include (1) when interest is paid to a company that is a resident of a tax treaty or an EU jurisdiction unless the interest is paid to that company in connection with a trade or business of that company in Ireland; and (2) based on the EU Interest and Royalties Directive, when payments of interest or royalties are made by an Irish company to an associated company of another EU member state, with association for this purpose requiring at least 25–percent common ownership. No branch profits tax or branch remittance tax is imposed on a nonresident corporation's withdrawals from an Irish branch.[130]

Avoidance or relief of double taxation

Foreign tax credit

Irish internal law does not include a general mechanism by which corporations are entitled to a credit against the Irish corporate tax for foreign taxes paid. Under various rules, however, Irish resident companies may be eligible for relief from Irish corporate taxes in respect of foreign taxes paid.

Tax treaties provide relief from double taxation. Those treaties are described below. In the absence of a tax treaty, a deduction for foreign tax paid generally is allowed against the income in respect of which the tax was assessed.

A foreign tax credit is allowed in certain circumstances. A foreign tax credit is available to offset Irish corporate tax on income from certain activities such as sales of computer software and the provision of computer services. Irish internal law also provides for credit for foreign tax imposed in relation to dividends received from nonresident companies. These credit rules for dividends implement the EU Parent–Subsidiary Directive as amended in 2004. Under the rules, an Irish resident company receiving a dividend from a five-percent owned (by voting rights) subsidiary that is a resident of a country with which Ireland does not have a tax treaty is allowed a credit against Irish tax on the dividend for any direct or withholding tax imposed on the dividend and for the portion of any foreign

---

130. International Bureau of Fiscal Documentation, European Taxation Analysis, Ireland, Corporate Taxation (detailed) at ¶ 8.4.3 (2006) (accessed through RIA Checkpoint internet-based research service).

tax imposed on the income out of which the dividend is paid.[131] This credit against Irish tax for foreign tax imposed with respect to dividend payments also is allowed to Irish branches of companies resident in the EU or in European Economic Area states with which Ireland has a tax treaty. An Irish company receiving a dividend from a five-percent subsidiary that has lower-tier subsidiaries is allowed a credit for the portion of any foreign taxes imposed on the lower-tier subsidiaries with respect to the dividend so long as the parent and the lower-tier subsidiaries are connected in a chain of ownership through at least five-percent indirect shareholding (based on vote).

Irish internal law allows cross-crediting (or "onshore pooling") for taxes on different dividend streams and permits unused credits to be carried forward indefinitely.

Tax treaties

Ireland has a network of more than 40 bilateral tax treaties. Under these tax treaties, any foreign tax on income and gains of an Irish resident company that is not otherwise eliminated by the treaty (for example, foreign tax on income attributable to an Irish company's permanent establishment in the other treaty country) generally can be credited against Irish tax imposed on that income or gain. The foreign tax credit may not exceed Irish corporate tax attributable to that income or gain. With limited exceptions, no cross-crediting is allowed under tax treaties.

---

131. This relief also is allowed even if treaty benefits are available for a dividend payment. The internal law credit mechanism in some cases could be more beneficial than the treaty benefits.

Index

†